THE HISTORY
=OF=
CHEROKEE
COUNTY

by

REV. LLOYD G. MARLIN, B.S., M.A.

Cherokee County Historian
Superintendent of
Holly Springs, Ga., Schools

Southern Historical Press, Inc.
Greenville, South Carolina

Please direct all correspondence and book orders to:
SOUTHERN HISTORICAL PRESS, Inc.
PO Box 1267
Greenville, SC   29602-1267

Originally printed: Atlanta, GA. 1932
Copyright 1932 by: Lloyd G. Marlin
New Material Copyright 2023 by:
    Southern Historical Press, Inc.
ISBN #978-1-63914-118-0
Printed in the United States of America

CONTENTS

PART ONE

APPENDIX

PART TWO

Family Accounts of:

Illustrations and Maps

PREFACE

One expects to find two things true of a preface: that it will appear in the front part of the book, and that it will express misgivings on the part of the author as to how the book will be received. This one is no exception.

When the first historian, back in the good old days of the Stone Age, hit upon the idea of chiseling on the side of a rock a few data concerning the history of his tribe, it is very likely that he had an impulse to apologize to the older and wiser among his neighbors— who had been there longer than he had—for the various mistakes which he felt sure he was about to make. For even our cave-man must have realized that a local history for local readers would be subject to criticism of a highly competent and admissable nature.

Very much the same attitude gave rise to a few misgivings on my own part when, in March of 1931, the grand jury appointed me historian for Cherokee County after I had lived in the county for only a year and a half. During that time, however, as a Methodist minister and a school teacher I had come in contact with many fine people in all parts of the county, and had formed a high respect for their traditions. In common with many others, I considered the preservation of the county's historical lore a worthy and desirable object—particularly since no previous attempt had been made to collect this material into book form. To the assignment of the grand jury I could bring a genuine enthusiasm for the subject, as well as a life-long interest in historical matters generally. There were even, it seemed to me, certain advantages in the fact that I had not lived in the county for a long period of years—such as the possibility of a fresher approach and a more objective viewpoint. And so I accepted.

"The result of my labors," as the old books say, is now before you. It has taken a large part of the last two years to compile the material for this book and to fashion it into what I hope is a readable record of Cherokee County's century of progress. It must be borne in mind that the limitations of space, which were, under the circumstances, beyond my control, have not allowed as full an inclusion of details or even of general topics as might have been desired; it has even been necessary to leave out material actually prepared for the book. In arbitrarily choosing those topics which have been included, I have, however, tried to select the facts of major interest and to present them in an organized manner.

The reader will note that this history is arranged topically rather than chronologically, although the time sequence is roughly observed in the plan of the book. The topical arrangement, which may seem a little odd in a history, makes it possible to present in each chapter the related details of a certain phase of the county's life; and I feel that a more connected and possibly a more interesting book has resulted, in this particular case, than if all events had been listed strictly in order of time.

The official character of *The History of Cherokee County* has been touched on. This book is a part of the statewide preparation being made for Georgia's Bicentennial Celebration in 1933. Realizing that much interest would be shown in historical matters during that year, the legislature on August 23, 1929, passed a resolution requesting all the counties in the state to have their histories written by Georgia Day—February 12—in 1933.

Acting on this recommendation, the grand jury at the March, 1931, term of the Cherokee County Superior Court appointed me to write the history of Cherokee County. The project was immediately indorsed in resolutions passed by the Canton Chamber of Commerce and the county board of education. At the winter term of court in that same year, three of the grand jurors—Ben F. Perry, A. P. Bobo, and J. J. Groves—were appointed to aid in the preparation of the history and to approve the manuscript, on behalf of the county, when it should be completed. These facts are noted here as a permanent record of the progressive attitude which the county has officially shown in the matter.

Without this cooperation and the cooperation of many individual citizens of the county, the present volume could not have been written. No previous work of this kind exists on the county, and it has been necessary to go to original sources for the information contained herein. In the compilation of material for the book I have been aided by more people than I could name here.

but I wish to take this opportunity to thank them publicly for their assistance. The county officials have made available to me all necessary public records, and a large number of persons have loaned valuable family records. To all who have helped in the preparation of this book I am deeply grateful.

Particularly do I wish to acknowledge my indebtedness to Miss Ruth Blair, Georgia's able state historian, for much valuable assistance and advice; to Judge W. A. Covington, of Atlanta, for his highly interesting sketch of the "Hill people" which appears in Chapters IX and X of this book, and for the wealth of other information which he has imparted to me about his "native heath," the Hills of Cherokee; to the three gentlemen of the grand jury's Historical Committee for their helpful cooperation; to the Walter W. Brown Publishing Company, printers of this book, for their interest in the attractive presentation of the material contained herein; and to Messrs. E. A. McCanless, L. R. Thomason, Smith L. Johnston, E. M. Barrett, Carl W. Groover, and L. L. Jones for their aid in making possible the publication of this book.

And now, I only trust that the reader will get as much pleasure out of reading the book as I did out of writing it. I can imagine no more colorful historical background than Cherokee County has had, and the material with which I have dealt has had an endless fascination for me. The story of the county's pioneers—and they have existed in all periods and in all walks of life—I have found not only interesting but definitely inspiring.

I hope you will find it that way.

LLOYD G. MARLIN.

Waleska, Ga.
October 1, 1932.

PART ONE

THE HISTORY OF CHEROKEE COUNTY

CHAPTER I

THE SETTING

O NE hundred years ago—just halfway along the march of years since Oglethorpe founded colonial Georgia—a great new county was formed from the domain of the Cherokee Indians and added to the roster of the Empire State. It was named Cherokee.

Indian and pioneer days seem not far behind to one who contemplates the wild grandeur of Cherokee's North Georgia scenery. And, although it has been nearly a century since the red man finally made his exodus to the plains beyond the Mississippi, the lands which he left constituted the last original territory remaining in Georgia, and are now, therefore, the state's youngest in civilization.

Lacking in mouldy antiquity, the county boasts instead the freshness and virility of her ancestry. The spiritual heritage of her pioneers, preserved in the industry and resourcefulness of her present citizens, remains as unfaded as the natural heritage of the Indians—a beautiful land of mountains and valleys, breathing of peace and health and plenty.

Before we take up the lives and activities of those earlier ones, it will be of convenience to review the nature of the territory which formed their setting and which now furnishes the environment of their legatees and descendants. This chapter will briefly describe the geology, topography, climate and other natural characteristics of Cherokee County.

Location and Size

Situated in the western part of northern Georgia, Cherokee County has a latitude of 34 degrees 14 minutes north, and a longitude of 84 degrees 30 minutes west. It is bounded on the north by Pickens County, on the east by Forsyth and Dawson counties, on the southeast by Little River and Milton

1

County, on the south by Cobb County, and on the west by Bartow County.

With an area of 429 square miles, Cherokee is slightly larger than the average county of Georgia. It is exactly as long as wide—23 miles—at its greatest length and width, although not square-shaped.

Geology

The county is situated in what geologists call the Crystalline area. This formation is of broken character, and although not yet definitely classified as to period, is known to have resulted from ancient vast upheavals. It is composed of igneous and metamorphic rocks, such as granites, gneiss and mica-schists. Igneous rocks are those which were once melted and have solidified. Metamorphic rocks include the marble deposits of the section. The Crystalline belt is the gold-bearing formation of Georgia, and provides the county also with copper, iron, asbestos, graphite, talc, mica, soapstone, and other minerals.

The soils of the county are of a gray, sandy, or gravelly nature, with the exception of a belt of red clay lands running from the southwest to the northeast corner.

Water is nearly all freestone, though mineral springs of medicinal value occur.

Topography

The land-surface of Cherokee County is mainly broken and irregular. This is especially true of the northwestern half, the general contour becoming somewhat flatter in the southeastern portion. In spite of the roughness of the country, however, little of its area is unsuited by topography for cultivation, especially with the aid of terracing.

In various parts of Cherokee rise wooded peaks of the Cohutta range of foothills—a part of the Georgia Blue Ridge, which is the southernmost ridge of the Alleghenies. Prominences of note within the county are Pine Log Mountain, with

SCENE ON THE ETOWAH RIVER, NEAR CANTON

an elevation of 2,410 feet, and Hickory Log (or Bird) Mountain, 1,600 feet. The average elevation of the county is about 1,100 feet.

Rivers and Streams

A profusion of small creeks and branches, many of them fed by springs, irrigate every part of the county and flow into the Etowah River or its system of tributaries. The Etowah enters the county at the northeast corner and pursues a southwesterly course through the middle. Some of the more important streams are Little River and Mill Creek in the south, Shoal Creek in the west, Salacoa Creek in the northwest, Bluff and Sharp Mountain Creeks in the north, Long Swamp and Conn's Creeks in the northeast, Cave Creek in the east, and Town Creek in the central part.

Climate

The different factors entering into climate—temperature, elevation, and rainfall—make Cherokee County a healthful place in which to live; they influenced many early pioneers to settle here, and have continued to exercise their drawing power. A mean temperature of 56 to 62 degrees, differing with locality, is sustained annually. The following account of seasonal variations is accurate:

"Winters are short and usually not severe. January is generally the coldest month, but its occasional spells of sharp cold are of short duration. Snow is seldom seen and rarely remains on the ground for more than a day. Spring comes early, and autumn weather extends almost to Christmas. While the midsummer days are quite warm, there is generally a breeze, especially at night."*

Owing to elevation, the air is clear, pure, and exhilarating.

From 52 to 55 inches of rain fall annually, this being about the average in North Central Georgia.

Flora and Fauna

Because of the equable climate and diversity of elevations, al-

---

*Bulletin, Canton Chamber of Commerce, 1927.

most any plant indigenous to the state can be grown, and nearly all of them are found, in Cherokee County. Distinctive of the section are the heavy growths of pine and oak that cover the hillsides in all parts of the county; the profusion of native nut-bearing trees, such as walnut, hickory, and chestnut; the clusters of sumac, berry bushes, ivy, dogwood, and mountain laurel that make the woods delightful the year round.

In the days of the Indians, fauna of Cherokee County included the beaver, raccoon, wild deer, opossum, fox, squirrel, mink, wildcat; pheasant, wild turkey, crane, wild goose; catfish, sucker, perch, trout—all in profusion. The inroads of civilization have not yet succeeded entirely in wiping out any of these species in the county; even deer and wild turkeys have been reported bagged by hunters in comparatively recent years.

Such—except for the boundaries—are the features of Cherokee County that have remained unchanged since the days when Indian war-whoops rang through its forests and deer stood unafraid on its hills.

Thus the setting.

CHAPTER II

INDIAN DAYS

CHEROKEE COUNTY is named for its earliest owners and inhabitants, the Cherokee Indians. The origin of the word "Cherokee" is variously accounted for; it is not a word belonging to the tribal language of the Indians, who called themselves *Yuniwiya,* or "real people," but entered their tongue later, in the form of *Tsalagi.* According to Prof. James Mooney, a government ethnologist who spent years in research among the Indians, there is no ground to connect "Cherokee" with any Indian word for "fire," as is sometimes done. His own explanation is that "Cherokee" was a corruption by traders of the Choctaw word *choluk,* meaning "cave-dweller," "the Allegheny region being a cave country in which rock shelters containing numerous traces of Indian occupancy are of frequent occurrence."*

Other examples of the Indian influence in nomenclature are found in Cherokee County. The name of the Etowah River (sometimes modified to "Hightower" by early settlers) is taken from an Indian settlement on its banks called Itawa. Salacoa Creek derives its name from the Indian *selu-egwa*—"big-corn." *Sutali* meant "six," and apparently both "Sutallee" and "Sixes" come from this word. Hickory Log, Pine Log, and Ball Ground were all named by the Indians; the present names being translations, of course. Waleska was named for the Indian maiden Warluskee.

The story of the Cherokee Indians is a fascinating one, and as far as the Georgia clans are concerned is entirely pertinent to the history of Cherokee County, since the original county included all the Indian territory remaining in Georgia at the time it was created. But the Cherokees, because of characteristics unusual in a so-called savage race, have been subjected to thorough study and research and there is already a large mass of printed data concern-

---

*Myths of the Cherokee, by James Mooney, in 19th Annual Report of the Bureau of American Ethnology, p. 20.

ing this tribe. Only the more significant events of Cherokee tribal history, therefore, will be given here—particularly those leading up to the creation of Cherokee County. In addition, an effort will be made to depict briefly the life and customs of this interesting people who played such a large part in the early history of the county.

Early Tribal History of the Cherokees

When our nation was very young, the lands of the Cherokees stretched between the Ohio and Tennessee Rivers and extended southward almost to the site of the present Atlanta, comprising about 40,000 miles of the Allegheny region and now included in seven states.

During the Revolutionary War the Cherokees took sides with the British, and as a consequence lost a large tract of their northern territory. In the Hopewell (S. C.) Treaty of 1785, however, they received an official confirmation of title to the balance of their land, their title before that time having rested only in occupancy. Further cessions and treaties followed, and the Cherokees settled to the southward, into a territory that by the latter days had shrunk to a relatively small area in Georgia, Alabama, Tennessee, and North Carolina, the greater tract lying in Georgia. The land which now comprises Cherokee County was well within their southern boundary.

In 1802 Georgia ceded to the United States the lands now comprising Alabama and Mississippi, with the provision that the federal government should extinguish the Indian titles to all lands in Georgia, "as early as the same can be peaceably obtained on reasonable terms."

The United States was a bit slow in carrying out its part of the agreement. It was twenty-five years before the Creek Indians of middle and southern Georgia were removed, and thirty-six years before the Cherokees were officially escorted from their North Georgia homes.

However, steps followed at Washington, after 1802, to speed migrations to the Indian Territory west of the Mississippi. Land in what is now Oklahoma was promised in return for the eastern holdings of the emigrants, and monetary inducements were added.

There commenced a gradual thinning out of the Cherokee ranks which continued up to the final removal; but it was the more northerly Cherokees, somewhat industrialized, who made up the greater number of emigrants; the Alabama and Georgia clans were more nomadic and preferred to cling to their old hunting-grounds.

Generally superior in civilization to the average run of American Indians, the Cherokees had always proved most amenable to the negotiations of the white man. In 1813 they rendered valuable service to General Andrew Jackson in helping him to subdue the hostile Creeks. Even the sixteenth-century DeSoto, searching for Georgia gold, had been struck by the friendliness and "civilization" of the Cherokee Indians, who guided him through North Georgia but failed to steer him to what later became Dahlonega.

In 1817 and 1819 cessions were made by the Cherokees of lands in the eastern part of North Georgia. The treaties involved were bitterly criticized by most of the Indians, and further negotiations for their lands proved futile for the next sixteen years, although several presidents of the United States and several governors of Georgia made strong efforts to bring about another cession. The definite and urgent causes which led to the ultimate removal of the Cherokees in 1838 were not yet in evidence.

The territory left to the Indians in Georgia after 1819 was all the northwestern part of the state, bounded on the east by the Chattahoochee River and on the south by a line a little above the present Atlanta—approximately the area of the first huge Cherokee County, to be described later.

Having thus briefly* carried the history of the Cherokee nation up to the time when white settlers began to dot North Georgia, we can turn aside for a glimpse at the customs and manners of the tribe at that period.

Customs and Life of the Indians

As pioneers knew them during the first third of the nineteenth century, the Cherokees were not dissimilar in appearance and dress

---

*For complete and authoritative history of the Cherokees, the reader is referred to **Myths of the Cherokee**, by James Mooney, in 19th Annual Report of the Bureau of American Ethnology; or to **Removal of the Cherokees**, by Wilson Lumpkin.

to other tribes. They adopted some of the white man's apparel, but disposed such garments on themselves, we are told, with less idea of utility than eye for effect. The gaudier and, apparently, the more unsanitary their clothing was, the more they admired it. Cleanliness was not one of their strong points.

Although some of the Indians had good frame houses, most of them lived in huts bare of comforts. Indian "towns" were really widely scattered collections of dwelling-places, with a council hall and a court where feasts and dances were held. In what became Cherokee County there were at least four sizable Indian villages. White* gives two: Old Sixes Town, located about seven miles southeast of the present Canton, headed by Chief Stop; and Little River Town, fourteen miles southeast of Canton, headed by Chief Chicken. In 1833 the former village is said to have held four hundred Indians, the latter three hundred. Mooney gives two more towns: Long Swamp and Hickory Log; both situated near the present Ball Ground.

Other Indian chieftains of the period were Tiuska, who lived on Cane Creek in the upper part of Cherokee County, where he built a large frame house and raised a large, respectable family; and Old Still, who lived on Mount Etowah, near Canton. When the Maddox home was built at the latter place in the '80's, many relics, such as pipes and primitive utensils, were found in an Indian grave on the hill. There was also Chief Foekiller, in whose honor a small stream now in Milton County seems to have been named. He lived near the present Waleska and was on friendly terms with the settlers of that section.

It has been said that "every foot of Cherokee County is linked to the past by Indian memories." Even today one may find Indian relics in any part of the county. Arrowheads, pottery, flint and bone tools and weapons, and even ball-play sticks bear witness to the county's first inhabitants. Ancient idols also have been discovered, but it is agreed by students of the Indians that none of the Georgia tribes ever worshipped idols, and these may date back to the mound-dwellers, whose existence is supported by certain Cherokee myths.

---

*Historical Collections of Georgia, by Rev. George White.

Of the religion of the Cherokees, Mooney said: "Owing to their predilection for new gods, their rituals and epics fell into decay." Possessed originally of a full set of creation-myths and sun-worshiping rites, they later turned in large numbers to the teachings of the missionaries, who worked among the Cherokees as early as 1803 and who formed a civilizing influence on them.

The main pursuits of the Cherokee men were hunting and fishing. Fighting, the other Indian concomitant, was never very popular among the Cherokees. Their food was chiefly game from the woods and maize from their patches. Deer, wild turkeys, squirrels, and 'possums formed a large part of their diet, but as game grew scarcer they were forced to rely more on agriculture and stock-grazing for a living. They made poor farmers, usually, and they never tilled an acre of poor ground. Generally the men let the women do the farming. Among the crops raised by their crude methods were corn, beans, pumpkins, sweet potatoes.

The favorite Indian pastime was "ball-play," a game similar to our modern lacrosse. The ball was not knocked but caught in a net on the end of a stick and thrown. The object was to put it between the goal posts, a pair of which stood at each end of the field. Great excitement always surrounded a "ball-play" between skillful players; sometimes crowds would come from miles around and stay for days at a time. Usually some of the players sustained broken arms or legs, and deaths were not infrequent in this rather athletic game. Tradition has it that on the site of the present Ball Ground a "ball-play" was once held between Creeks and Cherokees to decide the ownership of a sizable tract of land which is supposed to have included the present areas of Cobb, Paulding, and Polk Counties. The Cherokees won.

Another sport of which the Indians were fond was racing their fast little ponies. The river-bottom field near Canton bridge used to be an Indian race-track.

A great event of tribal life, and one that has been often described, was the green-corn dance, held annually after the "roasting-ears" had matured. Much ceremony was observed at one of these important functions, and the braves danced as long as they could hold out.

The marriage rites of the Cherokees were very simple, but the brave and his squaw nearly always lived together faithfully. The method followed by a young buck who wanted a wife was to build and stock a cabin and then negotiate with the relatives of his chosen bride, after which the bride was informed of the matter and installed in the cabin.

The Civilization of the Cherokees

Much has been written concerning the civilization of the Cherokee Indians. "General Carroll, who visited them in their picturesque highland country in 1829, reported to the Washington government substantially in this wise: 'The advancement the Cherokees have made in morality, religion, general information, and agriculture astonishes me beyond measure. They have regular preachers in their churches; the use of spirituous liquors is in a great degree prohibited; their farms are worked much after the manner of the white people, and are generally in good order.' They were supplied with looms and spinning wheels, as well as farm implements. One of their gifted men, Sequoyah, had invented an alphabet of eighty letters, which has been described as the most remarkable feat of its kind since Cadmus. At their capital, New Echota, they published a newspaper, the *Phoenix,* in their own language. They insisted that they were a sovereign nation, over whom Georgia had no jurisdiction.'"* In addition, the Cherokees who could afford it owned slaves. A census of their nation taken in 1825 showed: native Cherokees, 13,563; white men married into the nation, 147; white women married into the nation, 73; negro slaves, 1,277.†

The advancement of the Cherokees in the arts of civilization has been ascribed to the teachings of the white men who went among them for the purposes of trading, preaching, or hiding from justice, and to the intermixture of blood which resulted in some cases. In justice to the Indians, it must be said that they took quickly, as a nation, to advanced ideas; but the

*From **The Atlanta Constitution,** March 10, 1932; editorial commenting on the news that the Oklahoma Cherokees were agitating for a removal to Mexico where they could "return to nature and escape the ills of civilization."
†**Myths of the Cherokee,** p. 112.

rank and file of the Cherokees continued to follow the irresponsible and unilluminated lives of their forefathers, even to the final removal. Their chiefs and leaders—the wealthy, educated, slave-owning class of Indians—nearly all had a certain amount of white blood in their veins.

Two things which have probably little bearing on the history of Cherokee County but which illustrate in an interesting fashion the progressiveness of the race for which the county was named, were the Cherokee alphabet and newspaper.

The invention by Sequoyah, a mixed-blood known to the whites as George Gist, of the Cherokee alphabet, or syllabary, has been pronounced one of the greatest achievements of the human intellect. The alphabet is phonetic, being made up, not of letters or of hieroglyphs, but of symbols for all the eighty-five different sounds found in the Cherokee language. It took Sequoyah twelve years to finish it, and it was so simple and efficient that shortly after its adoption by the Cherokee council in 1821, thousands of hitherto illiterate Indians had learned to read and write in their own language.

This alphabet led to the publication of the Indian newspaper, *Tsalagi Tsulehisanunhi,* or *Cherokee Phoenix.* Under the supervision of a missionary named Worcester, special type was cast in Boston and a printing-shop set up in 1827 in a log house at New Echota, the Cherokee capital, which was in Gordon County near the present Calhoun. The editor, an educated Cherokee named Elias Boudinot, was assisted by Worcester and two white printers, and the paper was issued periodically in both languages for about six years, and continued by the Cherokees after their removal to the West.

But the civilized methods of the Cherokees were to get them into hot water when they applied them to government. In 1827 there occurred at New Echota a political event unparalleled in the history of any sovereign state. The Cherokees, having put their literary talent to work to evolve a written constitution and a set of laws denying the jurisdiction of Georgia's laws over their territory, passed on the constitution, adopted the laws, and became—according to their solemn announcement—one of the distinct, autonomous nations of the earth!

Georgia was very galled. It was bad enough to have to harbor this tribe of savages at all—worse to reflect that a large part of northern Georgia seemed destined to become a permanent Indian reservation—but worst of all to have a foreign nation try to set itself up within her boundaries! This superb effrontery—as Georgia naturally regarded it—really marked the turning-point in the state's Indian problem, for it led to the abandonment of diplomacy and the employment of more effectual weapons, chief of which was mail-fisted legislation. Thereafter Indian affairs were handled by the state with very little evidence of kid gloves.

Thus, in the same year (1827) that marked the removal of the last Creek Indian from Georgia, the Cherokees brought about the first serious crisis in the chain of events leading to their own removal, which will be treated in a later chapter.

Also by their action they helped pave the way for the creation of Cherokee County.

CHAPTER III

CREATION OF THE COUNTY

THE official birthday of Cherokee County was December 26, 1831.

On that day there became law of Georgia "an act to lay out and organize a new county, to be comprised of all the lands lying west of the Chattahoochee River and north of Carroll County line, within the limits of Georgia, ... to be called Cherokee."*

The new county, it is seen, was a huge one. It contained some 6,900 square miles, in contrast to its present 429. Georgia, the largest state east of the Mississippi, would hold not quite nine counties the size of the original Cherokee!

There were some other interesting things about the new county. Its territory comprised all the Indian lands then remaining in Georgia; no more, no less. It was created of lands which—theoretically, at least—belonged to the Cherokee tribe of Indians. And lastly, it was not an original county!

Status of the Territory

If the second statement appears debatable, it must be borne in mind that there had never been any passage of title to these lands from the Indians. True it is that there were white men living in Cherokee Georgia in 1831, plenty of them; and that by right of occupancy or purchase most held title—and effective title, whether legally recognizable or not—to the lands they lived on. There were still more men there in 1835, and to their rights of occupancy and purchase they had added the right of state patent, in many cases. There was never any question, furthermore, that Georgia's boundaries included all the first huge Cherokee County. And yet—the Cherokee Indians, to whom the lands had been confirmed repeatedly by United States

---

*Acts, Georgia, 1831, p. 74.

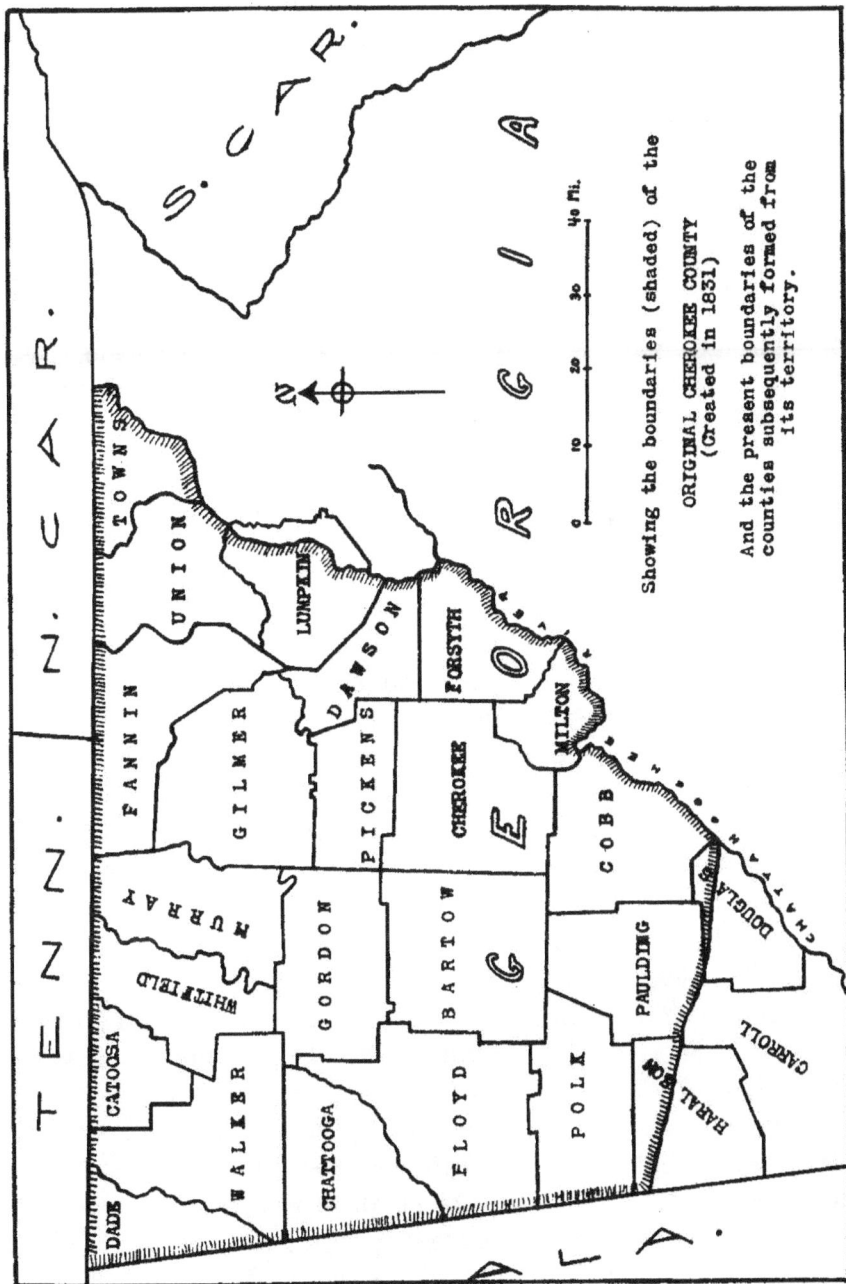

Showing the boundaries (shaded) of the
ORIGINAL CHEROKEE COUNTY
(Created in 1831)

And the present boundaries of the
counties subsequently formed from
its territory.

THE ORIGINAL CHEROKEE COUNTY

treaties, had not before the year 1835 ceded away an inch of the holdings left to them under the Treaty of 1819. Nor had they promised to do so. The promise which Georgia held that Indian titles within her boundaries would be extinguished had not been given to her by the Cherokees, but by the federal government in return for certain favors whereby the Indians had benefited not at all. Therefore, it appears that the first Cherokee County *was* made from lands belonging to the Indians.

Of course, there are at least two sides to every argument, and to this one there were three. As the affair progresses historically, and especially when it reaches the point at which the Indians were removed from the state, many past and present historians have waxed warm in their declarations of culpability—lacking in unanimity, however, as to the culprit. The grasping selfishness and heartless cruelty of Georgia have long been a theme, in this connection, of certain historians outside the state; the obstinate and willful refusal of the Cherokees to aid the march of progress and accept a fair price for their holdings has been duly criticized; while the fact has been brought out by still other and equally acute commentators that the United States helped to complicate matters with a promise to deliver to a second party what belonged to an unwilling third, and was ambiguous in the promise, at that.

A continuation of the feud is not intended here; it is mentioned merely as a spotlight recurrently thrown back on certain phases of the early history of Cherokee County. When the removal of the Indians is taken up, the reader will have to form his own opinion about the justice of that step.

In the meantime, nothing has been said of the four years intervening between the Indian declaration of autonomy and the creation of Cherokee County. These four years are important; they witnessed lively times in North Georgia. They saw a gold rush that was America's greatest before 'forty-nine. They saw in action the builders of the nation: the Pioneers. They saw, on one hand, a lawless rabble gone primitive in a primitive setting, and on the other, a stern, law-abiding, hardworking group whose ideals no setting or situation could affect. They were times of intensity. Times of blood and sweat, of fighting and toil, of bitter defeats and joyous triumphs. Pioneers' times.

Frontier days in North Georgia did not end in 1831—the work that was to be done was only getting started then; although the formation of Cherokee County in that year helped, more than anything before had helped, to restore law and order to the environment and to wipe out some of the odds against the pioneers. Nor did frontier days in Cherokee Georgia start in 1827, although there were not many permanent settlers before that time. But probably in no other four years has the section felt such far-reaching and lasting influences of change as in that intense period which culminated in the creation of Cherokee County.

Events Leading Up to the County's Formation

Georgia's first law countering the Cherokee's adoption of a constitution was an act passed in December, 1827, extending the authority of the state over Cherokee territory within its borders, and placing that territory under the jurisdiction of the courts of Carroll and DeKalb Counties.

The statement that Cherokee is not an original county has a "believe-it-or-not" flavor, but it has been easily and quite publicly verifiable for a hundred years. The assumption that the county was made from original territory arises, no doubt, from the fact that Cherokee is the mother-county of practically all Northwest Georgia. But that it is not an original county will presently be clear.

The act of December, 1827, did not add the Cherokee territory to the two counties mentioned; it only extended their legal jurisdiction over it. In the following year, however, Cherokee Georgia *was* divided into counties by an act entitled "An act to add the territory lying within the limits of this state, and occupied by the Cherokee Indians, to the counties of Carroll, DeKalb, Gwinnett, Hall, and Habersham; and to extend the laws of this state over the same."*

These preliminary steps in the extension of Georgia's au-

---

*Acts, Georgia, 1828, p. 88. (Act approved Dec. 20, 1828.)

thority over the Cherokee lands were taken for two reasons: To protect the lives and property of the settlers that were already there; and to improve conditions so as to induce further settlement and colonization of the Indian territory. Indian depredations, however infrequent, and the lawless activities of a certain class of white men who had come into the territory were both sources of annoyance and danger to the settlers with whom Georgia hoped to fill up her frontier territory as an aid to getting rid of the Indians. Courts could now be held in the territory to mete out justice to offenders.

But the next year a situation was to develop with which the courts of Carroll, DeKalb, Gwinnett, Hall, and Habersham, plus the combined police forces of three governments—the United States, Georgia, and the Cherokee nation—were not able immediately to cope.

Gold was found in North Georgia.

Dr. Knight* describes the situation: "Gold was discovered on Duke's Creek [in Habersham County] and in the neighborhood of Dahlonega. There followed a rush of adventurous argonauts into the forbidden land of the Cherokees. It is estimated that by the summer of 1830 there were at least 3000 whites from various states digging gold at the sources of the Chattahoochee. To quote Mr. Phillips: †"The intrusion of these miners into the Cherokee territory was unlawful under the enactments of three several governments, each claiming jurisdiction over the region. The United States laws forbade anyone settling or trading on Indian territory without a special license from the proper United States official; the State of Georgia had extended its laws over the Cherokee lands, applying them after June 1, 1830, to Indians as well as white men; and the Cherokee nation had passed a law that no one should settle or trade on their lands without a permit from their officials.'

"Such was the impetuosity of this mad rush to the gold mines that all of these governments combined did not possess police power requisite to deal with the situation."

*Georgia and Georgians, Lucian Lamar Knight, p. 556.
"†Georgia and State Rights, U. B. Phillips, pp. 72-73."

With regard to the influence which the discovery of gold in their territory had on the removal of the Indians, Dr. Knight says: "It operated as a spur to hasten the departure of the Cherokees toward the west, and created an eagerness on the part of the white population to possess themselves of the red man's home among the mountains;"* and Prof. Mooney wrote: "About 1828 gold was found . . . . . near the present Dahlonega, and the doom of the [Cherokee] nation was sealed."† ·

But the immediate result of this gold activity was to center the attention of the legislature on devising improved means of controlling the territory. Accordingly they passed laws prohibiting the mining of gold, except under certain strict regulations, either by white men or Indians, and even a law prohibiting white men from going into the territory or living there at all without first taking the oath of allegiance to Georgia.

All this, however, is already familiar to the student of Georgia history. What is important for our purposes here is that one of these legislative efforts at control took the form of an act passed in 1830 authorizing the survey of Cherokee Georgia. That difficulties were anticipated in this move appears in the title of the act: "To authorize a survey and disposition of the lands within the limits of Georgia in the occupancy of the Cherokee tribe of Indians, ... and to authorize the governor to call out a military force to protect surveyors in the discharge of their duties, and to provide for the punishment of persons who may prevent, or attempt to prevent, any surveyor from performing his duties, or who shall wilfully cut down and deface any marked trees or remove any landmark which may be made in pursuance of this act, and to protect the Indians in the peaceable possession of their improvements and of the lots on which they may be situated."‡

The difficulties were in fact encountered, and the surveyors made little progress. So in 1831 another act was passed order-

*Georgia and Georgians, Lucian Lamar Knight, p. 561.

†Myths of the Cherokee, James Mooney, p. 116.

‡Acts, Georgia, 1830. (Act approved December 21, 1830.)

ing "the immediate survey, distribution, and occupancy of the Territory"—thus revealing the main purpose of the survey—and requiring the governor "to order out the district surveyors for completing the surveys of said territory, with as little delay as possible; and when the survey shall be completed, and returns thereof made in conformity with the provisions of said act, it shall be the duty of the governor, in case he shall deem it for the interest of the state, to cause the lottery commissioners to assemble at Milledgeville, to commence the drawing of the lottery as contemplated by this act."*

This act, which went into effect the following April, finally brought about the desired results; but without waiting to see whether it did or not, the legislature passed another act four days later creating Cherokee County out of the entire territory.

The title of the act has already been given (see beginning of this chapter). Besides laying out the boundaries of the new county, the act authorized the erection of public buildings, the creation of militia districts, the election of militia officers and justices of the peace, and the impanelment of jurors. In addition, it set the time and place for the first court to be held, and allotted the county to a judicial district and a militia brigade.

The act follows in full:

Act Creating Cherokee County

Sec. 1. *Be it enacted,* [etc.], That all the territory, lying west of the Chattahoochee River and north of Carroll County, within the limits of Georgia, and which is now attached to and forms part of the several counties of Carroll, DeKalb, Gwinnett, Hall, and Habersham, shall form one county, to be called Cherokee. That on the first Monday of February next, the persons who may be in said county, and who may be entitled to vote for members of the General Assembly, may meet together at the house of Ambrose Harnage, and under the authority and superintendence of three Justices of the Peace, elect five Justices of the Inferior Court for said county, a Clerk of the Superior Court, a Clerk of the Inferior Court, a Sheriff, a Coroner, a Receiver of Tax Returns, a Tax Collector, and a County Surveyor.

---

*Acts, Georgia, 1831, p. 141. (Act approved December 22, 1831.)

Sec. 2. *And be it further enacted,* That said Justices shall certify, under their hands, to the Governor, the persons so elected, who shall thereupon be commissioned to hold their respective offices until the next election for like offices throughout the State; *Provided,* that nothing in this act contained shall be so construed as to affect any commission heretofore issued to any officer now residing in said Territory.

Sec. 3. *Be it further enacted,* That the said Justices of the Inferior Court, as soon as practicable, shall fix on a site for the necessary public buildings, and shall have erected thereat such temporary public buildings as in their judgment may be for the public interest, and such as the public interest may require. And said Justices shall, as soon as practicable, lay off said county into Captain's districts; not more than two to be formed of each section — and when the same shall be defined, they shall give 15 days' notice of the time and place, in each district, for holding an election for Justices of the Peace, (and Constables, and one of said Justices or a Justice of the Peace,) and two other persons resident in the district, shall superintend said election, and certify the result of said election to his Excellency the Governor, who shall proceed to cause commissions to issue to the Justices elect, which said commissions shall continue until the time of election for Justices throughout the State.

Sec. 4. *And be it further enacted,* That it shall be the duty of the Justices of the Peace in each district, after they shall have been commissioned as aforesaid, to advertise in their respective districts the election for captains and subaltern officers, according to the Militia Laws of this State, and the captains after they are so elected and commissioned, shall as early as practicable, make out a complete roll of all persons in their respective districts liable to do militia duty, and return the same to the Inferior Court of said county, and the captains and Justices shall proceed to advertise and superintend elections for field officers, according to the militia laws now of force in this State.

Sec. 5. *And be it further enacted,* That the Justices of the Inferior Court shall proceed to draw grand and petit jurors, as directed by the laws now of force.

Sec. 6. *And be it further enacted,* That the time of holding the Superior Court of said county shall be on the fourth Monday in March and September, and the time of holding the Inferior Court shall be on the fourth Monday in June and December.

Sec. 7. *And be it further enacted,* That the place of holding the Superior and Inferior Courts shall be at the house of Ambrose Harnage.

Sec. 8. *And be it further enacted,* That said county be added to and made a part of the Western Judicial Circuit, and shall form part of the first brigade of the 7th division of the militia of this State.

ASBURY HULL, *Speaker of the House of Reps.*

THOMAS STOCKS, *President of the Senate.*

WILSON LUMPKIN, *Governor.*

Assented to December 26, 1831.*

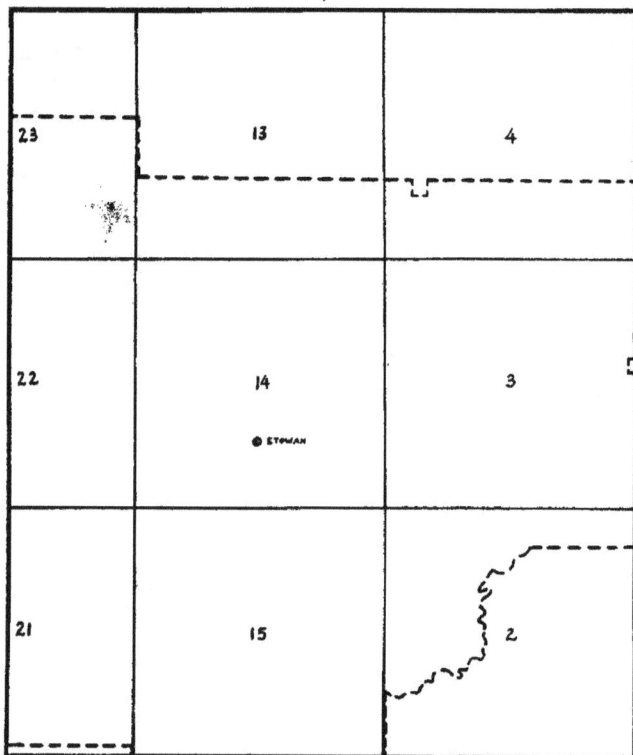

CHEROKEE COUNTY IN 1832

Boundaries of the second Cherokee. As cut out of the original county in 1832, it included the land districts shown (all in Section 2). Districts 21, 22, and 23 were halved by the line between Cherokee and Cass (now Bartow). Dotted lines represent present boundaries.

The territory shown north of the upper dotted line was given to form part of Pickens County in 1853; that shown below the dotted line in District 2 was given to form part of Milton County in 1857.

---

*Acts, Georgia, 1831, p. 74 ff.

But Cherokee Georgia did not long remain Cherokee County.

Created primarily as an emergency measure, the original county served the temporary purpose of holding the territory together under Georgia's laws while the survey was being made and while a more permanent arrangement could be worked out for its disposition into counties of normal size.

Accordingly, at the next session of the legislature, in an act approved December 3, 1832, the original Cherokee was divided into ten counties: Cherokee, Cass (now Bartow), Cobb, Floyd, Forsyth, Gilmer, Lumpkin, Murray, Paulding, and Union. The act, however, first added a small tract of land from Hall and Habersham Counties to the territory to be reapportioned. The same legislature, on the 24th of December,* added to Campbell County a small tract which had evidently been left over in the lower part of the original Cherokee.

Later divisions of these eleven counties formed in 1832 have increased the number of counties made from the original Cherokee to twenty-two and parts of two others (see map on page 15.)

Here follows the act of December 3, 1832,† quoted in part as it pertains to the creation of the present Cherokee County:

Act Dividing the Original and Creating the Present Cherokee County

An act to add parts of the counties of Habersham and Hall to the county of Cherokee, and to divide said county of Cherokee into ten counties and to provide for the organization of the same.

Sec. 1. *Be it enacted,* [etc.], That [here is described a small tract of land in Hall and Habersham Counties] shall form and become a part of [original] Cherokee County.

Sec. 2. [Outlines the boundaries of a new county to be called Forsyth.]

Sec. 3. [Same, Lumpkin.]
Sec. 4. [Same, Union.]
Sec. 5. [Same, Cobb.]
Sec. 7. [Same, Gilmer.]

*Acts, Georgia, 1832, p. 55.
†Acts, Georgia, 1832, pp. 56 ff.

Sec. 8. [Same, Murray.]
Sec. 9. [Same, Cass.]
Sec. 10. [Same, Floyd.]
Sec. 11. [Same, Paulding.]

Sec. 6. *And be it further enacted,* That the second, third, fourth, thirteenth, fourteenth, and fifteenth and such parts of the twenty-third, twenty-second, and twenty-first districts of the second section as lies east of a line to be run, commencing at the center of the north line of the twenty-third, and running due south to the south line of the twenty-first district, shall form and become one county, to be called Cherokee.

Sec. 12. *And be it further enacted,* That on the first Monday in March next, the persons who may be resident in said counties, entitled to vote for members of the Legislature, may meet together at the several places hereinafter designated in their respective counties, and under the superintendence of three suitable and capable persons, elect five Justices of the Inferior Court, a Clerk of the Superior and Inferior Courts, a Sheriff, a Tax Collector, a Tax Receiver, and a County Surveyor and Coroner for each county — who shall hold their respective offices, for and during the time hereinafter prescribed in the seventeenth section of this act.

Sec. 13. *And be it further enacted,* That the places of holding elections for said counties shall be as follows:

. . . . . In the county of Cherokee, at the place where John Lay now lives. . . . . .

Sec. 14. [Provides for certification and commission of county officers.]

Sec. 15. [Gives inferior court justices power to designate county sites and erect public buildings.]

Sec. 16. [Provides for the election of justices of the peace, two for each "captain's district."]

Sec. 17. [Provides that the county officers elected under this act shall hold office until January 1, 1834; and that a new election shall be held then.]

Sec. 18. [Provides for the organization of militia districts, with captains and subaltern officers for all districts.]

Sec. 19. [Continuation of same.]

Sec. 20. [Provides that the justices of the inferior courts shall select grand and petit jurors, as soon as practicable.]

Sec. 21. [Directs county surveyors to run lines of their counties and file plats.]

Sec. 22. [All ten counties are placed in Cherokee Judicial Circuit, the judge and solicitor-general to be elected.]

Sec. 23. *And be it further enacted,* That the times of holding the Superior Courts in the Cherokee Circuit shall be as follows: . . . . . In the county of Cherokee, on the second Monday in February and August in each and every year. . . . .

Sec. 24. [Provides that the places of holding court shall be the places designated herein for holding elections of county officers, until otherwise ordered by the justices of the inferior courts.]

Sec. 25. [Provides for the transfer of suits from courts of the original Cherokee County to courts of the new counties, when they are organized.]

Sec. 26. *And be it further enacted,* That all officers, civil and military, who have been heretofore elected and commissioned for the County of Cherokee, shall continue in office in the counties and districts into which they may be thrown until the expiration of the term for which they may have been commissioned, and that no election shall be held in the county or district where said officers shall reside, unless the same becomes vacant, until the regular time of elections throughout the State.

ASBURY HULL,
Speaker of the House of Reps.

THOMAS STOCKS,
President of the Senate.

WILSON LUMPKIN, *Governor.*

Assented to December 3, 1832.

CHAPTER IV

LEGAL BOUNDARIES AND DIVISIONS

THERE is a classic story about a Kentucky mountaineer whose cabin and corn-patch lay in a tract of territory that was transferred from Kentucky to an adjoining state. Asked how he liked living in the new state, he replied he liked it fine; he'd "always heerd Kentucky was an onhealthy place to live, anyhow."

It is presumed nothing like this ever happened in Cherokee County, where the charge of "onhealthiness" would be inapplicable. A review of the county's boundary changes, however, shows that a considerable number of its inhabitants, since the original Cherokee was laid out in 1831, have at one time or another suddenly found themselves living in a brand-new county. The record was set by one or two persons who resided in the southeastern corner of Cherokee before that part of the county was cut off in 1857 to help form Milton County, and who lived to see Milton made a part of Fulton County in 1932.

The same tract had also been in DeKalb County from 1828 to 1831, and in the original Cherokee County from 1831 to 1832.

Also subject to change are the lines of the county's militia districts, the present boundaries of which are shown in the map on page 30.

There is another subdivision of the county's territory, but of a different nature and with more permanent lines. The land districts of Cherokee County will be described in this chapter, along with the militia districts and the various changes that have been made in the county's boundaries.

County Line Changes

The two acts of legislature quoted in the preceding chapter give legal descriptions of the original Cherokee County and the Cherokee County cut off therefrom in 1832. These descriptions show that the original Cherokee was made from all the territory north of the Carroll County line (in 1831) and west of the Chattahoochee River; and that the second Cherokee County was formed from the second, third, fourth, thirteenth, fourteenth, and fifteenth land districts, and the eastern halves of the twenty-first, twenty-second, and twenty-third land districts, all in the second section of the original Cherokee. At the time the original county was laid out, there were no land districts in Cherokee Georgia, the survey not having been completed.

The maps on pages 15 and 30 show these first two stages of Cherokee County. In the second stage the county contained 607½ square miles. It continued with practically the same boundaries from 1832 to 1853.

In 1853 came the first major line change. In that year Pickens County was created, by a legislative act approved on December 5 and entitled "An act to lay out and organize a new county from the counties of Cherokee and Gilmer, and for other purposes therein specified."* To aid in the formation of Pickens County, Cherokee contributed about 130 square miles of its northernmost territory, a little over a fifth of its total area.

The second and last major line change came four years later. On December 18, 1857, an act was approved creating Milton County, which was laid off from Cherokee, Cobb, and Forsyth.† Under this act Cherokee gave about forty-eight square miles, something like one-tenth of its remaining area. The land contributed was in the southeastern corner of the county, and comprised all the second land district southeast of Little River.

Since the creation of Milton County in 1857, no important change has been made in the boundaries of Cherokee County. At various times in the past, however, minor changes, involving only one or two land lots at a time, have been approved by the legislature. It is not necessary to list these minor alterations here, particularly since some of them were repealed later. The present lines of the county, as shown by the official county map, are given in the map on page 30.

*Acts, Georgia, 1853-4, p. 306.
†Acts, Georgia, 1857, p. 36.

The Twenty-Four "Daughter-Counties"

As stated in the preceding chapter, ten counties were formed from the original Cherokee by the act of December 3, 1832; and twenty-four counties have later been formed wholly or in part from these ten. The map on page 15 shows this redistribution of lands into "daughter-counties" of the original Cherokee.

The following list gives the dates of formation of these twenty-four counties and the sources of the territory from which they were made:

BARTOW (first called CASS). Created December 3, 1832, from original Cherokee. Part from Murray, 1834.

CATOOSA. Created December 5, 1853, from Walker and Whitfield.

CHATTOOGA. Created December 28, 1838, from Floyd and Walker.

CHEROKEE. Created December 26, 1831. (See preceding chapter.) Laid out second time from original Cherokee, December 3, 1832.

COBB. Created December 3, 1832, from original Cherokee.

DADE. Created December 25, 1837, from Walker.

DAWSON. Created December 3, 1857, from Gilmer and Lumpkin.

DOUGLAS. Created October 17, 1870, from Carroll and Campbell.

FANNIN. Created January 21, 1854, from Union and Gilmer.

FLOYD. Created December 3, 1832, from original Cherokee. Part from Chattooga, 1840; from Paulding, 1847.

FORSYTH. Created December 3, 1832, from original Cherokee. Part from Lumpkin, 1850.

GILMER. Created December 3, 1832, from original Cherokee. Part from Union, 1856.

GORDON. Created February 13, 1850, from Floyd and Cass (now Bartow). Part from Floyd and Murray, 1852.

HARALSON. Created January 26, 1856, from Carroll and Polk.

LUMPKIN. Created December 3, 1832, from original Cherokee. Part from Hall, 1850; from Habersham, 1853.

MILTON (now part of FULTON). Created December 18, 1857, from Cherokee, Forsyth, and Cobb.

MURRAY. Created December 3, 1832, from original Cherokee.

PAULDING. Created December 3, 1832, from original Cherokee. Part from Carroll, 1850; from Cobb, 1851.

PICKENS. Created December 5, 1853, from Cherokee and Gilmer.

POLK. Created December 20, 1851, from Paulding and Floyd.

TOWNS. Created March 6, 1856, from Union and Rabun.

UNION. Created December 3, 1832, from original Cherokee. Part from Lumpkin, 1845.

WALKER. Created December 18, 1833, from Murray.

WHITFIELD. Created December 30, 1851, from Murray. Part from Walker, 1853, 1859.

Land and Militia Districts

In the present Cherokee County there are three whole land districts—the third, fourteenth, and fifteenth—and six fractional land districts—the second, fourth, thirteenth, twenty-first, twenty-second, and twenty-third; as will be seen by reference to the map on page 22. All of these districts lie in the second section of the survey of the original Cherokee County.

The size of the whole land districts is nine miles square. Each contains 51,840 acres, and is divided into lots of uniform size. There are, however, two sizes of land lots in Cherokee County. Thus the second, third, fifteenth, and twenty-first land districts contain nothing but forty-acre lots, while the remaining districts all contain one-hundred-and-sixty-acre lots. The reason for this difference is explained in the next chapter in connection with the Gold Lottery of 1832.

Land districts, which are a part of Georgia's system for the legal designation of land, have no organization, and their lines are fixed permanently by the original survey which in the case of Cherokee Georgia occurred in 1832. In both respects they differ from militia districts, which correspond to the townships of various other states and represent the ultimate unit of government in Georgia, except for the incorporated towns; and whose boundaries may be changed by local election and legislative act.

Although provision was made in the act creating the original Cherokee County that the justices of the inferior court should

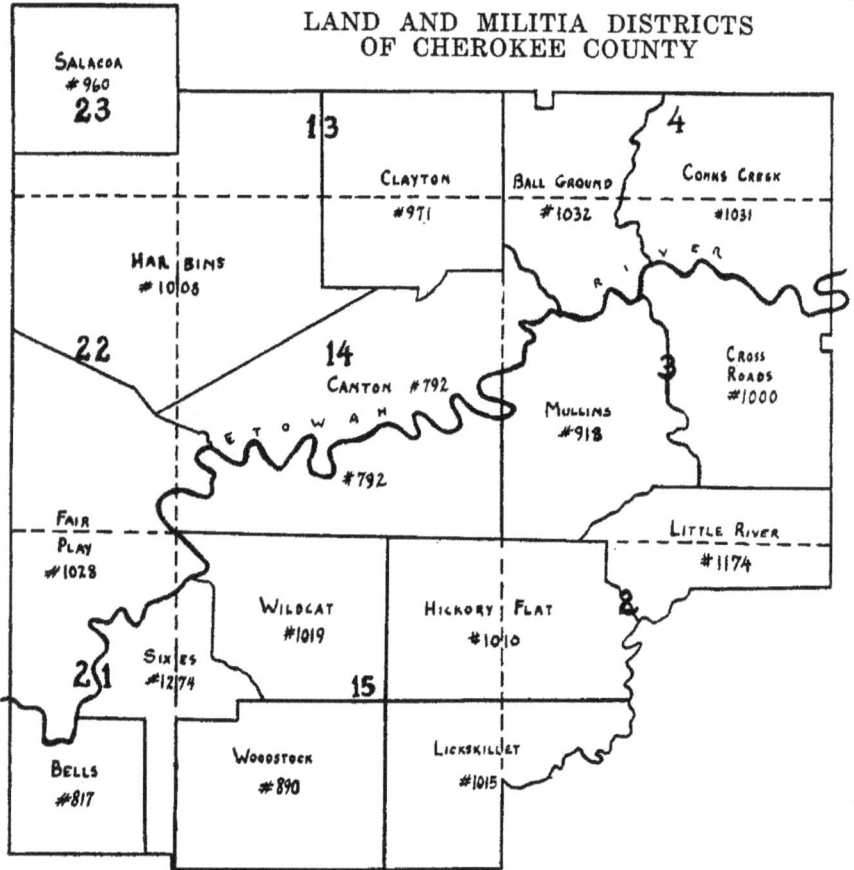

LAND AND MILITIA DISTRICTS
OF CHEROKEE COUNTY

Dotted lines and large numbers show land districts (all in Section 2) of the present Cherokee County. Solid lines represent the boundaries of the militia districts named and numbered.

lay out "captain's districts" (militia districts) as soon as practicable, there seems to be no record that any such districts were legalized until 1833, after the original county was divided up. In that year the legislature passed an act approving the militia districts of Cherokee County as laid out by the justices, and in the following year another act provided for new districts. This latter act was repealed in 1840, but again declared in force in 1858, at which time the district lines made since 1840 were also legalized.*

The militia districts of Georgia date from a time soon after the War of 1812, when the necessity became apparent for a standing army quickly available in emergency. Each county was divided, by statute, into "Georgia militia districts," and the able-bodied men resident in each district were organized into a military company by a captain, who was duly elected by the district. "Musters" of companies and of larger military groups were held five or six times a year. For several decades the militia flourished bravely. Its chief service to the state occurred during the difficulties arising with the Creek and Cherokee Indians.

The militia system lasted until the Civil War period, but for a number of years before that time Georgia's "standing army" had degenerated, in most localities, into a standing joke. Many humorous incidents are told of the old "musters" of this later period, when drilling was likely to be held up for an hour or two while some of the privates finished a game of horse-shoes or attended to some other urgent personal business. No two soldiers ever dressed alike or bore the same kind of weapons, at one of these affairs, and their movements in the drill usually showed a similar discrepancy.

Although militia districts no longer serve any military purpose, they still retain the civil functions allowed to them by the original statute. In addition, they serve as a useful subdivision of the county in the operations of various state departments, such as the bureaus of health and agriculture; in the taking of the census; and in the holding of elections. The latter is today probably the most important purpose served by the militia district. Besides corresponding in every case with election districts, the militia divisions also correspond in some cases with school districts.

The civil officers of a militia district consist of a justice of the peace and a notary public, who have, among their official capacities, the power to try a limited variety of court cases; and a "lawful constable" (L. C.), who contains police powers.

---

*Acts, Georgia, 1833, p. 95; 1840, p. 52; 1851, p. 161.

"Court day" in the militia districts used to be a more or less lively occasion in Cherokee County, with generally several imported lawyers pleading in criminal and civil cases before the local justices, and a generous sprinkling of citizens out to enjoy the ceremonies. In more recent years, however, the judicial powers of these local courts have been exercised in increasingly fewer cases.

CHAPTER V

SETTLEMENT AND ORGANIZATION

I N THE year 1832 there occurred a great many things of importance to this history. The first election of Cherokee County officers was held; the first court of the county sat; the survey of Indian territory was finished and the Gold Lottery of 1832 begun; and the original county was divided up—to list a few of these events.

Overflowing into the following year were: the first court and first election of officers of the *present* Cherokee County; the designation of Etowah (now Canton) as county seat, and its incorporation; and a steady influx, started the year before, of settlers from lower Georgia and adjoining states who had drawn fortunately in the Gold Lottery.

The division of the original county has already been discussed, but the other events will be taken up in this chapter.

How did the settlers of Cherokee County obtain their lands? This interesting question seems not to have been fully explained by the historians, and the following account is as full and accurate as it has been possible to make it.

Lotteries and Land Grants

An explanation of the lottery system of distributing new territory is first in order. According to Brooks,* the Oconee River is the boundary line between two systems of land distribution. Lands to the east of that river were granted by the "head rights" system, under which the head of a family was given two hundred acres, plus fifty for each dependent, and was allowed to choose his own tract. Since the immigrants naturally chose the best lands, the head rights system resulted in sparse settlement, uncertainty as to land lines, and, sometimes, collusion in fraud or speculation.

"Dissatisfaction with this system became so widespread that when the new cession [of Indian lands in 1802] was obtained, the

*History of Georgia, R. P. Brooks, p. 185.

33

legislature bestirred itself to invent a new system. In 1802 an act was passed establishing a 'Land Lottery.' This institution does not appear to have been used in other states. The act provided that all new lands and all subsequent lands to be acquired from the Indians should be surveyed at public expense and divided into small lots of uniform size. Each lot was then given a number, and a map of the whole was deposited in the surveyor-general's office. Slips of paper with numbers representing the lots were placed with many blank slips in a box and people were allowed, under certain restrictions, to draw for lots. The Land Lottery system proved much more satisfactory than the older system."*

A further description of land-lottery procedure is given by Dr. Knight:† "As set forth in the act, those entitled to draw were: 'All free white males, 21 years of age or over, who had been residents of the state for twelve months.' These were entitled to draw once. 'But every white male person having a wife, with one child or more under age; all widows having children under age; and all families of orphans under age, were entitled to draw twice.' To prevent improper manipulation, lists were carefully drawn in each county by legal officers. These were then sent to the governor, who ordered a drawing to be held under the supervision of five managers. Some inevitably drew blanks. To those who were fortunate, grants were issued, each bearing the governor's signature, attested by the great seal of the state, which was stamped on a wax pendant and attached to the deed by means of a ribbon. Within twelve months after receiving his grant, each person was required to pay into the treasury a nominal sum of $4 for every one hundred acres of land contained in his lot; and on failure to comply with this requirement, he forfeited his titles to the land deeded."

All of Cherokee Georgia is supposed, and by some stated, to have been apportioned by the lottery system; but that this was the case is very doubtful. To begin with, there were *two* lotteries of the lands contained in the original Cherokee County: a fact that has been rather shy about occupying its place in Georgia his-

---

*History of Georgia, R. P. Brooks, p. 185.
†Georgia and Georgians, Lucian Lamar Knight, p. 451.

tory. The first one, which was called the "Gold Lottery," began after the survey was completed in 1832, and drawing continued until May of the following year. The second lottery started on January 1, 1838, and lasted only three or four months. It was called the "Cherokee Land Lottery," or simply the "Land Lottery." Although a good many original grants of land in Cherokee Georgia were made by the state in the interval between these two lotteries—a fact leading to the mistaken conclusion that there was only one lottery, a continuous one—it is indicated that accessions of original land during that interval were by individual state grants obtained without any preliminary drawing.

In the division of the Cherokee lands into lots for distribution to settlers, the influence of the gold-fever then current was illustrated in an interesting way. The land districts in the southeastern part of the territory, all of which were thought to contain gold, were laid off into lots of only forty acres apiece, while the remaining districts, in the northwest part, were laid off into lots of one hundred and sixty acres apiece. The lot lines, which of course remain the same today, show that the forty-acre or "gold lots"— as they were called—roughly lie in what has since been verified by geologists as the gold belt of Georgia. In 1832 these "gold lots" were considered very valuable—and indeed several of them did reward their owners handsomely—therefore they were made only one-fourth as large as the lots outside the gold belt.

The proportion in which the original Cherokee County was divided into gold-bearing and non-gold-bearing districts holds true, incidentally, of the present smaller Cherokee County, the map of which shows forty-acre lots in the southeast half and one-hundred-and-sixty-acre lots in the northwest.

As indicated by its name, the Gold Lottery of 1832 (and 1833) disposed of the "gold lots." It is known that several of the one-hundred-and-sixty-acre lots located in the present Cherokee County were granted before May of 1833, but whether they were drawn in the Gold Lottery or not is a question. At any rate, the great majority of the larger lots were not drawn until 1838.*

---

*A very rare old book, **Cherokee Land Lottery,** compiled by James F. Smith in 1838 and giving the names of fortunate drawers and numbers of the lots drawn in the lottery of that year, shows this statement to be true.

The lottery system may have been a vast improvement over the head rights system, but it did not by any means insure that the fortunate drawers would be the actual settlers. As it turned out, they often sold their rights to persons who had previously settled on the land involved, and never even came to North Georgia. Also, in many cases, absent owners lost their lots by making incorrect tax returns, not knowing of the act of 1832 dividing Cherokee County.

For these reasons, the state documents pertaining to original land grants are of doubtful value in ascertaining the names of actual settlers. And since no grants at all were made prior to 1832, such records could not in any event show who the first settlers were. Other sources, however, supply this information in part.

Early Settlers of Cherokee County

A list of the first settlers of Cherokee County (the county as cut off in 1832) is given by White,* an excellent authority on this period. His list includes persons known to have been in the section several years before the first county records were opened; and is given here in full: "Daniel H. Bird, John P. Brooke, John Wagner, Gen. Eli McConnell, John McConnell, John B. Garrison, R. F. Daniel, James Daniel, William Grisham, John Epperson, Washington Lumpkin, Henry Dobb, Charles Christian, John Maddox, Thomas Johnston, William Greene, Samuel Tate, Peter Kuykendall, John P. Winn, James S. Dyer, Martin Evans, John M. Chambers, James Donaldson, Merrick Ford, E. Putnam, T. Chamlee, M. Chamlee, S. Rucker, James Dorris, David Rusk, John Hunt, Sen. John Leonard, William May, William Key, James Maddox, B. Bailey, John Mullins, John Pugh, John Henson, John Wheeler, Henry Wheeler, P. C. Boger, E. Dyer, and others."

The jury lists given in the older court records of Cherokee County contain the names of many early settlers. The first grand jury, which met in March of 1832, of course represented the original Cherokee County and not the one cut off from it in De-

---

*Historical Collections of Georgia, Rev. George White.

cember of that year, but their names are given here, especially since those members who did reside in what became the new Cherokee were all prominent in the affairs of their section. The entire jury: James Hemphill, John Dawson, James Cantril, Franklin Daniel, Green B. Durham, Robert Fowler, John Jack, Reuben Sams, John P. Brooke, Charles Haynes, George. Baber, Noble Timmons, John S. Holcomb, Leroy Hammond, Samuel Means, William H. Ray, Hubbard Baskin, William Smith, William Lay.

Jurors for the first term of court in 1833, held in February, had been chosen at the second term of 1832, held in September, before the original county was divided. This jury never met, since many of its members did not live in the new Cherokee.

The second term of court in 1833, held in August, therefore furnishes us with the first list of jurors drawn exclusively from residents of the new Cherokee County. Nearly a hundred names were drawn by the inferior court justices sitting in May of that year, as grand and petit jurors for the August term; and although only about half of them were called on actually to serve, all their names are given here, as those of early residents of Cherokee County:

Archibald Bradford, Squire Herren, James Chambers, Ferdinand Bailey, E. I. Maddox, Martin Evans, Ignatius A. Few, Lewis Winn, Stephen Harvey, John B. Garrison, Moses Perkins, Noble Timmons, A. C. Avery, Elias Putnam, James Willson, Henry Maddox, Jesse J. Leonard, Tilman Chamlee, John M. Chambers, John P. Winn, William Lay, William Lawless, G. R. Glenn, John Waites, Emanuel Corbin, Valentine H. Cain, Peter C. Boger, John Cannon, John Daniel, Wiley King, George Brock, John G. Maddox, Wiley Hammett, John Nix, Felix Moss, Larkin A. Ragsdale, Jabez J. Holcombe, Samuel Nelson, Aaron Moore, Hardy Moss, I. E. Brock, Seaborn Jones, William Priest, Rhea Paxton, John Timmons, Jonathan J. Johnson, James Couch, Joseph Bradford, John Blake, Jesse Stancil, John Nix, John Linley, Adam Barnett, Joel Leathers, George A. Bolch, William Aaron, Joseph Cagle, Seaborn Maddox, L. Peak, Lewis S. Langston, Joel Chandler, Martin Chamlee, Phillip McIntyre, Amos Chaffin, G. H. Trout, Ed Maddox, E. Dyer, James Fetze, George Cox, Surry Eaton, William Kinningham, William Nix, James Neilor, William Tate, F. M. Lumpkin,

Edward Mims, R. C. Blythe, R. F. Fowler, N. McInear, N. Moore, Albert A. Winn, John Lindley.

Among the very earliest settlers of what is now Cherokee County should be mentioned the names of John Epperson, John and Noble Timmons, Henry and Thomas H. Holcomb, John B. Garrison, R. Frank Daniel, and Eli McConnell. There were doubtless others as early as they, but no evidence of any earlier bona fide

R. F. ("UNCLE FRANK") DANIEL, one of the first white men to come to what is now Cherokee County. Mr. Daniel took a leading part in county affairs for many years. (See also chapter on Canton.)

settlers has come to the attention of the author, at least. The three last-named men came to the section in the middle 'twenties of the last century; the Holcombs were well established on Conn's Creek before 1830; the Timmonses are said to have arrived about 1820; and John Epperson, who at first had no white neighbors whatsoever, traded with the Indians at a post he had established, according to family records, as early as 1815. Garrison, Daniel, and McConnell were all very active in early county affairs, and the impression prevailed in the earliest newspapers published in the county that they had been the three first settlers. There is, of course, room for some little controversy on a point so difficult to establish. It is safe to say, however, that any person who had settled by 1830 in what is now Cherokee County was one of a very small and select group.

The first white child born in what later became Cherokee County is thought to have been a son of John B. Garrison; the first white girl, a daughter of Eli McConnell.

Regarding the nature of the people who came to Cherokee County in the early days, it may be inferred from the names already given in this chapter that most of them were of English, Irish, Scotch, Dutch, or German stock, with English predominating. The settlers were hardy, adventurous, generally honest and law-abiding, and generally unburdened with means. Very few of them, at least, carried any large amount of wealth with them on the wagon-trek to their new homes; although it did not take some long to exhibit an enterprise and ability that gave them a financial edge on their fellows. But the land did not appeal to persons who desired to live in ease and luxury; nor was there much in the rugged new country, at that time, to attract capital.

Most of the settlers came from North and South Carolina: if not directly, at least via Wilkes, Franklin, Hall, or some other older county of northeast Georgia. Tennessee, South Georgia, and Virginia were the other main sources of Cherokee County's early population.

The principal period of immigration to the county was during and immediately after the Gold Lottery of 1832-3. Prior to that the chief stimulus to population had been the gold rush in 1830, though few permanent settlers were attracted at that time.

Before 1830 there were very few white persons living in the section. But there is no question that before 1832, when the state made its first grant to lands in the Cherokee country, a number of settlers had substantial holdings in what is now Cherokee County, and it is interesting to consider the resourcefulness which these men must have exercised in obtaining lands from, and in living among, a tribe of Indians which regarded their ancestral legacy as jealously as the Cherokees did.

More will be said about the settlers in the next chapter. In the meanwhile, the county having been created and partially populated, the next step was to organize it, in accordance with the instructions of the legislature and the desires of the voters.

The County Is Organized

When Cherokee County was created in 1831 from Carroll, De-Kalb, Gwinnett, Hall, and Habersham, several officers of the latter counties lived in Cherokee. There was, for instance, William Grisham, of Canton, who was clerk of the superior court of De-Kalb County. Such officers continued in their positions, but it was necessary to elect a whole set of officers for Cherokee County. This was done, according to the provisions of the creating act, on February 6, 1832, the house of Ambrose Harnage being used as a poll. Elected as the first officers of Cherokee County were the following:

Oliver Strickland, clerk of the superior court; William T. Williamson, clerk of the inferior court; John Jolly, sheriff; Jesse Watkins, surveyor; Asa Keith, coroner; John McConnell, John Witcher, Robert Obarr, Genubath Winn, and Henry Holcombe, justices of the inferior court.

It might be mentioned at this place that the inferior court was then, and until the creation of the ordinary's court in 1850, the governing body of the county. Its five justices administered most of the official business and included in their province the duties of the present ordinary and commissioner of roads and revenues.

The whereabouts of Harnageville, which seems in 1832 to have been composed chiefly of the house of Ambrose Harnage mentioned in the creating act, has been the subject of considerable speculation on the part of those persons who have taken an interest in the proceedings of the first court of Cherokee County. Harnage must have been a man of some importance in the county, and his name appears several times in the early court records as plaintiff in civil actions for property; but nothing definite

40

has been found out concerning this individual himself; it is even claimed that he may have been a well-to-do Indian, which appears unlikely. And the location of his house, which is more important here, has been credited to several different localities, including a site near Ball Ground on the old Harnage Road between that place and Waleska.

The true location of Harnageville, however, was not in the present Cherokee County. According to Colonel Sam Tate, of Tate, Ga., "the first civil court held in Cherokee County was held where the Tate homestead is. I do not know just when the postoffice was established at Harnageville, but when I was a boy it was called Harnageville and letters came to this office. I think it was abandoned soon after the Civil War."

At Harnageville, then, the first and only election of officers for the original Cherokee County, and the first of its two superior court sessions, were held.

The county being divided up into ten counties by the act of December 3, 1832, however, another site became necessary for the official transaction of business of the new Cherokee, and this site was designated in the dividing act as the house of John Lay, who lived in or near Canton (then Etowah). On Monday, March 4, 1833, as also provided, there was held at this place an election of the first officers of the new Cherokee County, the following men being chosen:

Reuben F. Daniel, clerk of the superior court; William Grisham, clerk of the inferior court; John P. Brooke, sheriff; Roger Green, surveyor; Lewis S. Langston, coroner; John McConnell, Randal McDonald, Elias Putnam, William Lay, and William Baker, justices of the inferior court.

Also at the house of John Lay was held the first superior court of the new Cherokee County, which was now in the Cherokee Judicial Circuit. The first courts of the county are of interest from several standpoints, and will be described briefly here.

Early Courts of Cherokee County

"On the 26th day," says the first court-minutes book, "it being the fourth Monday in March, in the year 1832," the first superior court was "begun and holden at the house of Ambrose Harnage,

41

now Harnageville, in and for the county of Cherokee, in the state of Georgia." Present were the Hon. Charles Daugherty, judge of the Western Circuit; T. H. Tripp, the solicitor-general of that circuit; and the grand jury aforementioned. The first case was against one John Agnew, who was accused of illegally residing in the Cherokee nation, but who was exonerated and discharged by the grand jury. The second prisoner fared worse: against Jeremiah Towns the jury found a true bill for the same offense. Third case: true bill against Thomas Cantril, Enoch Earley, and George Downs for the crime of hog-stealing. And so on. Of the nine cases to come before the grand jury at this term, four were for illegal residence and one for digging gold.* Business disposed of, the jury made this illuminating recommendation:

"We, the grand jury chosen and sworn for the county of Cherokee, [cannot?] refrain from the expression of our gratification of the organization of the country into a county. We know that new as our county is, the extent of its territory and the few persons yet citizens of it, much cannot be done towards the improvement and repair of our roads. We would, however, recommend the inferior court to use all the means within their control to have this object attended to. The roads in the county have been so long neglected that they are in some places almost impassable, and knowing as we do that during the ensuing summer an unusual number of persons will visit the country, we would respectfully urge the inferior court to the accomplishment of a purpose so interesting to the whole community.

"The opinion of his Honor, Judge Daugherty, upon the right of the state to organize the country into a county and to legislate for it and over it merits our approbation."

Court was again held in September of the same year (1832), with the same judge and solicitor present, and still under the auspices of the original county, but this time at "Cherokee Courthouse," which was the name Canton was known by before its incorporation as "Etowah" in 1833. A number of cases were tried at this term, but the most unusual penalty inflicted was upon John and Butler Kimball, who were convicted of horse-stealing and sentenced to receive thirty-nine lashes apiece on their bare backs

---

*See page 19.

on each of three successive days, and thereupon to remain in jail for twenty days longer. To recuperate, probably. At this term of court the grand jury made another interesting recommendation, in which they expressed their views on the great John C. Calhoun's doctrine of Nullification, which was then causing a historical uproar. The recommendation:

"We cannot refrain from an expression of opinion in regard to the excitement created of late in regard to the 'Tariff Act' and its effects. We view the law passed at the last session of Congress as a small concession [sic] of the odious and unequal mode of taxation. We also view said act as unjust in principle and unequal in its operation; yet cannot but express our decided disapprobation of a resort to Nullification, secession, or any other mode that will in the least have a tendency to weaken the bonds of our Federal Union."

To these sentiments nineteen of the grand jurors subscribed, but the other three recorded an exception "because"—they put it— "we think the Tariff extremely oppressive [sic], unjust, and unconstitutional, and because we prefer the interests, rights, and freedom of the state of Georgia to all other interests whatsoever." Perhaps these three men lived to see their views shared by the entire state some thirty years later.

The next term of court was held in February, 1833, also "at Cherokee Courthouse." Present were the Hon. John W. Hooper, first judge of the Cherokee Circuit, and William Ezzard, solicitor-general. This was the first court held in the new Cherokee County, and because the jurors had been chosen from the original Cherokee they could not serve. No cases, consequently, were tried, and all cases pending were transferred to the fall term of court in the counties "to which they properly belonged."

At the August term, 1833, the status of the current courthouse is exposed in the grand jury presentments, and it is brought out also that no townsite, by which is probably meant no county site, has yet been determined on:

"We, the grand jurors, have . . . . a just cause of regret, to-wit: the situation of our courthouse—if, indeed, we might be said to have any. We therefore recommend to our inferior court, and hope they will without further delay proceed to select a site for the town . . . . with due regard to the beauty, eligibility, and central situation for the public buildings of our county."

With a characteristic interest in politics, this jury also could not "refrain from an expression of opinion" on the actions of the convention then altering the constitution of Georgia; this opinion having its inevitable dissenters. State and national affairs seem to have been a vital concern of the people of Cherokee County even then.

Scattered throughout the court records up to 1838 are many cases involving Indians and reflecting the relations between white residents of the county and their red-skinned neighbors. In no case does there appear to have been any official persecution of the Indians, although a case is shown where two white men who had beaten an Indian to death were acquitted through technicalities arising in the trial. In general, justice seems to have been done regardless of the color of the prisoner at the bar; witness the following from the grand jury presentments at the September term, 1834:

"We perceive with the highest approbation the determination of the people to protect the Indians in the enjoyment of their rights secured to them by law; the vicious white man is taught to know that injuries done them are not to escape unpunished, that prosecutions will be preferred and urged against all persons that do wrong to the Indians, either in person or property."

Some of the queer names by which the Indians went are given in these early records: Lucy Doghead, Colesnake, Six-killer, Tagah Togah alias Stand alias Standing-Up, Tutleracthee alias Toothache alias Two-Brick, Young Panther, Mushstick, Sparrowhawk, Bark Chicken, and Log-in-the-Water—who, according to an old newspaper item, was "floated off to the penitentiary" for horse-stealing, and was the first person ever to receive that penalty in Cherokee County. Some of the crimes imputed to the others were assault and battery, hog-stealing, simple larceny, and gold-digging.

These early records also show that the old legal standbys, John Doe and Richard Roe, had not yet come into prominence, their equivalents then being Caleb Goodtitle and Peter Holdfast.

The early "courthouse" mentioned in the record as being

near the house of John Lay in Canton was the site of all the early superior court sessions except the first one. This location had been designated by the legislature, in the dividing act of 1832, as the place at which the first official affairs of the new Cherokee County should take place; but power lay with the justices of the inferior court thereafter to fix the county seat at some other location, if they chose to do so.

Establishment of the County Seat

The justices decided, however, to let Etowah remain the county seat, and the town received its corporation charter in 1833. There

JUDGE JOSEPH DONALDSON, early settler and business leader of Cherokee County, and one of the founders of Canton. (See also chapter on Canton.)

were several reasons why Etowah was selected: it was in the center of that part of the county which was most thickly settled; it was currently being used for official gatherings; and its citizens showed a bit more enterprise in working for the coveted honor. Some discussion was had of moving the county seat permanently to Hickory Flat, another thriving settlement seven miles to the east, but the influence of Etowah's pioneer settlers, including William Grisham and Judge Joseph Donaldson, prevailed in the matter.

Etowah was incorporated by an act of the legislature approved December 24, 1833.* This act also confirmed the selection of Etowah as the county seat of Cherokee County, and named the town's first commissioners. They were William Grisham, Howell Cobb, Philip Croft, M. J. Camden, and James Burns.

It is not generally known that Canton, besides having had the early name of "Etowah," was also known at one time as "Cherokee Courthouse." Records of the federal postoffice department show, however, that the first postoffice the town ever had was established July 18, 1832, under the name of "Cherokee Courthouse, Ga." The early court records of the county also mention "Cherokee Courthouse," naming it as the place at which the second court session (September, 1832) and the five sessions after that were held; but on account of the nature of the name no one seems to have guessed that its use here referred to a town and not to a building.

William Grisham was appointed first postmaster of the town, and when the legislature changed the name of Etowah to "Canton" Mr. Grisham sent the new name in to the postoffice department and the name of his postoffice was likewise changed. The town became "Canton" on December 18, 1834;† the postoffice, on January 13, 1835.

Mr. Grisham and Judge Donaldson were probably the two earliest residents of Canton, and both had engaged in the silk industry on coming there in about 1831. It is not known which of these two settlers the new name originated with, but from their activities in the silk industry it is clear that "Canton" was adopted from the name of China's great silk-center, and not from Switzerland's famous "cantons"—the latter having been said, with perhaps a little exaggeration, to resemble Cherokee County in topography, and therefore suggested as the source of Canton's name.

---

*Acts, Georgia, 1833, p. 331.
†Acts, Georgia, 1834, p. 263.

It is interesting to reflect that Canton's first industry was the same as Georgia's first. The colonists of Oglethorpe, who had come to England to settle on the seacoast of Georgia a century before the founding of Canton, had brought with them visions of riches to be attained from silk culture, for which the climate of Georgia was then thought to be singularly fitted. The failure of their project was not conclusive enough to prove to certain later Georgians, including Donaldson and Grisham, that the silk industry could not be made to pay. Whether these two found it profitable is not recorded, and their venture does not seem to have lasted many years, but they both became quite prosperous in a community where wealth was not the rule.

Judge Donaldson is said to have brought 100,000 silkworms to Cherokee County. Mr. Grisham also had a large number, and he conducted his business in one little room where he raised the silkworms and spun silk cloth. Both men put out many mulberry trees for the nurture of their silkworms; there are still a number of mulberry trees in Canton.

When the question of permanently locating the county seat was being argued by the justices, these two men and another early settler of Canton, John P. Brooke, are said to have contributed practically the whole townsite to influence the choice of their village. Unfortunately the county records are incomplete for this period, but it is assumed that town lots were surveyed and platted from the land donated by Brooke, Donaldson, and Grisham; and that the county received at least a part of the proceeds from their sale. William K. McCanless, a pioneer wheelwright and builder of the section, is stated to have been the first person to buy a town lot in Canton.

CHAPTER VI

PIONEER LIFE

WHEN the Census of 1840 was taken, Cherokee County had 5895 inhabitants, as compared to its present 20,000. No earlier figures are available than those of 1840, because at the preceding census date the county had not yet been created. It seems unlikely, however, that the county as cut off in 1832 contained more than a few hundred inhabitants, the immigration resulting from the Gold Lottery having then only got under way.

It is safe to assume that a considerable part of these 5895 persons did not come to the county until late in the decade preceding 1840; with a jump in population following the Land Lottery of 1838. The additional fact that Canton never contained as many as two hundred people until as late as 1870—according to census figures—confirms the idea that the early population of the county was very sparse and scattering, and almost entirely of an agricultural character.

The settlers who flowed into the county in a steady stream after drawing began in the Gold Lottery of 1832 came usually in wagons or ox-carts piled high with their families and worldly goods. Poor roads—sometimes the total lack of roads—made the new homesteads hard to reach, and hard to leave. Neighbors were well-spaced. Communication and social life were limited mostly to log-raisings, religious gatherings, and rare trips to "town." For the most part pioneer life was an unceasing round of labor for both men and women, with these bright spots all the more welcome and eventful for the contrast.

Various accounts and records, handed down from one generation to the next and illustrating the daily affairs of the county's earliest inhabitants, have been drawn from for this chapter; and particularly well does one such—an autobiography—illuminate the ordinary events of life in the first days of the county. Of both historical and human interest is the diary once kept by Nathaniel

Frank Reinhardt, who was born in Hall County in 1833, the year before his father, Lewis W. Reinhardt, moved to Cherokee County as one of the first settlers in the northwestern part.

This diary, which was started when its author was past 20 and stopped when he went to the Civil War, in which he was killed at 28, includes reminiscences of his early childhood in a period ending with the close of Cherokee's first ten years as a county. Clear and formal in the style of eighty years ago, this autobiographical portion is presented here with but slight revision. The topics covered are many: home life, early agriculture and industry, the old "field school," Indians, social customs. In fact, no more inclusive or authoritative account of Cherokee County pioneer life has been found.

Quoting:

Diary of Nathaniel Reinhardt

"My father, Lewis W. Reinhardt, was born in North Carolina in 1804. His parents moved to McMinn County, Tenn., and from there he moved to Hall County, Ga., in 1830, where he married my mother. My father is of German descent, his grandparents on both sides having emigrated from Germany to the United States prior to the Revolutionary War. My mother is of English descent. Her parents were of the Missionary Baptist faith; my father's parents were of the Methodist Episcopal faith.

"When I was thirteen months old, we moved in the early part of the year 1834 from Hall County to Cherokee County, my father having bought lands there. And he built a mill on Shoal Creek and opened a small farm. At this time this portion of the county was settled almost entirely by the Cherokee Indians for whom Father ground their grain, and bartered also with them to some extent.

"In 1835—Father bought a tract of land on the old Pinelog Road some two miles from his mill-place, improved it and in the latter part of 1835 he moved on it. On our arrival at the new location I remember seeing a pine-knot fire in the yard and several persons standing around it, some Indians I think and some white persons. My memory dates from this day.

"1836—Father remained on the place he settled on the Pinelog Road and raised a crop. He also kept a house of entertainment for travelers, and kept stock. I remember seeing a large yoke of oxen he owned; they were unusually large and gentle. We called one Bully and the other Brandy. A large snake attacked a hen with some chicks, and devoured the chicks, but was killed and the next day his carcass was devoured by a large sow we had.

"One day passing by the Tom Foekiller old Indian cabin on the hill above where Father lived, I saw a number of green gourd vines growing at the back of the chimney, and some of them running up the chimney. I remember also being at Grandfather's in the fall while the chestnuts were ripe, and some of us crossed over the mill-pond in a canoe and gathered chestnuts.

"1837—I was at a large Indian ball and dance, in the fall season of the year, at the Indian ball-ground near Father's. The exercise opened by a game of ball in which the men participated actively. The trees over and around the playground were filled with women, children and spectators looking on.

"1838—A very cold winter. An immense number of pigeons flocked over the woods; the Indians killed great numbers of them. Father brought me a bowl of Indian connahaynee of which I was quite fond.

"In the spring many U. S. soldiers were passing through the country for the purpose of collecting and removing the Cherokee Indians to the West. They frequently lodged at night at Father's. Saw old Foekiller, a neighbor Indian, just after he had been arrested by the soldiers, who were carrying him to Fort Buffington. They treated him rather cruelly, which excited my sympathies very much in his favor. The old Indian desired to see father, who solicited better treatment in his behalf. He left all his keys with Father. After the Indians had been collected by the soldiers and started on their final march off, they came near our house the first night and camped. I caught the measles from a soldier who lodged with us that night, and had them severely. One of the neighbors came and stayed the night at Father's from fear of injury by the Indians.

"1839—Father kept a house of entertainment, took in a great many travelers and stockdrovers. This year he made a large crop of corn. He hired a great·deal of work done on his farm. He kept up some fish traps on Shoal Creek in which he caught a good many fish. In the summer, however, the watercourses nearly all dried up, and many had to beat their corn into meal for bread.

"1840—Father rented out the most of his corn land; one tenant was taken in, boarded and everything found him, and he paid two-thirds as rent. In the summer some of us took a 'coon hunt. I enjoyed the sport of the chase finely.

"In the latter part of the summer I was sent to school, for the first time, being then over 7 years old. I had almost learned the alphabet at home. Mr. Morrison was the teacher—a tolerably clever "old field-teacher." Some of the older pupils stole my provisions and made sport of me, yet I liked to attend school very much. I went there about a month, then in the latter part of the year I went to school to Grandfather Reinhardt at the old Methodist Church, for about two months.

"With our two dogs Maje and Lion I hunted squirrels and rabbits; I was also successful in trapping birds—caught several partridges and frequently a jay. I also fished some, though not allowed to venture much about the creeks.

"1841—Father sold his plantation for $1000 with the expectation of leaving the county, and made a short trip or two to suit himself in some other place, but finally bought land again in, the same neighborhood and settled on it in March. The place he bought had no cleared land on it. He commenced clearing off a field in April, enclosed about sixteen acres, and cleared and cultivated the most of it. Father worked exceedingly hard and hired but little. After the crops were laid by he commenced work on a dwelling-house, stables and barn.

"During this year I went to school some to Mr. Morrison, not more than two months, I think. I studied spelling and reading. Spelled in Webster's Elementary Spelling book, and I suppose if I read any, read in it also. I advanced very well.

"I was frequently sent to mill on horseback with small bags, or turns, of grain. Generally rode a sorrel horse called Jim, and went to William Ward's mill, the same old mill first built by Father on Shoal Creek. My parents were tolerably tight over me, but not too much so by any means. Went to Canton for the first time I remember ever to have been in a town. I rode behind Father on horseback. He took me into the courthouse and seated me on the steps. A lawyer was pleading whom I supposed to be a preacher preaching, this being the only kind of public speaking I had any idea of. During this summer Father bought me some dozen marbles, with which I was highly delighted. I was not usually furnished by the purchase of many playthings. Our yellow dog Maje was bitten by a large rattlesnake and died within a few minutes.

"1842—Father employed much of his time in building his stables, barn, and dwelling-house. He planted out a number of fruit trees. He had several house-raisings, etc., having commenced a large log double-house. During this year I aided daily in the crop, the spring gathering, piling and burning limbs and brush, chopping sprouts, hoeing corn, and did nearly all of our milling on horseback. Father cultivated ten or twelve acres in corn, it being all the field he had cleared off.

"I went to school to Mr. Morrison a few weeks in the summer and fall. Father bought me a reading-book, the New York reader No. 2, and I was quite proud of it, having previously learned to read easy pieces in my spelling-book.

"During the summer I met with the misfortune to chop off one of my small toes with the ax, while chopping wood early one morning before school. It did not come completely off and was banded back toegther, but mortification set in and the only remedy was to cut it off entirely. This Mother did with a razor, she generally doing the little necessary jobs of this character.

"Helped Father saw off shingle blocks, while a man whom he had hired rived and shaved the shingles. We moved in our new house in the fall. It was covered, the floor over the back half of one room was laid, and some large flat rocks were set up for the back and jams of the wooden chimney only just begun; in this condition we entered the house and finished it afterwards."

Indians as Neighbors

This old diary brings out at first hand not only the remembered high spots of a boy's existence back in those early days but also many of the details that wove themselves into the pattern of adult pioneer life. Building houses from hand-hewn logs, clearing up virgin timber-lands and laboriously tilling the new soil, living without what would now be utter necessities, and taking hardship and effort "in one's stride"—all these things went along with existence in every part of the county. Another concomitant of life which present generations would view with distaste, not to say alarm, was dwelling among Indian neighbors.

The Reinhardts differed in no important respect from many other good families of Cherokee County, and a further incident or two from their records will be given here, as typical of life among the surroundings described, before other representative families are taken up.

Lewis W. Reinhardt, head of his "clan," was a large, well-built, energetic man of German stock, intensely religious—not an uncommon quality in those days—and described by one of his friends as a "typical shouting Methodist." He founded Reinhardt Chapel, the first Methodist church in the upper part of Cherokee County, shortly after settling in Harbin's District in 1834. The town of Waleska is now situated on his old homestead.

Mr. Reinhardt was greatly respected by the Indians for his fairness and generosity to them, and in token of their esteem was called by them "Suli,"—meaning "buzzard"—on account of the gray suit he usually wore. On one occasion this suit prevented his death at the hands of an Indian friend, who was waiting in "Suli's" cabin, at dusk, for another Indian whom he was "after" and whom he expected to call at the cabin for sanctuary. Instead of the enemy, "Suli" himself walked in, and was astonished to see a huge Indian swing a tomahawk at his head, then suddenly deflect its course to avoid hitting him. After explaining the situation and telling "Suli" that his gray suit was all that had saved him in the dim light, the big red fellow completely broke down over the near mishap to his white friend.

At another time, all of Mr. Reinhardt's red neighbors for miles around joined in a chase after another Indian who had come into the community from outside and stolen a "shoat" from "Suli." Only at the insistence of the latter did the Cherokees, after catching the hostile Indian, relent to such a mild punishment as driving him out of the country.

Some of the Cherokees themselves, however, were dishonest and stole property from the settlers. Lost Town, it is said, was so called because the Indians there stole cattle, and when a cow wandered into their hands it was a lost cow. Once a group of Indian women entered Mr. Reinhardt's home, apparently for a social visit, and engaged Mrs. Reinhardt in neighborly conversation. Presently they offered to swap her a dozen eggs for some salt, which they prized very highly. The good housewife felt the warmth of the eggs with suspicion, but good-naturedly gave her

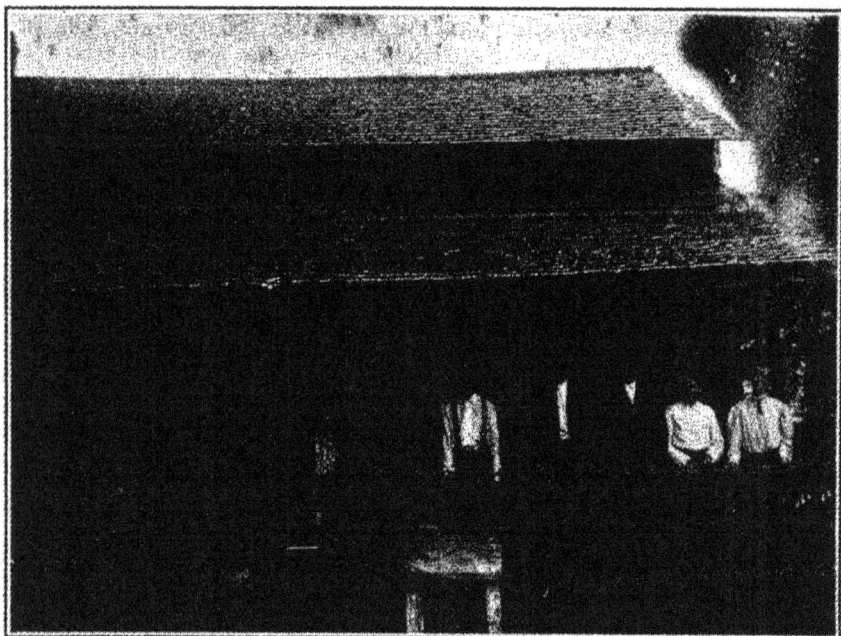

HOME OF AN EARLY SETTLER. This old house, built in 1837 by Joseph Knox, early pioneer and first school-teacher of Cherokee County, was one of the first homes built in Sutallee District. It is still standing.

callers some salt and sent them away, and then placed the eggs back under her own setting hen, whence they had a moment before been taken.

Drinking Indians were a menace to settlers, but a sober Indian usually accompanied his boisterous mates to restrain their behavior. On one night such a party called to see "Suli," and on being rather tremblingly informed by his wife that he was away, one of the drunks broke a chair and started in to "raise cain." He was promptly thrown out of the house into a puddle of mud by two perfectly sober warriors. The carousing, yelling crowd then melted away into the night without further harm to the house or its occupant.

Regarding the relations in general between the early settlers and Indians, it may be said that the attitude of the whites was in the main one of tolerance and even protectiveness, while the Indians were quick to show their appreciation of any kindness done them. Although the Cherokees occasionally made raids and even perpetrated massacres in white settlements in some parts of their territory, there is no record of any such hostile displays in Cherokee County, where the two races seem to have got along very well together.

An example of Indian hospitality was the big kettle of "connahaynee" (hominy soup) which stood outside the door of every Indian cabin and from which white visitors at any hour were urged to partake. In spite of the manifest friendliness of the invitation, white persons often found it necessary to overcome a natural squeamishness at the sight of dogs eating from the same kettle or at the general dirtiness of Indian cookery, before they were able to return the compliment by eating some of the connahaynee; but that dish was said to be quite palatable when such sanitary shortcomings were disregarded.

Probably the simple curiosity of the Indians was at times of as much annoyance to the settlers as their small depredations. It is said that John Epperson, already mentioned as one of the first white men in Cherokee Georgia, used to tell how he sat in suspense at night while Indians crept around his cabin, peering in the windows and generally taking in everything. Their suspicions and curiosity finally subsiding, however, the Indians became good friends to the Epperson family.

In all parts of the county barter and trade was carried on between whites and Indians, and a number of the settlers had grist mills at which the Indians had their corn ground into meal. Reinhardt's old mill and the one operated by Jeremiah Field, another prominent settler who lived east of Canton, were two of these; and there were many others.

Pioneer Diversions

The everyday occupations of the settlers—mostly farming, sometimes milling, storekeeping, building—were occasionally broken into by such social and religious events as corn-shuckings, log-raisings (or log-rollings), quiltings (for ladies only), camp-meetings, ordinary church-meetings, and old-fashioned singing-parties and spelling-bees. These various events, more or less common to every pioneer section, have long been famous in song and story, and need little description here.

Most practical of all were the first three named, and yet possibly the most hilarious. When a settler had cut and trimmed the logs for his new house, he issued invitations to all the neighbors to come out and help him raise the logs to their intended positions in the structure; and the enjoyment that was derived from the proceedings only went to prove that work for sport's sake is not work at all. The spirit of competition in strength and prowess that moved the perspiring men, not unaided by admiring glances from the fair spectators and the thought of the country supper waiting, were more than adequate reward for expended effort.

Corn-huskings were especially popular with the younger set, the female members of which probably watched for the red ears with as great fascination as did their escorts. Those husking-bees got a tremendous amount of corn husked.

Early schools and churches also played an important part in the lives of the pioneers, but discussion of these is reserved for subsequent chapters.

CHAPTER VII

SOME EARLY EVENTS IN THE COUNTY

THE decade that followed the removal of the Indians in 1838 witnessed few extraordinary events in the history of Cherokee County, but it was a period of steady growth and consistent progress. Population doubled. From 5895 persons in 1840, it jumped to 12,800 by 1850—the largest increase, both numerically and in per cent, shown by any census period in the history of the county.

The Land Lottery of 1838, held in the early part of that year and already described, contributed to the population of Cherokee before 1840; but the increase after that was due not to artificial stimulation but to the inherent advantages of the county. Roads were beginning to open up, law and order had become well established, the land had shown its productiveness, and the undesirable aborigine had been removed to the West.

How this latter fact was finally accomplished is Georgia history—though not history according to the cynic's definition of that word as "facts agreed upon," for there is arguing among the historians as to the manner in which the removal was carried out. A brief review of the historical facts, and then some of the incidents of the removal as it affected Cherokee County:

Removal of the Indians

On December 29, 1835, at the Indian capital New Echota, a treaty was entered into between the Cherokees and the United States that ended Georgia's long struggle to dispossess the Indians, and named the terms of their removal from the state.

Court records of Cherokee County show that for several years prior to the signing of this final treaty, sentiment in the county had favored some measure that, while dealing fairly with the Indians, would insure their early removal from Georgia. Failure to obtain such relief, according to a grand jury presentment in

1834, "would fix down upon us a people whose language and manners differ with those of the whites, and who, should they remain a few years longer, will be doomed to drag out a miserable existence." Another presentment spoke of the "state of degradation to which the Indians are fast approaching," referring to the habit they were rapidly acquiring of addiction to drunkenness. White men's liquor has always played havoc with the Indians of North America, and the Cherokees were no exception.

The terms of the Treaty of 1835, while not entirely meeting the demands of the Cherokees, were eminently fair. The tribe ceded to the United States all their remaining lands east of the Mississippi River, for which they were to receive the sum of five million dollars and a large tract of land in the government reservation west of the Mississippi. The Indians were to be paid also for their houses and other improvements left behind, and the government was in addition to bear the expense of their transportation and to furnish them supplies for one year after their arrival in what is now Oklahoma. The treaty was to go into effect two years after its ratification.

Although representing the bargaining of years, this treaty was not recognized by the majority of Cherokees, who claimed it was signed by unauthorized persons without the approval of the tribe. They did not believe it would be carried out, and when the appointed time for their exodus, early in the year 1838, came around, they merely went about their affairs as usual with seemingly no intention of leaving their homes. It therefore became necessary for the United States to invoke the aid of military force.

On May 24, 1838, Georgia officially took possession of her Cherokee territory. General Winfield Scott, of the United States Army, was detailed to remove the Indians. His troops were assisted by two Georgia regiments under the command of General Charles Floyd. In small detachments, the army scoured the territory and made prisoners of one Indian family after another, gathering them into camps. By June 3, 1838, the work was finished and the Indians were taken to Ross' Landing, in Tennessee, from which point they started for Indian Territory, under military escort. More than 15,000 Cherokees were so removed.

It is with regard to the behavior of the soldiers and the treatment accorded the Indians during this removal that accounts differ. For instance:

"No one has ever complained of the manner in which the work was performed. Through the good disposition of the army and the provident arrangements of its commander, less injury was done by accidents or mistakes than could reasonably be expected."*

"The history of this Cherokee removal may well exceed in weight of grief and pathos any other passage in American annals. . . . . Troops were sent to search out with rifle and bayonet every small cabin hidden away in the coves or by the sides of the mountain streams, to seize and bring in as prisoners all the occupants, however or wherever they might be found. Families at dinner were startled by the sudden gleam of bayonets in the doorway and rose up to be driven with blows and oaths along the weary miles of trail that led to the stockade. Men were seized in their fields or going along the road, women were taken from their wheels and children from their play. In many cases, on turning for one last look as they crossed the ridge, they saw their homes in flames, fired by the lawless rabble that followed on the heels of the soldiers to loot and pillage. . . . . 'The Cherokee removal was the cruelest work I ever saw.' "†

The statements made here by Mooney are contradicted by an actual witness;‡ on the other hand, at least two eminent Georgia historians have characterized the removal by such epithets as "a blot on the fair name of the state which time will not efface."

The weight of testimony seems to show that the Cherokees were treated with unnecessary harshness while being collected and transported. This side of the matter is borne out by the autobiography of Nathaniel Reinhardt already quoted. It is further told that Lewis Reinhardt, who was only one of the many citizens of Cherokee County that acted as friends and advisors of the Indians during the removal, was called on by Chief Foekiller to decide for him and his hundred warriors whether or not to surrender at Fort

---

*Historical Collections of Georgia, Rev. George White.
†Myths of the Cherokee, James Mooney, p. 130.
‡My Autobiography, Rev. W. J. Cotter, p. 48.

Buffington. On being advised to do so, they gave themselves up peacefully. A few days later, Mr. Reinhardt saw the old chief being cruelly beaten by the soldiers for returning late to camp after a leave of absence; and humanely interfered in the prisoner's behalf.

Fort Buffington was the location in Cherokee County where the Indians were collected. There were some half-dozen forts in all used for this purpose in Cherokee Georgia during the removal. Fort Buffington is about six miles east of Canton.

At Sixes, also in Cherokee County, a company of soldiers was detailed at the time, but it is not thought that any Indians were held at that place. Sixes was then an Indian village of some size.

Another of the settlers of the county who helped the Indians to move in 1838 was Captain Nehemiah Garrison, a native Virginian, who then lived near Fort Buffington. The records show that he put in a claim for timber damaged by the soldiers there during the removal, on which his son, John B. Garrison, fifty years later realized the sum of $750 from the federal government. This timber is thought to have been that from which the stockade was built. This old log structure stood for many years, and is remembered by a number of the older residents of Cherokee County.

A few of the Cherokees succeeded in escaping from the soldiers by hiding out in the mountains, living on roots and berries until the searchers had left. These homeless Indians drifted into North and South Carolina, and their descendants are today provided for by the government at a reservation near Murphy, N. C., where several hundred Cherokees now reside. But most of the Indians were removed to the "land of the setting sun," as they called it; and in the West they have prospered fairly and, in large measure, have adapted themselves to the ways of the white man's civilization.

A Famous Criminal Case

It was just before the Indians were removed from the state that a white man named Thomas Copeland was shot to death near Canton. Because it was thought at first that the Indians had revolted and were responsible for the act, great excitement prevailed for a while and many citizens of the county feared for their lives, until it was found that a white man named Joseph Wofford was the actual murderer. Wofford was tried and sentenced to death at the February term, 1839, of the superior court of Cherokee County, and was hanged in Canton on April 12, 1839.

Because of the fact that this was the first legal execution ever to take place in the "Cherokee purchase," the Wofford case has achieved more or less note, and a brief account of it is given here, drawn from the court records and old newspapers of the county.*

The murder took place on the night of April 19, 1837, at Copeland's home. His wife testified that the family were all sitting around the fireplace after supper, when a shot was fired in at the door by an unknown person, wounding Copeland in the neck. He lived eight days; unable to speak, he wrote, at first, that he thought a strange Indian had fired the shot, but later that he thought Wofford had done it.

The cabin in which Copeland lived was situated on the south bank of the Etowah River close to where the Canton bridge now stands. This old cabin remained a landmark until 1883, and was torn down in March of that year.

Some of the other witnesses at the trial were R. Frank Daniel, Daniel H. Byrd, George Brock, Joseph Knox, Langston Worley, Larkin Ragsdale, and William Grisham. The evidence was wholly circumstantial. It was brought out that there had been bad blood between Wofford and Copeland; that they had engaged in a fight three years earlier following which Wofford, though allegedly the instigator, had caused the arrest of Copeland; that the grand jury had returned the case a "malicious prosecution" and taxed Wofford with the cost. Several of the witnesses swore that the prisoner had made threats against Copeland's life previous to the killing. Unable to establish an alibi, Wofford was convicted of murder in the first degree.

The foreman of the jury which heard this case was Samuel Tate. John K. Moore was one of the other members. The judge was Turner H. Tripp; the solicitor-general, William Ezzard. The

---

*Cherokee Advance, June 16, 1881, and March 6, 1884.

murdered man had been in charge of the ferry which Judge Joseph Donaldson operated before he built the first bridge at Canton; and Judge Donaldson prosecuted the case.

Wofford languished in the county jail for about two months after the trial, and was then taken out and hanged by due process of law at a place described by a newspaper of 1884 as "the hollow back of where John Bell now lives and where two or three hollows come together."

The penalty imposed on Wofford attaches a certain amount of interest to the following paragraph from the presentments of a previous grand jury of Cherokee County, that of September, 1835:

"There is one part of the penal code which we most earnestly submit for the consideration of the next legislature, which is the confinement in the penitentiary for life for the crime of murder where the evidence is wholly circumstantial, as we believe that most murders are committed where nothing but corroborating circumstances can be had to convict the murderer. We are of the opinion that all murders should stand upon the same footing, whether they be made to appear by positive or circumstantial evidence."

It was forty-five years before anybody else was hanged in Cherokee County.

The War with Mexico

In the year 1846 an opportunity came to hardy men of Cherokee to take up arms against an enemy of the United States with the outbreak of the War with Mexico. To the small quota of soldiers required of Georgia by the government, Cherokee County promptly contributed a company of ninety-one men,* called the "Canton Volunteers" and led by Captain Kennedy Gramling. Organized and equipped, this company left Canton on June 5, 1846, for the Texan front, as a part of the famous Georgia Regiment of Volunteers.

The adventurous character of the early settlers is nowhere shown better than in the enlistment of this company of volunteers, many of whom were men with families. No common enemy threat-

---

*Names of these men will be found in the Appendix.

ened their homes; they stood to gain little but glory by their efforts in battle; patriotism and love of adventure furnished their only incentives for thus putting their lives in danger. Most of these men were sons and grandsons of soldiers who had fought under Washington and Greene, although unfortunately their cause was not like Washington's — the cause of human liberty.

The "Canton Volunteers" were absent from home for twelve months. Only about sixty returned; the rest died of wounds or disease or were killed in battle.

As soon as the War with Mexico was ended, gold was discovered in California, and a rush began to the gold fields of the west that dwarfed into comparative insignificance even the Georgia Gold Rush of 1829. Here again, the sons of the Cherokee County pioneers went into action, and the county lost no inconsiderable number of its young men temporarily, and some of them permanently.

The 'forty-niners who went from Cherokee had their choice of several routes, all filled with danger and hardships. Some of them went to the Mississippi and trekked from there another two thousand miles across the plains and through the gaps of the Rockies. Others went to the Gulf ports and took ship-passage around Cape Horn; still others stopped at Panama, crossed the Isthmus, and waited for north-sailing ships to pass.

Among the "California men" from Cherokee County were two Carpenter brothers, Lewis and Adam, of Waleska; Clark McClean and E. Lenning, of Jasper (which was at that time a part of Cherokee); and three Timmons brothers, Cicero, Gus, and Jasper, also from that part of the county. There were many others. All the men named completed the perilous journey to California, made their "stake," and returned home to their families and friends in Cherokee.

Salacoa Settled

A final event to be recorded of the period with which this chapter deals was the settlement of the "Little Virginia" colony in Salacoa Valley.

In the year 1850 a number of Virginia families emigrated to Georgia and settled in the northwestern corner of Cherokee County.

These settlers were from the tobacco-growing regions of Virginia, and came from the best family stock of that state. Most of them brought along slaves.

Among the families who formed the "Colony" were the Mahans, Pattons, Fergusons, Hutchersons, Taylors, Jeffersons, and Richardsons. Other names also were represented.

Traveling in wagons, they arrived in the Valley during the fall of the year, and had to build log cabins at once against the on-coming winter. The following spring they began to plant what was then a new crop for Cherokee County — tobacco. Although Salacoa has always lived up to its name—which is Indian for "big corn," tobacco formed the principal money crop of the early Sala-coans. They prospered, and some of them erected factories at which leaf tobacco was pressed into plugs. A considerable industry sprang up in the main product of Salacoa, of which more will be said later in this book.

The tobacco industry has almost disappeared from Salacoa today, but the descendants of the original families, and the fertility of their Valley, remain. No part of the county has furnished men of more ability or note, among its products being Thomas Hutcherson, son of the settler, whose death ended a career that would undoubtedly have included the holding of the highest honors in the state.

CHAPTER VIII

THE WAR BETWEEN THE STATES

THE *Cherokee Mountaineer* published at Canton on October 19, 1861, carried this advertisement, among others: "J. M. Hutson, Tailor. Will execute all work in his line, either common or military styles."

And this masthead:

"For President (of the C. S. A.), Hon. Jeff Davis, of Mississippi; for Vice President, Hon. Alexander H. Stephens, of Georgia; for the Capital of the Confederate States of America, Atlanta, Ga."

Presumably Mr. Hutson, the tailor, found plenty at that time to keep him busy, particularly with his military patterns. Whole companies of Confederate soldiers were then being outfitted by wealthy men of Cherokee County. "Military styles" had dominated men's fashions, by October, 1861.

The *Mountaineer's* platform was but slightly less successful than Mr. Hutson's advertisement; it mispredicted only the site of the Confederate capital, which was soon after established at Richmond, Va.

In this early paper was much war news from outside, relating chiefly to operations between Northern and Southern forces in Missouri, on the lower Mississippi, and around Richmond. Also pertinent to the newly begun war were announcements wherein candidates for Cherokee County offices pledged that if elected they would give half their "commissions" to the cause of the South. A sense of nearness to the conflict pervaded the paper. Reflecting the remarkable morale of the period, the *Mountaineer* nevertheless gave its readers no room to doubt that a great and destructive war was beginning to take on grim reality.

Even by then Cherokee County had sent hundreds of men out to training-camps and the battlefields.

The Soldiers from Cherokee

The first company to respond to the Confederate call in 1861 was the "Brown Riflemen," a hundred strong, under the command of Captain Thomas E. Dickerson. This company was named in honor of Governor Joseph E. Brown, formerly of Canton. Soon other companies, commanded respectively by Captains J. J. A. Sharp, Jesse M. Burtz, Posey Daniel, A. M. Reinhardt, W. B. C. Puckett, John McConnell, Joseph McConnell, N. J. Perkins, John B. Garrison, A. J. Covington, Thomas J. Edwards, and others, were called into the field, having been made up, in most instances, by the captains. In addition, a large number of men joined the regulars.

Some twenty-three companies of Confederate soldiers enlisted from Cherokee County; official records show that in all, the county furnished over 1,800 men to the Southern cause— more than any neighboring county and considerably over an eighth of its own total population at that time! Most of the men were first sent for drilling to Camp McDonald, at Big Shanty (now Kennesaw), important training-camp of upper Georgia.

Of these twenty-three companies, ten were in the Georgia Infantry, one in the Georgia Cavalry, eleven in the Cherokee Legion (infantry and cavalry), and one in Phillips' Legion (cavalry). (Note: In the Appendix of this book are given the names, by companies, of all Confederate soldiers who went to the war from Cherokee County, and the names of officers *at enlistment*.)

Fancifully depicting the spirit of the men were such company names as "Cherokee Rangers," "Cherokee Lincoln Killers," "Cherokee Repellers," "Cherokee Revengers," "Salacoa Silver Grays," and "Cherokee Stone Walls." It was by these names, instead of by the official but more prosaic letters, that each man spoke of his own company, and many a Confederate veteran has since identified himself by them.

To review the many distinguished and brilliant records made by Cherokee Countians in the War Between the States would fill several books the size of this one. More somber was the county's death roll; hundreds of men were slain and hundreds more were maimed for life. Never has the South recovered from the loss of fine family stock that occurred in the

A YOUNG "REB" FROM CHEROKEE. Jacob Chapman, a Confederate soldier who lived near Holly Springs, armed and accoutred for action.

murderous Civil War, and nowhere was that loss more deeply felt than in Cherokee County.

Cherokee's Part in the War

In considering the part of Cherokee County in the Civil War, it should be remembered that many people in the hills of North Georgia were in sympathy with the Union; it is not remarkable, therefore, that in the upper part of Cherokee there were good citizens who conscientiously disagreed with Confederate principles. When a nation can be so bitterly divided, why not a county? The hill people did not own slaves, were not in sympathy with those who did, and refused in some instances to cooperate with the South.

Cherokee as a whole went for secession, being influenced by the strong leadership of the governor it had just furnished to Georgia, Joseph E. Brown, and by the strong Southern feeling in and south of Canton. Many people of Mountain Georgia, though, rallied to the old flag, and enlisted with the forces of the Union. To the north, Pickens County practically seceded from Georgia, raising the stars and stripes on the court-

WILLIS TRUMAN KNOX, son of the noted pioneer Joseph Knox, was one of the Confederate soldiers from Cherokee County who served with distinction in the War Between the States.

house at Jasper, where they waved until after surrender. Even Cherokee furnished a few soldiers to the Union.

The upper Cherokee men who did enlist in the Southern army, however, made soldiers worthy of any opposition. In Scotland, every family grows into a clan, whose leader is called ''The,'' as ''The'' McGregor, etc. In the hill section of Georgia, before the war broke out, each family had its ''The''—a capable young or middle-aged man who was its acknowledged leader. At secession's call to arms, scores of "The's" rushed to the training-camps, and Camp McDonald drilled many "The's" of Cherokee County.

Of great assistance to the Confederacy in its struggle against the richer North were wealthy men of Cherokee County who showed their devotion to the cause of the South by furnishing arms and uniforms to Southern troops. Among such men were Judge Joseph Donaldson, a pioneer developer of Canton, who, being too old to go to the war himself, outfitted in 1861 an entire company of soldiers and sent them; and Jesse M. Burtz, Captain of Co. F, 28th Georgia, who spent a large part of his personal fortune on arms and equipment for 156 men. Others followed these examples as they were able, and a great many of the soldiers furnished their own outfits.

A curious fact was that Cherokee, which furnished more soldiers to the South than nearly any other county of "Indian Georgia," was never the site of a major Civil War battle, or even of an important skirmish. About the only military event of importance that took place in the county was the burning of Canton by a detachment of Sherman's men, in 1864; and even this was not in the nature of regular warfare but was a measure adopted in retaliation for guerilla warfare on Sherman's forces, as will be seen.

But though the war did not come to Cherokee County until the closing months, and then with less destructiveness than many other localities suffered, Cherokee at the very outset of the struggle made a contribution to the Confederacy—aside from her 1,800 soldiers—as notable as any part of the South was able to make. That contribution was Joseph E. Brown, war governor of Georgia.

"Joe Brown and His Little Red Bull"

One chilly November day in 1840, a poor, illiterate farmer boy of Union County, Ga., left home on foot to go 125 miles to school. Seventeen years later, at the age of 36, he was inaugurated governor of Georgia.

Joseph Emerson Brown attained such honors as Georgia has given to few of its sons. Four times governor of the state, judge of its supreme court, and senator to Congress, the "farmer boy of Gaddistown" is recognized as one of the greatest Georgians of all time.

A popular story has it that he was plowing a "little red bull" on his farm near Canton when notified of his first nomination for governor. This story, we are assured by the later historians, is purely mythical, like the tale of little George and his hatchet. The facts are, we learn, that he was not plowing at all but was binding wheat to help out his hired men in the rush season; and that the bull belongs to the Gaddistown period of his life. Nevertheless the legend, being as picturesque as the man, persists.

Governor Brown's connection with Cherokee County began when he was 23 years old, just out of Calhoun Academy, an old school located in Anderson District, S. C. He appeared in Canton on foot one day in 1844 and put up at R. Frank Daniel's old hostelry. Soon he obtained his first office of public trust, teacher of Canton Academy. Stimulating the attendance there from six to sixty in the first year, he made five or six hundred dollars and paid for his education.

While teaching this school young Joe Brown was studying law at night, and in September, 1845, without ever having read a day in a lawyer's office, he was admitted to the Canton bar by the Hon. Augustus R. Wright, then presiding. With the aid of Dr. John W. Lewis, he borrowed enough money to go to Yale Law School, where he graduated in 1846. Next year he married Miss Elizabeth Grisham, of Canton.

After 1849, when he was elected state senator from Cherokee and Cobb, honors began to come thick and fast to Joe Brown. In 1852 he was a presidential elector; in 1855 he was elected judge of the superior courts of the Blue Ridge District. While in this office he was nominated for governor by the state democratic convention, without knowing that his name was being used. His election followed in October, 1856. He was reelected in 1859, 1861, and 1863.

It is said of Governor Brown that he never lost a race for office. When first nominated for governor, he was practically

BROWN PARK, CANTON. MONUMENT TO WORLD WAR AND CONFEDERATE VETERANS AT RIGHT. RESIDENCE OF P. W. JONES AT LEFT.

unknown. "Who is Joe Brown?" became the question of the hour. Some of his women neighbors in Canton made a quilt for him, which his opponents referred to as "Joe Brown's crazy-quilt," also not forgetting the "little red bull" or the obscurity of the "Gaddistown clodhopper." This attempted belittlement only endeared him to the hearts of the common people, who rallied to his support.

Governor Brown's executive record has been minutely recorded by others—he belonged to a state, not a county. Because he used his tremendous influence, during the historical Secessionist Convention of 1861, to swing Georgia from the Union when Georgia was the pivotal state of the Confederacy, he has been accused by some with having precipitated the Civil War; but none has ever questioned the sincerity of his motives or the expediency of his actions during the struggle which ensued.

It was Brown's gift for expediency that caused him to fall into popular disfavor when the war and his last term as governor were over. Foreseeing the era of the carpetbaggers, he aligned himself with the Republican party and advocated submission to the victorious North. That he was able by this policy to make reconstruction easier for Georgia is now undisputed, but his about-face won him much contemporary bitterness. It was some time until Georgia saw that Brown had been right, and then it took him back to its bosom and made him its chief justice for twelve years and a United States senator for ten years, after which he declined further honors.

Successful in business as well as politics, Governor Brown —or Senator Brown, as he was of course later called—accumulated much property and became a man of considerable wealth. He was a liberal supporter of his church, the Baptist, and of other worthy causes. Part of his property was in Cherokee County—a fine river-bottom farm near Canton and a beautiful home on the Etowah, where he spent some time each year during his latter days. On November 30, 1894, he died in Atlanta, full of years and honors.

Some Unique History

Since no battle of importance between Confederate and Union forces occurred in Cherokee County, it is of especial interest to note the "unofficial" warfare which took place in the county.

Most worrisome to Northern forces of all guerilla fighters in North Georgia was probably a small band of Southern sympathizers, called "McCollum's Scouts," which originated and operated chiefly in Cherokee County during the closing year of the war, and which had the aim of thwarting Sherman's foraging squads and the local Union sympathizers.

Not outlaws, McCollum's Scouts were a peculiar product of the local environment with its mixed sentiment. To some persons they seemed murderous fiends; to others they were avenging angels. It depended on the viewpoint.

References to guerilla bands in the Civil War are plentiful; authoritative accounts of them are not; and it is fortunate that details concerning McCollum's Scouts have been preserved by a distinguished son of Cherokee and a historian at heart, Judge William A. Covington, now of Atlanta. Of his own family's connection with this phase of the war, Judge Covington relates that two of his distant kinsmen were executed by Scouts; on the other hand, his grandfather's farm on Shoal Creek near Waleska was raided by Sherman's foragers, who "made a clean sweep of everything they could carry off, my grandfather being old and his sons being with Lee in Virginia."

The following full account of McCollum's Scouts, published here for the first time and of definite historical importance, is from the pen of Judge Covington:

McCollum's Scouts

"There were many people in the hill country of Cherokee, Bartow, and Gordon Counties who, while having sympathies with one side or the other, did not join either the Union or Confederate armies and who resisted conscription.

"As Sherman, in the spring of 1864, pressed forward from Chattanooga to Atlanta, he passed down through Bartow

County, fought a battle at Resaca, and remained for a while at Cartersville. When Hood interrupted his supply trains from Chattanooga, he proceeded to reinforce his supplies by foraging on the country, for thirty or forty miles from Cartersville. Naturally, he did not want to forage on Union sympathizers, and so his wagons were directed by such sympathizers to the farms of the Confederates, many of whom were fighting Grant at Richmond.

"Just as naturally, about this time a group of Southern sympathizers organized themselves in Cherokee County, making it their business to fire into Sherman's forage wagons and guards from the adjacent woods, and to lay waste the homes and property of the Union sympathizers. This band of unofficial 'home guards' was called 'McCollum's Scouts,' after Ben McCollum, their leader and organizer. McCollum was a man of good connections who should have been in Lee's army, with the twenty-five or thirty young men under him. In justice to McCollum, it is very likely that he was the Benjamin F. McCollum who the records show enlisted in the 'Brown Riflemen' and was soon discharged for being under age; but he was three years older in 1864.

"The Scouts established a rendezvous, or camp, about three miles up the river from Canton, on the same side of the river. In no time they were carrying terror into the hearts of the Unionists in upper Cherokee and Pickens. When they would catch one of the guides who had directed any of Sherman's wagons, he was given short shrift. One favorite way of disposing of them was to go up into Pickens and upper Cherokee and capture some of this class, bring them down to the river near the camp, and shoot them off their horses into the running stream.

"They went up into Dawson County, and captured two young men who were at home on sick furloughs, carrying them swiftly across the boundary line to a place near the present town of Tate. The sisters and mother of the men came wailing after them but found them dead, at the ends of ropes.

"They caught a man named Jim Pitts, over about Salacoa, put him on a horse and swept through Beasley's Gap, in Pine

Log, into Bartow County, where they impressed into service a local Methodist preacher named Fletcher Weems, and along with him a convenient rope. Stopping on the road up near Adairsville, they told Weems to do his stuff quickly, which he did. Jim Pitts preserved the indomitable courage of his race, consistently cursing them all and singular except the preacher, till they choked down the soul they could not conquer.

"Martin Chumler lived at the southern end of Pine Log, near the Wolf Pen. He was active in assisting Sherman's folks, and helped them to 'gather' corn for many an absent Southern soldier. Finally he heard of a young Confederate soldier from Texas, who was lying ill at the home of someone who lived just east of Moore's Mill, on the lower part of Shoal Creek. Chumler went over and arrested the boy and started to Cartersville with him, making him walk as much as he could. Over near the White place, in Lost Town, they were intercepted in a lane by McCollum's Scouts, and Chumler fled across the country. When the Scouts learned the situation from the weeping boy, they followed and captured Chumler, and strung him up. The news got out, but in those terrible times men were afraid to do any act that seemed to show them in sympathy with such a corpse. Finally a lot of women, many of whose homes Chumler had assisted to plunder, accompanied by a single man whose sons were at Petersburg, went and dug a grave just under the swaying corpse, and let it down to its rest.

"Three men—one from Cherokee and two from Pickens— were particularly active for Sherman's foragers. Finally, just after they had left a detachment of troops near Ball Ground and were riding together toward Sharptop, in Cherokee, they were captured by McCollum while their horses were drinking at a ford on Sharp Mountain Creek. The captors did not know whom they had caught, but finding a roster of the detachment of Sherman's troops on the person of the Cherokee County man, and being dissatisfied with his explanation of having found it in the road, they proceeded with the three men in the direction of Jasper. On making inquiry of an aged blacksmith there, they satisfied themselves that the two Pickens men were harmless and discharged them—more readily, perhaps, because they were Masons, as was, incidentally, McCollum. But the Cherokee County suspect they held, and soon they found that he had been with a foraging squad of Sherman's when it came to Jasper the week before. So the Scouts carried him to the top of a mountain, where the Jasper road crosses it about three miles south of Jasper, hung him up, and fired two pistol balls through his heart. Next day, the dead man's wife came walking across the hills from Cherokee, borrowed a little cart and a yearling from a nearby farmer, and with the assistance of the farmer's son went up to the mountain top and cut down the corpse; then she drove away alone with her dead, back to Cherokee.

"Sherman struck back at the Scouts in characteristic fashion. One afternoon he sent out a burning squad which reduced to ashes every residence on the public road from Cartersville to Ford's Furnace, near the Bartow-Cherokee line. On another day he telegraphed to his military commander at Chattanooga, in substance as follows:

" 'Send a detachment of troops down to Calhoun, in Gordon County, and have them burn every house in it. If they manage to have to kill a few men I shall not be displeased. I am tired of the shooting into my night trains at that town.'

"This order was possibly countermanded, since Calhoun was not burned.

"Otherwise as to Canton. Directly in reprisal for the acts of McCollum's Scouts, Canton was almost completely destroyed by fire in a single day. One of the houses left standing was the residence later occupied by Dr. John M. Turk and now the site of the office of The Georgia Marble Finishing Works. The man of this house was with Lee in Virginia, but a neighbor woman excitedly snatched from the walls his framed certificate of membership in the local lodge of third-degree Masons, and running into the yard met the squad that was entering to fire this residence. She happened to thrust the certificate under the nose of an officer who was also a member of that order, and he instantly reassured her and set a guard over the premises to prevent harm thereto.

"There is no way of knowing the names of the Scouts. It is known that his two chief lieutenants went west after the close of the war. McCollum was admitted to the Canton bar, and published a series of articles in the *Cherokee Advance*, in justification of his acts during the war. Presently he removed to Hampton, Ga., and hung out his shingle. One day, crossing the decision of the local policeman in some way, he was informed flatly that if he repeated the act he would be killed. The next day he repeated the act, and the policeman promptly hunted him up, beat him to the draw, and emptied right into his front the contents of a double-barreled shotgun, of the effects of which McCollum, then and there lay down and died. It was murder, of course; but the policeman went off to the West for a while and nothing was ever done about it. 'He that taketh by the sword shall perish by the sword.'"

The Burning of Canton

As above explained, the burning of Canton by Sherman's men late in May, 1864, was at least partially in reprisal for local interference with the Union foragers. "In districts where Sherman's army was not opposed, mills, gins and houses were not to be molested; but they were to be destroyed wherever the march was interrupted."* It seems, therefore, that Canton had McCollum's rashness, as well as Sherman's relentlessness, to blame for the conflagration.

It has been suggested that Sherman ordered Canton burned because it was the old home of Governor Brown. The reprisal theory sounds more reasonable, but either circumstance —or both—may have been responsible.

Available records differ as to the amount of damage done by Sherman's men in Canton. Accounts in different newspapers two or three decades later seemed to agree that only one or two houses were left standing, but since these accounts name several different residences as the "sole survivors," it looks as if the writers were misinformed. Some of the older residents of Canton say that only about half of the town was

---

*History of Georgia, R. P. Brooks, p. 291.

burned, and Mr. George I. Teasley, of Canton, is able to recount at least twenty-five buildings, including four or five stores, that were left standing. In 1860 Canton had only about two hundred inhabitants, so it is likely that there were not more than fifty or sixty houses there before Sherman's men came, and that the extent of the damage done by the soldiers has been somewhat exaggerated.

The method used by Sherman's squad of burners was to fire individual dwellings on every street in Canton, but not to fire a whole section anywhere. Whether they acted on information against the occupants is not known.

It is known, however, that a few of the individual householders were able to prevail on Sherman's men to spare their homes. Judge Covington has already related one such instance, in which a Masonic certificate played a leading role. The old Garrison home, which had been rebuilt from a former Methodist church building, was also preserved intact, through the entreaties of a good woman named, properly enough, Barbara Jamison Garrison; like the more celebrated Barbara who persuaded Stonewall Jackson to spare her country's flag, Mrs. Garrison showed a good deal of courage in protecting what was dear to her.

In this connection it is interesting to note the humanizing influence of Masonry during the Civil War. Many stories are told of courtesies exchanged by Masons of opposing armies.* In the northeast part of the county, near Ophir, a squad of Sherman's foragers entered the home of Martin Roberts, father of the late Henry W. Roberts. One of the men found some Masonic regalia, including an apron, in one of the dresser

---

*Sherman relates in his Memoirs that, on one occasion he ordered an officer to take his men and clear a section of woods of the Confederates who were occupying it. He listened for the sound of gunfire impatiently, until the officer returned and reported: "General, those woods are full of Masons, and I have a lot of them, too; and they got so close together that they recognized this fact, and so neither side will shoot at the other."

drawers of this house, and presented them to the leader of the squad. The latter, a Mason, ordered his men to stop searching and leave the house.

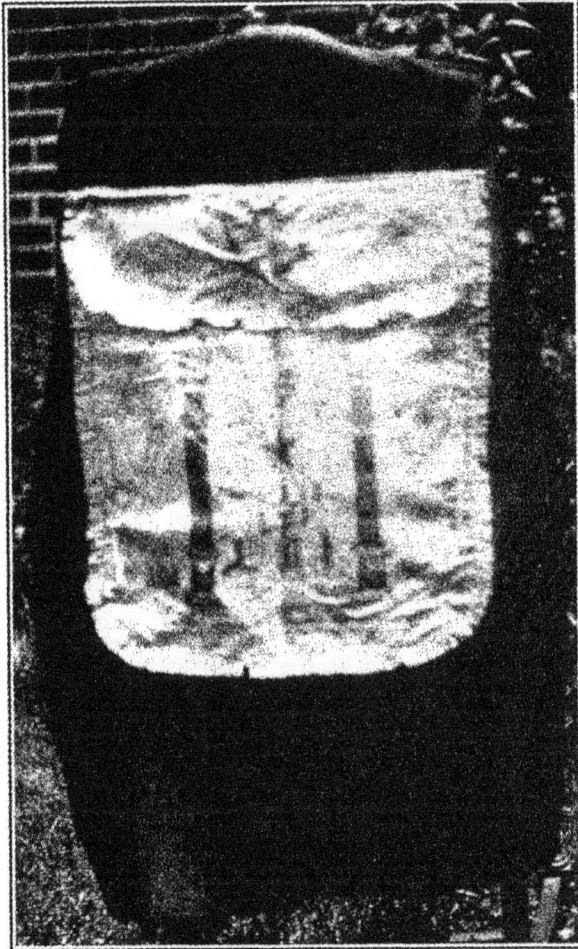

MASONIC REGALIA which saved the home of Martin Roberts, near Ophir, during the Civil War. (See text.)

It must have been just before the burning of Canton that Wilson M. Barton, who had enlisted from Cherokee County in the 43d Georgia, on getting a much-needed furlough walked most of the way from Vicksburg, Miss., to Canton with some important Confederate papers in his possession. Being tired when he reached Canton, he sat down to rest near the well on the left of the old courthouse door, in the center of the town. Mr. Barton saw a squad of Sherman's men approaching, and in a flash he destroyed the papers by throwing them into the town well nearby. The Federals arrested him, but after he gave the Masonic sign he was released.

More than likely the hundred or so Canton citizens who were rendered homeless by Sherman's burners failed to regard the event as a blessing, even on a warm spring day; but it must have hastened civic improvement. Twenty years later the *Atlanta Constitution* reported:

"Canton was destroyed during the war except for one old house(?). Its backwoods atmosphere is now gone, and Canton is a town of new and modern appearance. Most of its buildings are of brick."

Camp Skid Harris

Probably on account of the pressure of reconstruction, it was not until long after the war that any serious attempt was made to bring the Confederate veterans of Cherokee County into a reunion association. On August 31, 1883, about 100 survivors of the 23d Georgia Regiment gathered in Canton, and deciding to make the reunion an annual affair elected their old lieutenant-colonel, John J. A. Sharp, as president.

The 23d had been composed of ten companies from North Georgia—two of them from Cherokee; and all of its 1,500 men had been mustered into service at Camp McDonald on August 31, 1861. This regiment had fought in the historic battles of Yorktown, Seven Pines, Richmond, Antietam, and Manassas, and probably 1,000 of its original number had been killed in the war.

In the next few years reunions of other regiments were held in Cherokee County, and as the number of survivors dwindled these formed what was called the ex-Confederate Association of Cherokee, headed by Captain H. W. Newman, a Canton lawyer who had distinguished himself in the war. In 1890 the state ex-Confederate Association recommended

that the local reunion take the name of one of its former officers, and the *Cherokee Advance* suggested that of the dead
Colonel Skid Harris.

Skidmore Harris' record was, briefly, as follows: A min-
eralogist of note before the war, he had sunk the shaft at Copper Mine Hill near Canton; he entered the war as first lieutenant of the county's first company, the "Brown Riflemen";
was promoted to lieutenant-colonel of the 2d Georgia Regiment
and shortly thereafter to colonel of the 43d Georgia; commanded more men than any other officer from Cherokee County
and was one of the best-loved officers in the army; was killed
at Boker's Creek the day after the siege of Vicksburg, in
May, 1863.

So Camp Skid Harris the association became, and the following were its first officers: Commander, Capt. H. W. Newman; Adjutant, John G. Heard; Chaplain, Rev. W. J. Johnson;
Surgeon, Dr. John M. Turk; Sentinel, W. N. Willson; Treasurer, Capt. Mark S. Paden; Historian, Harrison Black.

For some years Camp Skid Harris flourished, and the veterans gathered annually to revive old scenes and re-fight old
battles. One by one the warriors fell as the years went by.
It has now been sixty-seven years since the war ended, and in
the whole of Dixie no sizable band of Confederate veterans
could be brought together. Cherokee County's you can count
on the fingers of one hand; and soon the story of their memora-
ble struggle can be gleaned only from the pages of history.

CHAPTER IX

THE "HILL PEOPLE"

THE farming regions of northwestern Cherokee County lie in what is known as the "hill section" of Georgia. Foothills of the Blue Ridge chain present a rugged aspect in many parts of upper Cherokee, and the environment has produced a rugged, honest citizenry. From the "Hills" have come some of the most noted men that Cherokee County ever gave to Georgia and the nation.

The hill region of Georgia contains a type of people about whom a great deal has been written, some of it by persons to whom the locality was evidently unfamiliar. There is available, therefore, a considerable quantity of misinformation on the present and past inhabitants of North Georgia.

Particularly have the hill-dwellers of the last century suffered from inaccurate portrayal, arising not so much from lack of observation as from lack of what may be termed "reportorial sympathy."

The folio of sketches presented in this and the following chapter are not open to either charge; and may be accepted as an authentic record of life in the hills of Cherokee County—"the Hills"—during the last century. They are written for this book by Judge William Alonzo Covington (see preceding chapter), who spent his years up to manhood in the northwestern part of Cherokee County, and who knew and understood the people of whom he writes, having been one of them. Unfortunately, no similar historian has come forward for other parts of the county. The writing of these most readable sketches, however, comprises a very real service to the descendants not only of the people involved but of all settlers of North Georgia.

By Judge Covington:

Character of the "Hill Folks"

"The population of the hill sections of North Georgia, after the removal of the Cherokee Indians, was very largely Anglo-Saxon.

Welsh, English, Scotch, Irish, Germans—all these strains were represented among the First Settlers. Slavery was not a popular institution, and there were practically no 'free persons of color.' During the contact with the Cherokees, there was some inter-marriage with that race; but the issue thereof either went West with the Cherokees or failed to persist as a race, when left, owing to inherent constitutional weakness.

"In the hill section of Cherokee, from the earliest settlement, the community idea was highly developed. Just as their ancestors had done a thousand years before along the bleak shores of the North Sea, these pioneers grouped themselves into 'Settlements,' whose motto might well have been 'one for all and all for one.' In those tasks of the individual citizen which transcended his powers, the neighbors were called in to help. For instance, houses and barns were thus erected, corn was shucked, and logs were 'rolled' and burnt from the clearings. When a man wanted to build a house or 'roll logs,' the adult men and stronger boys came to do the heavy work. The married women came along to assist in the cooking of a substantial feast. At the close of the day the 'young folks' put on an old-fashioned dance, to the music of local 'fiddlers.'

"There were whole settlements in which practically no one could read or write. This writer was reared in one such, after the close of the Civil War. His 'Aunt Sis' was the only person in it who could write a letter of correspondence, and she did the letter-writing for the whole community. Mail came once a week by star route from Cartersville, twenty-five miles away. Some families did not get a letter for years, and when a letter did come, it usually meant that some relative who had moved to Arkansas or Texas had died. And so letters were received with a dodgy feeling.

"The young men of this section were bashful to the last degree. It required a year to get up to hand-holding terms with their sweethearts. So, in a great many cases, the smitten young man would go to 'Aunt Sis' and get her to write a letter to his Dulcenea, informing her how she stood with him and setting forth the honor-able nature of his intentions. As soon as this letter was received the young lady would hot-foot it to 'Aunt Sis' to get it read and answered. My aunt knew exactly how to handle the situation, and how to write the answer 'in such cases made and provided.' Thus would be closed the correspondence, and a wedding and a 'houseful of children' would result.

"The original settlers of Cherokee, so far as they belonged to any church at all, were generally Methodists and Baptists. At the end of the War, the hill section especially found itself greatly upset and shaken. Sherman's raiders and guerilla warfare had impoverished the country. At such times people easily become interested in things religious; and when the revival fires which were running through the South struck upper Cherokee, there was instant response, in spite of the wounds of the Civil War and the bitterness developed during its four years. An evangelist who asked to be called 'Davenport' conducted a series of meetings, with the result that hundreds 'turned to the Lord,' became good Methodists, and so continued till the day of their death—and their children after them. Then, one day, a sheriff from somewhere in East Georgia came along looking for 'Brother Davenport' and he passed onwards toward the West. Not exactly ideal 'apostolic succession'—but 'twill do; for did not Balaam the son of Besor utter some of the loftiest things in religious literature?

"In post-bellum days, the Methodists divided on political lines. The *Northern Methodist Advocate,* in the campaign of 1876, had pictures of Hays and Wheeler at the head of its editorial page. And there were divisions among the Baptists — not, however, so much along political lines. Generally the line of cleavage among them was as to doctrinal and polity points, such as instrumental music in the churches, and missionaries and Sunday schools. Then there was the great war between Methodists and Baptists as to the method of baptism.

"There was one thing, however, on which general unity prevailed among all the church people—everywhere dancing and other 'worldly amusements' were banned for church members. The young folk would be gathered into the fold, during the camp-meetings and revivals in 'fodder-pulling time'; and as surely as Christmas approached there would be yieldings to the impulses of the flesh— 'falling from grace,' as we Methodists call it. Lord, how pathetically barren were our lives during the short period of youth, and how cruel it now seems that the preachers consigned the unrepentant dancing girls and boys to endless perdition. Especially for the girls, soon to settle down to the business of tending babies, washing dishes, and milking the cow—for fifty years.

"Public roads were scarce in that section of Cherokee for the first fifty years after the Indians were removed; and two-thirds of the families lived away from such roads, on blind settlement-roads. It is hard to exaggerate the terrible monotony of existence under such conditions, especially for the women. It was necessary for the men to go to mill, to the postoffice, and to the country store, from time to time, thus enabling them to maintain some social contacts; but their wives were forever grinding on in the same endless, changeless routine. Maybe they managed to get out to church services, once a month; and sometimes the mother would take the children and, in sheer desperation, go to stay all day with a neighboring housewife, with whom she could 'talk about' the other 'neighbor-women' to their hearts' content. When a stranger chanced in at night for the purpose of 'spending the night,' the mother and children could hardly keep their hands off him—they wanted to paw on him, like setter pups.

"For these contacts, rare as they were, saved the women from despairing at their loneliness. These and—sometimes—tobacco. One could hear these poor women remark often, 'Terbacker shore is a heap of company.' Even some of the girls 'dipped snuff' on the sly; with their mothers using it more openly or, possibly, chewing plumply like their men. After babies were over, they took the accustomed seat in the chimney-corner and either chewed or smoked a pipe. I think it is different now, and I keep in touch with the 'Hills.' At about 45 'Grandma' shortens her skirts, bobs her hair, and gets a permanent wave.

"Notwithstanding all statements to the contrary, there was a good deal of drinking of intoxicating liquors in this section, during the pre-War period and for a generation afterwards. It is not thought, however, that the legalized sale of liquor was found in Cherokee after the early 'seventies. One Shade LeGrand seems to have run the last 'grocery' in Canton, some time in the early 'seventies. It was in the old days of 'good liquor,' but there lingered a long time the expression: 'As mean as Shade LeGrand's liquor.' The 'grocery' left Cherokee for the reason that the town charters were without authority to regulate the sale of intoxicants, and under such circumstances the ordinary of the county had the power to refuse a license. In the 'seventies the people elected such an ordinary and no other kind was ever elected afterwards. There has been less and less 'moonshining.'

"Big families were the rule in the 'Hills.' Some of them looked, when lined up, like a long flight of stairs, or a 'shoot the chute.' Babies got into the world cheaply—a dollar or two spent at the country store for red flannel and pink calico did the business for a layette, and the 'granny woman's' fee was anything from a setting of guinea eggs up to a side of meat. And the poor little things died in droves, of teething, malnutrition, and forty other diseases. The measles, the mumps, and the hookworms did not get us all, but they gave each one of us more than one close shave.

Education in the "Hills" After the Civil War

"About the year 1870 a public school system was organized in the state, but it did not get to going well until 1872; and it was in this year that public schools were first taught in Cherokee; although subscription and 'poor schools' were known before that time. I know that Aleck Rhine taught a subscription school at 'Swayback' Church, about two miles north of Waleska, as early as 1858; and that Miss Mollie Reinhardt taught a subscription school at the Waleska cross-roads in the year 1870. Not until 1873 was the first public school taught in northern Cherokee. Miss Julia Crawford was the teacher, and 'Swayback' was the location. In 1875, and possibly in 1874, Miss Julia Word taught a public school at 'Swayback.'

"In 1876, Joseph M. Sharp—father of Dr. Joseph A. Sharp of Young Harris fame—taught the 'Swayback' public term. My mother had already taught me to read and spell; and I carried down to this school my 'blue-back speller' and a 'McGuffey's Second Reader,' and announced myself ready to ride. There was a bunch for you. Pupils were present from as far off as eight and ten miles—that being the distance to the nearest school in any other direction from their homes. I know some who walked five miles. In ages they ran from 6 to 20 years. Children from two or three families were seemingly well-fed; but the great majority of us had never known anything about a 'balanced ration' and were accustomed to eat what was put on our plates, and glad to get it. When we ran out of 'taters,' meat, or anything else, we did not have any more until the new crop came in. Anyhow, there we were, eager—most of us—to find out what Mr. Sharp could tell us.

"In those days, and for a hundred years before, in the poor white sections of the South, the schools were called 'blab schools.' That is to say, as soon as the roll was called, or we had come in from play, each pupil recited his lessons aloud to himself. If this was disconcerting to the arithmetic students, they might take their slates and books outside, and occupy benches in the grove hard by. When it comes to remembering a lesson, there is merit in the 'blab system.' The only schooling Abraham Lincoln ever had was five months in a 'blab school.'

"One day Mr. Sharp, in some excitement, announced to us that on the following Wednesday the Honorable Warren Hudson, then county school commissioner, was going to visit us. He told us that when this great man arrived, he would go out and help him unhitch his horse, and they would come to the doorsteps together; and showed us how, when he introduced him, we were to jump up and bow. In fact, he rehearsed the business with us, not once but many times. We were all greatly excited, as it was reported that Commissioner Hudson lived at Canton, where the houses were painted white, and where many of the houses had lofts in them. Mr. Hudson arrived on schedule, and we handed him, I think, the biggest assortment of awkward bows that was ever seen since the world began.

"Our school closed with an 'Exhibition.' It was held at night, from a platform outside the schoolhouse, fronting the audience seated as best they might be. All the pupils who wished were on the program. Redding Lyons Cook, a six-footer from away up on Shoal Creek, recited:

> 'Twinkle, twinkle, little star,
> How I wonder what you are,
> Up above the world so high,
> Like a diamond in the sky;'

pronouncing 'are' like 'air,' and 'diamond' as if it ended in a 't.' A pretty girl of about sixteen summers and dressed in white with a big red girdling ribbon, recited in a voice vibrant and sweet:

'The Curfew shall not ring tonight.' A little girl with face so washed that it shone again, and hair tightly platted down her neck, gave them:

> 'The lark is up to meet the sun,
> The bee is on the wing,
> The ant its labors has begun,
> The woods with music ring.'

Barefooted, in a calico waist down the front of which ran two parallel rows of ruffles, I rendered a poem of eighty or a hundred lines entitled 'The Dying Soldier' and commencing:

> 'Two soldiers lying as they fell
> Upon the reddened clay;
> In daytime foes, at night in peace,
> They breathed their lives away;'

and as an endurance test, both for me and the audience, it was a perfect success.

"That was the end of the schools at 'Swayback.' The roof finally fell in. The spot where we triumphed is forgotten; but I believe I could locate it by the spring of cold water gushing up from a rock which supplied us.

"When my mother had taught me to read, early in the year 1876, little was found on which to exercise my new powers. There was nothing in our home in the way of books except the 'blue-back speller,' and there were not a dozen books altogether in the whole Settlement. There were a few in the home of Mr. Joseph O. Heard, who was a Mexican War veteran and had a history of that war. He had also a large family Bible, the frontispiece of which contained a picture of the Devil—an immense dragon with prominent horns and teeth, cloven feet, and barbed tail. My mother having previously stressed the fact that he was out after me, I accepted the picture as accurate. Not long afterward I ate meat for supper, and that night this monster gave me a hot chase. I avoided him by running into a piece of woods, where he was foiled by the thickness of the trees. This family Bible was too big to borrow; so I did not read it.

"In my hunger after knowledge, I had recourse to my mother's 'patterns.' In that section, in those days, a young housewife was called on to make her husband's clothes, generally from cloth that he had woven; and this applied to the children also, as they came along. The patterns were obtained by borrowing from the neighbors and cutting out new ones, from such scraps of paper as might be accessible, such as vagrant newspapers. As soon as I learned to read, I noticed the printing on some of my mother's patterns, as they hung on the wall, and so I got them down and read all I could. Rarely did I find any complete literary production, owing to the scrappy nature of the stuff; which was disappointing, necessarily.

"But in 1878, I think it was, my father was induced by someone to subscribe to the *New York World*. It came weekly by star route from Cartersville to Sharp's Store at Waleska, where we went three miles to get it. In the latter part of the year, my interest picked up in the *World*. Along about fodder-pulling time, a serial story commenced, by the title of 'A Divided House, or, The Red Manse Mystery,' written by an author with some such name as 'Colonel Prentice Ingraham.' The scene was the mighty West; there were cowboys, Indians, and bucking bronchos aplenty; and the thing was written in a way to stimulate and increase interest to the end.

"Before long the whole Settlement knew about this story; and of Sunday afternoons the adults and larger children gathered at our house to hear me read the installments. None of us had even heard of fictional literature, and to all of us the story was intensely real. There would have been no way to convince us that the author, or anyone else, could ever have invented, or been allowed to publish, such an elaborate lie.

"Finally, just before the expiration of our subscription, an installment, instead of winding up with the customary 'To be continued in our next,' changed to 'To be concluded in our next.' Also, the very status of the story required that something pop. The hero was beleaguered by peril. It was for him a funeral or a wedding, with the odds in favor of the funeral.

"The paper came to the Store, on Friday afternoons, and so at noon of the ensuing Friday my father stopped the plow and told me to 'go for the mail.' When I reached the Store, I saw quite an unusual crowd. I hitched and went up on the store-porch; and found the crowd was made up of my audience for the run of the story. The instant I saw their faces, I knew they had beat me to it, and had had the paper read by the clerk; also, that the story had ended in tragedy. Finally Tom Costner, a bachelor of 35 or 40, approached me, and said:

"'Lon, he's dead.'

"Then he walked away to conceal the evidences of his grief.

"Long afterwards, I read that two hundred years ago when Richardson's novel *Pamela* was being read serially in a backwoods community in England, and when, at his conclusion, he brought his heroine, a poor work girl, triumphantly through temptation into honorable and desirable marriage, the generous and sympathetic backwoods readers rushed tumultuously outdoors and rang the town bell.

"In the year 1855, or thereabouts, three Sharp brothers settled at Waleska from Walhalla, S. C. There was nothing at Waleska, at that time, except a crossing of the roads. John J. A. Sharp and White Sharp started off the town with a country store, a cotton gin, and a tobacco factory. After the Civil War, in which they served throughout, they found themselves 'flat' as a result of Sherman's raids in this section.

"These two men were distinguished by what we are accustomed to call a liberal social philosophy. And so while they envisioned a big material development of their section, with Waleska as the center, and worked to it, they never lost sight of the social and moral well-being of the surrounding people, especially of the children. White Sharp organized the first Sunday school ever organized in that section. Lewis Reinhardt was superintendent. Colonel John J. A. Sharp owned perhaps fifty good books, which he pressed to loan to any of us children who would read them. Joseph M. Sharp, the other brother, was in no wise behind in enthusiastic interest in the children of his neighbors. I have never known a man who better filled the definition of 'gentleman.' He and his wife raised an excellent family of children, among them the late, great Dr. Joseph A. Sharp.

"History owes something to Colonel John J. A. Sharp. He believed in the eternal value of every boy and girl in that section— believed it actively, day and night. As the gold-miner scans the dirt for the pure metal, so he was constantly on the alert to detect all active ambition among the poorer children of that section. He organized a debating society and a local lodge of the 'Georgia Christian Temperance Union,' at Waleska. Out of the latter was to come Georgia's statute against the manufacturing and selling of intoxicants as beverages, passed in the year 1907.*

"Of course, the crowning work of the Colonel was in connection with the establishment of Reinhardt Normal College, in which he collaborated with his brother-in-law, Captain A. M. Reinhardt. The first work—the literal 'breaking of the ground'—for this enterprise was in the summer of 1883. I saw the first saplings dug up. That was all that was done in 1883, however. In the following year Prof. J. T. Lin, a graduate of two colleges, was induced to commence the college by opening school, in an old shop of considerable size on the edge of town, on the Fincher mill road.

"That was the end of an era for that section. The thick clouds of intellectual and spiritual poverty began to give way before the rising sun. The rock was smitten, and abundant and fructifying streams gushed forth; and these streams continue to flow this day—to the uttermost parts of the earth."

---

*Author's note: One of the bills sponsored in the legislature by Judge Covington.

CHAPTER X

FURTHER SIDELIGHTS ON LIFE IN THE "HILLS"

IN THE DAYS before educational opportunity came to them through the establishment of Georgia's public school system and, later, the founding of Reinhardt College at Waleska, the people of the "Hills" harbored a number of curious beliefs. Indeed, some of these ideas persist to the present day, not only in the hills of Georgia but in many other parts of the United States. Superstitions have not disappeared even in this enlightened age.

No tame and colorless fetishes, such as those dealing with ladders and mirrors and the number "thirteen," however, are the ones described in the following account by Judge Covington. Superstition prevailed, with the hill settlers, in matters of life and death and sickness and crops, and was occasionally even mixed up with religion. If a "Saga of the Hills" should ever be composed, it will not be complete without mention of the strange beliefs here recorded.

By Judge Covington:

Superstitions of the "Hills"

"The hill folk set great store by superstitions, and their belief in 'signs,' 'warnings,' ghosts, and haunted places took rank with their religious creeds. I can not think, as some do, that all this originated from their contacts with negro slaves, for the reason that such contacts were not sufficient to have produced such results. It seems most probable that such superstitions had their origin far back and far away in the past history of the ancestors of these people. But I set out with the idea of listing some of the commoner superstitions that prevailed in the locality where my first years were spent. Here are some of them:

"The overwhelming majority of the farmers planted their crops with reference to the phases of the moon. Certain crops were to be planted only when the moon was on the increase, while others could be prudently planted only at or near the 'new moon.' Occasionally a man could be found who was a reckless disbeliever in such custom; but he was thought to be 'curious in his head.'

"The astrological beliefs originating in Egypt and 'Ur of the Chaldees,' and persisting through all the centuries, were in full practical force and effect. Many activities were regulated by the 'Signs'—meaning signs of the zodiac; such as soap-making, killing and curing meat, and various operations on domestic animals. Nor was it necessary to take a long course of study in such occult matters as the principles of astrology. *Grier's Almanac,* which from year to year hung on a nail over the fire-board in the living-room of every house, rendered all that unnecessary, with its picture of a naked young man surrounded by the various signs of the zodiac.

"I believe the Egyptians held cats sacred. While not exactly sacred among us, cats had certain privileges, powers, and exemptions. It was bad luck to kill a cat. He might be given away, or carried such a distance from home as would render it improbable that he would find his way back; but it would not do to kill him. Also, when a family moved its habitat, it was allowed to carry along chickens, dogs, goats, and all other domestic animals—except cats. No matter how valuable a cat he might be, nor how long he might have been, so to speak, a member of the family, he must be sacrificed to the unrelenting furies ready always to spring upon the mover of a cat.

"If you were on the road and a rabbit crossed it in front of you, you were in for an unprofitable trip. Trouble lay ahead. But this could be headed off by immediately tying a knot in something.

"To kill the ugly toad made the cow go dry—which was no minor disaster to happen to a whole family.

"To spin a straight chair on one of its legs was simply begging for misfortune; and getting his ears smartly boxed for this was a part of the education of every child.

"Children were also brought up not to carry through the house an axe or other edged tool, under pains and penalties in such cases made and provided. The ordinary run of hard luck was enough, without inviting more.

"To turn back for any temporary purpose when one had started anywhere, no matter how short the distance to be traversed, was certain to make the main trip turn out disastrously—unless, before turning back, one made a cross mark on the ground, and spat on it.

"The beautiful cooing dove—he of the love note sweet and low—was never killed. Did not one of his predecessors bring hope to the Ark, and has not the dove in all lands and ages symbolized peace?

"For a screech-owl to broadcast to a home signified big trouble; but this could be warded off by sticking a fire-shovel in the live embers of the hearth. In fact there has never been a case recorded of a screech-owl persisting to cry a minute after the shovel went into the fire. The victory over him and the forces he represented was always complete and instantaneous.

"For a whippoorwill to perch himself on a house in which a person lay sick, and 'hand out his line,' or do the same from a nearby tree, meant death without bail or mainprise. Prayer nor physic, mummer nor magic, could avail anything after that.

"A drought could be broken by killing a snake and hanging it from a limb or something, belly upwards. Results were both immediate and satisfactory. Once this writer and his brother wanted it to rain so they might go fishing, and their father did not want it to rain because it would interfere with his plowing program. We hung up a snake, in due and ancient form. That same night there fell a torrential storm that washed the rack logs out of the creek and the very dogs out of the yard. Our father made an investigation that developed our culpability, whereupon he wore out a handful of switches on us, and admonished us to 'quit meddling with the elements.' We did, then and there.

"Ghosts had been seen by practically all our elders, who regaled us, of nights, with hair-raising accounts of such appearances, rendered with circumstantial detail. Various places enjoyed the reputation of being haunted—particularly abandoned graves and scenes of violent deaths. We younger ones used to pass by those places at night with heads averted, and by no means loitering. It has been a matter of fifty years since I saw those unhallowed spots, and no one knows better than I that there is nothing to the stories told of ghosts appearing at them. But I have no hankering to be about them at night. I got my accounts about them from good people.

"Conjurers there were, in my day, who could do various things by secret rites. My mother gave me, when I was a child, an account of a desperate horseback ride made by a young white man to the home of her father for the purpose of getting him to stop the flow of blood from a foot of a young negro, who had cut his foot over on the west side of the county. Her father could 'stop blood,' and he did, just in time, by the exercise of some necromantic art, as he stood in his tracks. So the rider found when he returned to the wounded man.

"The 'thrash,' a mouth disease of babies, was subject to the conjurer's art also. The mother went to the conjurer, in secret, and was told what to do. She must never tell how it was done, and never did. I have seen mother so circumstanced going to the conjurer's home.

"Children in our settlement were subject to a kind of inflammation of the back part of the roof of the mouth, causing more or less pain and inconvenience. I had it once, and was sent by my mother to the home of an old man—quite a prominent farmer, he was, and a veteran of the War with Mexico. I told him what I wanted, and he gravely set me down in a heavy straight chair, and told me to gather hold of the rounds at the sides with my hands. He then took hold of a handful of my rather longish hair and lifted me bodily, chair and all, from the floor; and so held me considerably longer than was comfortable. This was 'lifting the fallen palate of my mouth.' It was also, I am convinced, a temporary 'face-lift.' Of course, the process must have been quite without effect on my trouble.

"Death was a tremendous thing with us, especially in the case of the young. And we died young, lots of us. It seemed that the proverb, 'Death loves a shining mark,' was working all the time. The mother of the dead child always wailed aloud at the burying. The preacher, if there was one, usually put the responsibility for the death on the good Lord: 'The Lord needed a flower for his garden, and so He took little Johnnie.' Well, all right, maybe so.

"These funerals were not what you would call cheerful affairs. There was no choir murmuring, 'Asleep in Jesus, blessed sleep.' Always, a few cracked voices wailed:

> 'Hark from the tombs, a doleful sound;
> My ears, attend the cry;
> Ye living men, come view the ground
> Where ye must shortly lie,'

to a tune appropriate to the sentiment. There were three more stanzas just like it. It is out of the hymn-books now; it was sung by three generations of mountaineers before it was abandoned.

"Death was in numberless cases heralded by 'warnings'—such as the ringing of the 'death bells,' by which we designated any roaring sensation originating and remaining in the ears. When you heard them ring, you would soon learn of a death of someone you knew. I have not heard the 'death bells' for forty years; but I did hear them numbers of times when I was a child.

"My Grandfather Covington was a good carpenter, and he made the coffins for the community. They were not as elaborate as the commercial products of this day; but they would hold you. And frequently, just before the death of a friend or relative, one might hear at night the sound of the coffin-maker's hammer driving in the nails. I recall that once when a corpse was lying in the community, I heard the knocking of the hammer, throughout a long, dreadful night."

Some Very Short Stories

In lighter vein are some of the stories recalled by Judge Covington concerning the people among whom he grew up. The following incidents which he relates bring out in humorous fashion a number of "Hill" characteristics:

"Three sisters, all old maids and all totally illiterate, lived near us—'Shug,' 'Betsy,' and 'Puss.'

"A little after the War, a poor preacher came to that section, and one night he held services at their home. A few of the neighbors went in. The preacher was reading a chapter, and one of the men present, who was just 'lit up' enough to be interested, got up and stood by him, and looked over his shoulder at the page. Finally he turned triumphantly to his associates and said:

" 'Boys, I'll be jumped if it ain't just like he's a-readin' it!' "

"And for years, in that section, when one wished to endorse some statement made by another in his presence, he would say:

" 'It's just like he's reading it to you.'

"It is a curious thing to note that these three sisters lived for years in the same house. As I said, they were all old when I first knew them. They did a little 'hoeing' among the poor farmers, who overpaid them as much as they were able. None of the sisters could count to a hundred. Once I was with my father when he called there for some purpose. A new tin washpan was in evidence; and my father said:

" 'Shug, what did your pan cost you?'

" 'Seventy-five cents,' said she.

" 'Now Shug,' remonstrated one of her sisters, 'you know it only cost twenty-five cents.'

" 'Well,' said Shug, 'I knowed it cost summers along there!'

"The Cutters were a poor white family, settled away up just this side of nowhere. Old Mrs. Cutter was a woman of great force and energy, and the head of her family.

"One day, when I was quite small, I heard noises that indicated distress on the part of Mrs. Cutter's boy Jim. I ran up there to look into it, and found Mrs. Cutter at work on him, with a brush-broom. She would 'frail' him awhile and then rest while she talked to him.

" 'I'll show you how to use bad words,' she was saying. 'I knowed how it would be when you was all the time playin' with them no-'count Jones children. I know where you learned that word. None of my people ever used such language as that, and I don't believe even your pa's folks ever did. Ef I cain't break you of it, I'll jest wear you out!'

"There was a lick at the end of every sentence; and every time the broom fell, Jim broadcast.

"Next day I got with Jim and asked him what it was he had said. At first he demurred flatly, but I kept on working with him. Finally he told me, having exacted a solemn oath of secrecy. The word was 'previous.' It is more than likely that Jim had used it in the wrong place; but that circumstance, even had it been recognizable to his mother, would not have influenced her treatment of him. The word itself was new and strange-sounding.

"In the Hills there was sometimes a child that was manifestly not 'all there' in his head. To a stranger the explanation of his condition was generally:

" 'Pore li'l feller, when he was little he went with his pa to the new ground on a windy day, and a limb of a dead tree fell on his head; and he has been queer ever since.'

"In our community there was such a character, whom we called 'Old John.' Being queer in the head, he said a lot of amusing things. Old John 'lived around' from place to place. When his welcome wore out, he would move on.

"One of his specialties was putting on a great show of 'getting religion' at every revival meeting. One Sunday Uncle Johnny Payne, a Campbellite preacher, was baptizing a number of persons at an appropriate place in the creek; and Old John was among them. When it came the latter's turn, Brother Payne stepped up to the bank and took hold of him, and led him down to the water, at which point Old John shied with energy.

" 'Come on, brother,' chanted the preacher; don't be afraid of the Lord!'

" 'I'm not afraid of the Lord, nor you neither,' said the candidate, 'but I'm scared as all git-out of that little moccasin snake over yonder!'

"The 'Hill folks' were a cautious set. Also, they were honest. As a result of these two qualities, they seldom exaggerated in their statements.

"I was present one night at a revival meeting, when a 30-year-old farmer got up to make a public statement of his spiritual condition—a usual preliminary to joining the church. He wound up by saying:

" 'And so, brethren, if nothin' don't happen, I expect to remain faithful to the end.'

"That is as far as he was willing to commit himself."

Waleska Camp-Meeting, 1884

That famous Methodist institution, the camp-meeting, has long been popular in Cherokee County; and more will be said of it later in this book. In the meantime, this series of sketches by Judge Covington on "Hill" life in Cherokee closes with an account of the Waleska Camp-Meeting of 1884 which is one of the most vivid descriptions of such a gathering it has ever been this author's privilege to read.

Quoting:

"At ' Briar-Patch Church,' or more properly Reinhardt Chapel, which is just south of Waleska, there was in my day a camp-ground at which meetings had been held from a time 'since memory runneth not to the contrary.'

"Camp-meetings were annual affairs, held usually in the summer before the fall gathering of crops. They furnished opportunities for the renewal of acquaintance by the older people, and also gave the 'young folks' a chance for a lot of good honest 'courtin'.' Of course, the principal object was the revival of religious fervor in the community, and to this end church services were held at the 'stand' at least twice a day, for four or five days.

"One meeting at 'Briar-Patch' stands out in my memory. It was on a Monday night during the camp-meeting of 1884. No signs of a 'revival' had so far appeared. Rev. J. T. Lin, an orator of great ability, was the regular preacher that year. He was, incidentally, the best 'hymn-liner' that was ever in the county, and highly emotional. Both Mr. Lin and the presiding elder had, on preceding nights, preached and 'failed.'

"Now, preaching at these meetings was strictly orthodox. Sin was preached both as exceedingly sinful and as universal, affecting all classes. Like Paul before Felix, the faithful preachers 'reasoned' with a dying race concerning 'righteousness, temperance, and the judgment to come'; and with the same results. As Felix 'trembled' under Paul's reasoning, so all classes brought under the influence of the revival preaching of those days shouted, trembled, cried aloud, or went into 'trances.' Such 'reasoning' is a condition precedent of religious revivals—always has been, always will be. Unless these things are true, there is no sense in getting excited about the future. Unless they are true, the Church has no business in the world.

"Well, as I said, Mr. Lin and the presiding elder had failed to awake these manifestations. So that night an old man named Carson was placed in the pulpit. Mr. Carson was at that time a local preacher of great age. Stooped as he was, and with his long white beard, he looked like Death with his scythe.

"The setting for his sermon was just right. The light from the tallow candles set on crossbeams of the 'stand'—as the covered shelter was called—was both 'dim and religious.' All around was a belt of woods, dark and dense.

"I was sitting just in front of the preacher, and could see his eyes shining in the uncertain light, like torches in sink-holes. His voice rattled as he 'lined' a hymn. It has not been in the Methodist hymn-book for many years, but it was there that night; and the first two lines, as the preacher rolled them out, were:

'My thoughts on awful subjects roll,
Damnation and the dead.'

The text was in keeping with the song—'He that being often reproved, hardeneth his heart, shall suddenly be destroyed and that without remedy.'

"The old preacher started out by saying:

" 'There are always a number of people in congregations like this who are simply "fillers"—men with whom the Holy Spirit of God has ceased to strive long ago. There are such present here tonight—men mortgaged to the devil for half a lifetime, escaping foreclosure for reasons inscrutable. Possibly he delays so they may "cut better." For you my message is not designed. Your bones have been bleaching out there in the plains of damnation for forty years; and while you sow, reap, vote, and otherwise pursue your temporal activities, the hell hounds are accustomed to come out, of nights, and lick them!'

"It was an awful thing to hear; and many in the audience who had all their lives resisted invitations of the Gospel, easily concluded that he was talking about them, and that they had committed the 'unpardonable sin.'

"With such a beginning, the preacher seemed to speak with supernatural power. His description of hell, as I now remember it, rivaled anything Dante ever wrote; and his insistent and remorseless pressure of this picture on the minds of the audience was a powerful thing. At times, discovering myself to be in great physical distress, I would thrust my fingers into my ears; but my finger-tips were insufficient to protect my ear-drums from the insistent pounding of the preacher's voice.

"Then, when the congregation was virtually frozen with horror, the powers of the preacher seemed to fail, suddenly. He took his seat, and someone tried to start the singing. There was a commotion down at the speaker's stand. Presently I saw them carrying someone out to a tent. I made my way to this tent, and met my uncle coming out slowly. My uncle was one of Lee's veterans, and the only man I remember there, that night, who was without visible excitement. I asked him who it was that they had carried into the tent, and he answered, 'Aunt Lotty Pitman.'

" 'She must be in a trance,' I hazarded.

" 'No,' said my uncle; 'she's dead.'

"And she was.

"There is no way to describe the dramatic effect of this death, coming when it did. Good old 'Aunt Lotty' was, we all realized, safe in any world; but her death brought home to the crowd the thing that the preacher had stressed—the uncertainty of human life—as nothing else could have done. The place was covered, pretty soon, with the 'slain of the Lord,' and the preacher prayed with the 'mourners' till near daybreak. More than ninety joined the church, some of whom lived to be greatly useful Georgians, both in church and state."

CHAPTER XI

GROWTH AND GOVERNMENT OF CANTON

WHERE the Etowah River curves in a mile-wide semicircle in the center of Cherokee County, the stream's eastern bank rises sharply to the strikingly attractive business district of Canton, the county seat. That is the northern approach. Coming in from the south, the pavement also climbs steeply, to burst upon the same brick and marble buildings with equally surprising abruptness. Whatever the approach, the visitor to Canton usually feels at once that here is no ordinary town; and the visitor, as always, is right. . . .

No county in Georgia offers a better example than Cherokee of balance between the three main branches of economic activity: agriculture, industry, and commerce. The fact is important, and explains to a large degree the consistency of Cherokee's growth in population and wealth.

Necessary to such a balance are natural resources which will permit, and reward, a diversification of effort. Also necessary is intelligent exploitation of these resources. Cherokee County has a host of natural advantages—desirable location, healthful climate, productive soil, and a rich supply of minerals, timber, and water-power. And evidence shows that able management has never been lacking

To the towns of Cherokee, and to the men who built and are building the towns, is due a large part of the credit for that integration of agriculture and industry which puts the county on its solid economic footing. Canton, in particular, has been a focal point for these two lines of activity. Never without an important industry, and now an important town in industry, Canton has for many years offered an excellent market for agricultural products and in turn has enjoyed the patronage of a surprisingly large rural area. Each contributing to the growth of the other, Cherokee

102

County and its capital city have progressed hand-in-hand during their common century-long history.

Most important of all contributions made by the towns to the county have been the leaders in trade and industry who, while building their own communities, have helped to build up the county as well. The history of Canton includes a number of such men; in fact, the economic development of Cherokee County has in every period been materially aided by the activities of those responsible for the growth and government of its county seat.

Less a history of Canton than a record of these men's names and something of their activities, this chapter will treat, in a necessarily brief and summary fashion, the development of the little city on the Etowah since the days when it bore that river's name.

Canton Before 1880

Reference to the population chart in the Appendix will show that Canton (which was not large enough even to be included in the census before 1870, and contained only 214 persons in that year) remained a very small village during the first fifty years of its history, and did not start to grow at all noticeably until after 1880. There were several reasons for the stimulus in population about that time, which will be taken up later in this chapter.

But even as a straggling little hill town, Canton served during these first fifty years as the chief—and almost only—commercial, educational, and social center of the county. It had, moreover, all the natural advantages it enjoys today, and it contained able and enterprising citizens. Despite the fact that it would have been hard to see in the Canton of, say, 1870, the Canton of today, foundations were being laid for later development.

It has already been told how Canton was incorporated in 1833 under the name of "Etowah"—the present name being approved by the legislature in the following year; and how the founders of the town had already established the silk industry there even before their village was incorporated.

A picture of Canton at that time would differ in few respects from descriptions that have been drawn of other backwoods villages of the period—except perhaps that its high location was more than usually picturesque. Such buildings as it contained, in those first years, were made of logs or rude hand-dressed lumber. Streets, of course, were mere dirt paths. The business part of the town then consisted chiefly of a postoffice and one or two general stores, which catered to Indians as well as white persons.

This postoffice, of which William Grisham was the first postmaster, served as distributing point for the mail of almost every-

EARLY CITIZEN AND OLDEST HOME. Pictured above is William Grisham, one of Canton's three founders and a noted early settler and developer of Cherokee County. At right is shown the house he built in Canton about 1838, one room in which he used for his silk business. Later on the house was occupied by Joel and Malinda Grisham Galt, and it is now owned by the family of William Galt. This historic residence is of Colonial architecture and is the oldest home in Canton.

body in the county, as the large four-horse coach that carried the mail from Gainesville to Canton was allowed to stop at only a few intermediate points. Riders came in from other settlements in the county to Canton once a week to get their mail and that of their neighbors, paying twenty-five cents for a single letter.

In 1833 a school and a church appeared in Canton. The school was incorporated by the legislature as "Etowah Academy," and it was considered an advanced institution of learning, receiving as pupils children of well-to-do settlers from all parts of the county. The existence of this school, in one form or another, has been continuous until the present day, the Canton public school system having absorbed it during the 'nineties. The church was of the Baptist denomination, and it was organized on August 20, 1833, with ten charter members.

William Grisham, aforementioned, was instrumental in organizing both these institutions, and was otherwise influential in the early life of Canton through his silk business, postmastership, and county officership. Of this early settler Dr. Knight* writes: "William Grisham . . . settled in Georgia from South Carolina during the early 'twenties; . . . subsequently removed to Cherokee County, where he cleared up the first farm land now at the edge of the city of Canton. He was a slave-owner and planter. He and Judge Joseph Donaldson were the first settlers in this locality, and introduced and became prominently identified with silk culture. He is given the credit for founding the First Baptist Church in Canton in 1833. He died in 1876 at the age of 75." Mrs. Grisham, who was one of the first white women to live in Canton, was very popular with the Indian women, and knitted little caps for them which they prized very highly.

Of equal prominence in the early affairs of Canton and Cherokee County was Judge Joseph Donaldson, who like Mr. Grisham remained one of Cherokee County's foremost citizens throughout a long and active life. Judge Donaldson it was who started the first ferry-line across the Etowah at Canton; and later he built the first bridge to cross it at that point. (This bridge was burned during the Civil War, but the original pillars are still standing and help to support the present structure there.) With large farming interests, he engaged also in building, milling, and commercial pursuits. He built the first Methodist Church in

---

*Georgia and Georgians, Lucian Lamar Knight, p. 2727.

Canton and contributed generously to its support. Judge Donaldson grew quite wealthy from his various enterprises, but was impoverished by the Civil War. He is said to have owned more slaves than any other man in the county, and he treated them so well that when they were freed after the war some of them refused to acknowledge their liberty and begged to stay on with him. His home across the Etowah River from Canton, built in 1856, was a headquarters for visiting persons of prominence, and he and Mrs. Donaldson were famous for their Southern hospitality.

Another early resident of Canton, also mentioned before, was William K. McCanless, wheelwright and builder. Besides erecting many of the old mills in various parts of North Georgia, Mr.

JOHN P. BROOKE AND WIFE

McCanless constructed the first buildings in Canton, including the first church and school building, and was influential in the early religious life of the community.

Likewise prominent among the first settlers of Canton was John P. Brooke, who was born on the Atlantic Ocean while his parents were sailing from Ireland to South Carolina, and who after winning political distinction in Hall County, Georgia, came to Cherokee County and helped to found Canton. He was the first sheriff of the county after it was cut off from the original, and he also served in the legislature from Cherokee. The official efforts and personal example of Mr. Brooke were considerable factors in establishing law and order in the new county; and he was for many years prominent in county affairs.

Of similar character was another early settler and resident of Canton, R. Frank Daniel, who was a "charter member" of the county and who exerted a great moral influence over the large number of lawless men who drifted into the section during the gold rush. First clerk of the superior court of Cherokee County after it was cut off from the original, Mr. Daniel also held other county offices and was postmaster at Canton for a time. He was widely known and much loved and respected; and when his death occurred in 1885 the funeral was the largest that had ever been held in Canton.

Of course, as the careers of these men and their contemporaries waxed and waned, the picture changed. Canton did not remain a backwoods town for long. Marked improvement was noted after the removal of the Indians in 1838, and in the ten or fifteen years that followed, Canton became more typically a "Southern" than a frontier village. Industry was springing up in various parts of the county, in the form of old-fashioned grist and flouring mills, carding and spinning "factories," saw-mills, and mining projects. Canton was the natural center of much of this activity, and profited thereby. In addition, the town's social and educational life flourished, as the pioneers began to sit back and enjoy the fruits of their toil.

A list of some of the more prominent citizens of Canton at this time, say about 1845, would include, besides the men heretofore mentioned, Jabez Galt, pioneer merchant who built Canton's first brick store building in 1839; James and John Maddox and George Hoyle, merchants; Rev. Bob Cowart, noted early preacher; Dr. John W. Lewis, wealthy farmer and physician who became the benefactor of Governor Joseph E. Brown; James Jordan and John B. Garrison, prominent county officers, the former a lawyer and the latter a very early settler; and others.

Another interval of fifteen years or so brings us up to a time just before the Civil War, and the picture changes again. An idea of the Canton·scene in the early part of 1861 may be drawn from the *Cherokee Mountaineer,* the county's first newspaper, launched in that year by W. J. Sloan. Canton attorneys were William A. Teasley, James Jordan, Samuel Weil, and James R. Brown. The brother of the latter, Joseph E. Brown, had in the meantime got

his start in the legal profession in Canton, and was now governor of
Georgia. About a dozen business houses existed at the time, including the stores of J. P. Daniel, Littleberry Holcombe, and E. G.
Gramling; in addition there were the usual livery stable, shoe and
harness shop, woodworking establishment, and tailor shop, and a
few other enterprises; and a courthouse and jail of sorts about
completed the business section of Canton at that period.

It has already been related how the town was damaged by fire
when Sherman's foragers passed through toward the close of the
Civil War. The setback was only temporary, and in spite of the

JOEL LEWIS GALT

further hardships encountered during the reconstruction period
that followed the War, Canton continued to grow steadily, attain-
ing by 1870 the hitherto unequaled population of over two hundred
souls.

For a number of years following the War the principal merchant of Canton was Joel Galt, son of the prominent early settler,
Jabez Galt. Mr. Galt, although refused for service in the Confederate Army on account of physical incapacities, returned to Canton

and soon built up a successful and, for that time, extensive business as a general merchant. His death in 1873 ended the career of one of Canton's most useful citizens.

Shortly after the Civil War one of Stonewall Jackson's veterans, Captain Joseph Miller McAfee, came to Canton from Forsyth County and entered the mercantile business. Starting on a capital of $200, he eventually built up an excellent trade, acquired other

CAPTAIN JOSEPH M. McAFEE

important interests, and became one of the most influential citizens in the whole of Canton's history. Some of his other activities were farming, milling, ginning, and building. In 1874 he built the town's first up-to-date hotel, a brick building on the site where the Hotel Canton now stands; and a few years later he started a brickyard where the brick were made for several buildings still standing in Canton. The long career of Captain McAfee—he was in the mercantile business for sixty-three years—will be touched on again here.

In 1870, three years after Captain McAfee's arrival, there came to Canton another merchant who was destined to play an important part in the town's commercial development. Benjamin Franklin Crisler established, in that year, a general mercantile business which survives to the present day and is the oldest business house in Canton. In addition Mr. Crisler operated a tannery and a shoe and harness shop; and became an extensive farm operator.

Also a merchant in Canton during this post-war period and for a number of years afterward was a man widely known for his other activities—Charles Marshall McClure, who was the first ordinary of Pickens County after that county was formed in 1853 from Cherokee and Gilmer; who later served as ordinary of Cherokee; who was a local (Methodist) preacher and a teacher of note; and who in his four capacities was valuable in Canton's religious, educational, civic, and business life.

Its development based on the efforts of men such as those already alluded to, Canton reached the year 1880 with a promising outlook; which was further brightened by several events that took place in the last months of 1879. In fact, the significance of these events, in the light of later development, is such as to suggest that here is the dividing point, for Canton, between the old and the new.

Causes for New Growth, 1879-80

In the decade following the year 1880, Canton's population increased from 363 to 659, almost doubling. This represented the largest *proportionate* increase shown by any census period in the town's history, with the exception of the decade following 1900—which also showed the largest *numerical* gain—when the population shot up from 847 to 2,002. The latter increase is largely traceable to the beginning of the cotton mill industry in Canton about 1900. But the launching of the mills was itself greatly influenced by certain events and ideas which had their origin during the "accelerated 'eighties." Some of these factors will now be presented, and a picture of this earlier period supplied.

During its first fifty years Canton lacked one very important aid to growth—easy contact with the outside world. The town had no railroad facilities until 1879. In the fall of that year the Marietta & North Georgia Railroad reached Canton on its way northward, and a new business era was inaugurated for the town and the county as well.

For good measure, about this time Canton got another store and a new weekly paper. The new storekeeper was a young man from Newton County by the name of Robert Tyre Jones. The new weekly was called the *Cherokee Advance,* and its 20-year-old editor and founder was one Benjamin Franklin Perry, late of Marietta. There was great furor over the advent of the railroad, less furor over the new citizens.

Which was only natural. How efforts had been made to bring a railroad to Canton and Cherokee County as far back as the 'fifties; how a handful of progressive citizens finally combined with certain forward-looking promoters and officials of the Marietta & North Georgia to bring about that road's entrance into Canton in 1879; and how this railroad gradually pushed northward through other towns of Cherokee County and finally through all of North Georgia, is sketched in a subsequent chapter. It is enough to say here that the efforts of Captain McAfee, Judge James R. Brown, Colonel W. A. Teasley, and their associates in this project were never better expended for the benefit of Canton than in securing this railroad. The immediate stimulation to business was noted in a grand jury presentment of 1880, which went on to say further: "Thanks to the new railroad, Canton now offers a market for the produce of all farmers of the county, for what is not consumed can now be transported by rail." This feature, of course, was to prove of vast importance to agriculture in Cherokee County.

Proceeding, we find the new storekeeper, R. T. Jones, beginning on a modest scale in this auspicious year of 1879. He started out with a small stock of merchandise and one employee named McNarin. Next year he hired another clerk by the name of Zebulon Walker, who is still with the Jones Mercantile Company. Expansion of the Jones store, in both force and clientele, was rapid, though based on sound principles. In view of the position now occupied among commercial institutions of the state by the Jones

111

Mercantile Company and its affiliated enterprises, any light on the methods of their founder is of interest. A newspaper writeup of the town's business houses in 1885, six years later, included the following item: "R. T. Jones now has one of the best-arranged stores and the most complete display system in town. His corps of clerks is lively and polite. His business is second to none in North Georgia." Further points in the Jones policy were careful buying, low and uniform prices, generous use of advertising, and a disposition to accommodate the public. All this, of course, in the days before huge retail establishments had made these points a standard part of merchandising.

A third factor of significance in the new growth of Canton at this period was the founding of the *Cherokee Advance,* a weekly newspaper started in January of 1880 by Ben F. Perry (Sr.). The town had already had three weeklies at various times in the past. The *Cherokee Mountaineer,* an able-enough little journal for its day, had been published there by W. J. Sloan in the early part of the Civil War period, its first issue having come out on May 18, 1861; but had been discontinued after a year or two, probably on account of the difficulty of obtaining ink and newsprint during those strenuous times. Early in 1875 Judge James O. Dowda launched the *Cherokee Georgian,* and under the competent editorship of Colonel John J. A. Sharp and P. H. Brewster the *Georgian* flourished for about four years; at the end of which time it was submerged into the *Cherokee Advocate.* The latter paper, edited by W. T. Laine and of a religious nature, was then published in Canton for about a year after which it was moved to Atlanta.

These earlier papers had all left their imprint on the development of Canton and Cherokee County, but none of them had identified itself with their progress to the extent that the *Advance* did. Coming at a fortunate time for the peculiar service it could render, the *Advance* made Canton "community-conscious." In a style so able as to place it among the leading Georgia weeklies of the day, it proclaimed the advantages of the town and the county, supported every movement designed to increase their prosperity and well-being; and introduced many important reforms and advances of its own. Its founder, Mr. Perry, may well be considered one of the most stimulating citizens Canton ever had.

Of course, the main function of a newspaper is to get the news; and in this field the *Advance,* under its successive editors, has never been behind its weekly contemporaries. Two remarkable feats of reporting accomplished by the early *Advance* deserve mention here. In 1885 a disastrous cyclone hit the upper part of the county, the day before the paper was due to appear. Mr. Perry held open the forms, rushed to the devastated area and wrote a four-column account of the damage suffered there, and the next day scooped the press of Georgia with his story; incidentally hastening the arrival of relief for the sufferers. In 1888 he secured for Canton the annual meeting and banquet of the Georgia Press Association, and his paper appeared the following morning with a full account of the meeting and a *verbatim* report of the important speeches, including the famous speech of Captain H. W. Newman on "The Georgia Cracker."

Still another service the *Advance* has always performed, in depicting contemporary history. Present-day readers can form something of an idea of the material progress that was made in Canton shortly after 1879—our dividing-point—from the following account given in the *Advance* of January 3, 1884:

"The growth of Canton during the past five years, although substantial and permanent, has been surprisingly rapid. Since the advent of the railroad in 1879 the town has made some visible improvement every day; and the trowel, hammer, and saw are still busy. Summing up the number of houses built and otherwise improved during and since 1879 we find 69 dwellings, 13 stores, 4 warehouses, 2 steam gins, 3 steam flour and grist mills, one millinery shop, depot, jail, church, schoolhouse, livery and feed stable, steam sawmill and planing-mill, furniture shop, and harness and shoe shop, 2 drug stores, 2 paint shops, one jewelry shop, and one *Cherokee Advance* printing office."

It is somewhere about this point that detailed descriptions of the town become unwieldy. Lists, as such, undergo a drop in historical value and become replaceable by statistics. Major additions to the Canton business scene, of course, require notice.

But before passing from the early 'eighties, it is necessary to examine yet another modern feature of Canton originating during that period—its form of government.

Canton's Government—Past and Present

On January 7, 1882, the legal voters resident in Canton went to the courthouse and held a municipal election. The event was significant because it represented the town's first step to obtain a *city* government.

No mayor was elected on January 7, but the voters named five councilmen: Benjamin F. Crisler, merchant; Henry W.

MANY CITIZENS OF THE COUNTY will recognize in this striking picture, taken more than twenty-five years ago, the faces of a number of men prominent in Canton and Cherokee County during the last century. In the front row (left to right) are Odian W. Putnam, William A. Teasley Sr., Judge James R. Brown, Ben F. Perry Sr. (kneeling), W. M. Ellis, George W. Brooke, M. A. Keith, and W. F. Ponder. In the back row (left to right) are J. B. Hawkins, George W. Evans, Dr. J. M. Turk, George I. Teasley, a Mr. Williams, J. M. Attaway, and W. T. McCollum. The old building represented in the picture was an outbuilding that stood near the old home of Governor Brown in Canton, in what is now Brown Park.

Newman, lawyer; Odian W. Putnam, county officer; Ben F. Perry, editor of the *Advance;* and J. P. McConnell, of the noted settler family.

Two weeks later, on January 21, this council met and elected Canton's first city officers. For mayor they selected one of their own number, Odian W. Putnam; for marshal, Sam Tate; for secretary and treasurer, Ben F. Perry.

Of these officers Mr. Perry is already familiar to the reader. Mr. Putnam was the son of one of the county's earliest settlers, David Putnam; and was already influential in the affairs of Cherokee County, having held the offices of superior court clerk and ordinary for several terms. Mr. Tate, then in his twenties, was later to become Georgia's leading figure in the development of the state's mineral resources through his marble quarries at Tate, Ga. Old newspapers tell of his efficiency and popularity as Canton's first marshal.

Other interesting "firsts" in the government of Canton were its earliest ordinances, passed by the council in January of 1882. They included bans on drunkenness, disorderly houses, public profanity, burial without permit, shooting fireworks and firing arms within fifty yards of a public street (this was Section 1); and provided for arrest and trial of offenders by the municipal authorities, the marshal prosecuting in the superior court for state offenses.

The officials named served for one year, and were succeeded by the following men: John D. Attaway, mayor; R. T. Jones, J. P. McCollum, E. B. Holland, B. F. Crisler, and Ben F. Perry, councilmen.

The first city tax ordinance, passed by council on December 21, 1882, provided for a rate of 12½ cents on the hundred dollars and brought in, the first year, the staggering sum of $190. Out of this amount the town paid the salaries of its officials, liquidated its public debt, and was still able to put money in the bank—or would have been if the town had boasted a bank.

Since 1838 the government of Canton had rested in a body of five commissioners, election of whom was provided for by an act of the legislature approved on December 31, 1838.* This was a corporation act amending the act of 1834 which had changed the name of the incorporated town Etowah to "Canton." But that

---

*Acts, Georgia, 1838, p. 132.

there was little need for government, by commission or otherwise, in the village before 1882 is evidenced by the lack of town ordinances before that year.

On December 8, 1882, another legislative act was approved to amend the charter of Canton. Although a mayor and council had been elected at the first of the year, the act was passed, according to its title, to "repeal conflicting laws, to provide for a mayor and council, to prescribe their powers and duties, and for other purposes."*

This act, besides ratifying the new government of Canton—providing, however, that the mayor should be elected by popular vote—also set new corporate limits for the town. The boundary line was thereafter to be "one mile from the courthouse in every direction, except that the Etowah River shall be the boundary of said corporation on the sides of said town where it runs." The territory thus included was about three times as large as that included in the old limits, set in the act of 1838, which had given Canton less than three hundred acres. The new part of town was, for the most part, away from the river, so that only a little waterfront was added.

Since 1882 several acts have been passed amending Canton's charter still further and increasing the powers of the municipality in accordance with its changing needs. Since 1905 council has had six members instead of five, and since 1919 the councilmen have been elected for two years instead of one. The mayor still enjoys a one-year term, but his salary was doubled by the act of 1919 so that he now receives $200 a year. Councilmen receive $25.† A recorder's court was established in 1912 to try cases formerly handled by the mayor and council, but this court was later discontinued. One of the few provisions of the 1882 charter still unchanged is that setting the corporate limits, which are the same today.

When Canton's charter was amended in 1882, a section was inserted in the amending act providing that nothing therein contained should interfere with the "local act prohibiting the sale

---

*Acts, Georgia, 1882-3, p. 255.
†Acts, Georgia, 1919, p. 878.

of intoxicating liquors within two miles of said town of Canton, passed by the general assembly of 1875." The act of 1875 referred to* is of interest here because it ended permanently the legal sale of intoxicating liquor in Canton, in a day when the retailing of intoxicants was unhindered by law both in Georgia and Cherokee County. The act also prohibited the selling of liquor "within two miles of Woodstock Academy," ten miles to the south.

Earlier in this book are discussed conditions arising from drinking before the passage of appropriate local legislation. Even on "court day" in the militia districts, one of the principal attractions was a keg of hard liquor, sold openly and presided over by the "tap-stick," who was usually a very popular man in his section. As late as 1882 it was the opinion of the grand jury that three-fourths of the crime in the county was due to drinking.

This, of course, was back in the days when similar conditions were general in the United States. But popular opinion in the county, even then, seemed to favor legislation that would control the traffic, this attitude appearing at temperance meetings held in Canton well before the Civil War. That such legislation appeared even by 1875 was a triumph for the churches and the temperance-advocating citizens of the county.

The prohibitive act of 1875 relating to Canton and Woodstock was soon followed by legislation forbidding the sale of liquor in the neighborhood of various churches and schools of Cherokee County. The grand jury in 1880 recommended that no licenses to retail liquor be granted by the ordinary, and a succession of able men in this office did much to put down its sale. Then, in 1891, the legislature passed an act prohibiting the selling of intoxicants within a three-mile radius of all churches and schools, with the exception of incorporated towns; and as the towns of Cherokee County already had secured prohibitive legislation the county was left entirely "dry" except for one little corner near Pine Log where no school or church was near.

As far as moonshining is concerned, there seems to have been little of it done in or near Canton at any time. With a part of Georgia's mountain population, however, moonshining has always been something in the nature of a family heritage; and the hills

---

*Acts, Georgia, 1875, p. 333.

of Cherokee County sheltered many an illicit still back in earlier days. Confinement in prison was no disgrace to the 'shiner, and no deterrent, and after "making" his six months or so he came back a hero to his friends and put up a new still. His neighbors' attitude was induced by the wretched jails of the period and by what they considered the hounding methods of the revenue agents. Laws prohibiting the sale of liquor did not visibly affect the moonshiner, who was already violating the U. S. revenue laws. For him it took another remedy, the gradual influence of education and churches.

It is significant that from one of these hill sections of Cherokee County came the co-author of Georgia's prohibition law passed in 1907, Judge William Alonzo Covington. Under this bill the state became "dry" ten years before the nation as a whole adopted the same course.

The act of 1875 helped Canton to establish and maintain a reputation as one of the most moral and law-abiding towns in the state, and so it continues to the present day. One of the earliest acts of the city fathers was to set the prohibitive tax of $1,000 on poolrooms in Canton; and in 1883 we find the *Advance* proclaiming that the town now had "no barrooms, poolrooms, or unemployed." Though Canton has had a considerable industrial population since 1900, it has maintained this record with admirable consistency.

Later Growth of Canton

The impetus to business which followed the entrance of the railroad into Canton in 1879 proved no mere flash in the pan; on the contrary, the full advantages of the town were only beginning to be developed.

One of these advantages was the richness of the outlying agricultural districts, which led to the development of Canton as a market and trading-center. It is not generally realized that Cherokee stands among the top counties of Georgia in per-acre production of cotton (the highest being Milton County, about half of which was formerly a part of Cherokee). Railroad facilities soon made Canton one of the leading cotton markets of North Georgia, the annual shipment by 1883 reaching 3,000 bales; and the figure continued to climb.

118

Another natural advantage which the railroad helped Canton turn to profit was its situation as a cool and healthful summer resort. The town became very popular, during the 'eighties and 'nineties, among lowlanders from the more sweltering sections of the South; and midsummer usually found the hotels and boarding-houses turning away customers. An added attraction was the alum spring about a mile southeast of the courthouse. Early in the 'eighties this spring was discovered to have certain medicinal properties, and visitors flocked to it from all over the state.

Trade flourished and small industries grew, and the population increased steadily. Conspicuously absent, however, were several features necessary for the town's fullest development. There was, for instance, no bank; and more important, there was no large industry.

Cantonites were not seriously inconvenienced by the fact there was no bank nearer than Marietta, because they had had, since 1880, the privilege of storing their surplus funds in the little iron safe that R. T. Jones kept in the back of his store; and, since 1883, the opportunity to patronize the exchange office which he established in connection with his mercantile business. Mr. Jones thus became Canton's first banker, but the town still had not obtained a bank.

In 1892 it did. Ben F. Perry, R. T. Jones, and others were successful in inducing an Alabama financier, William S. Witham, to add to his chain of banks by establishing one in Canton. About fifty leading citizens subscribed the $25,000 capital stock and elected as first officers of the Bank of Canton: William S. Witham, president; R. T. Jones, vice-president; Ben F. Perry, secretary; John B. Richards, cashier; P. P. DuPree, attorney. The charter was received in December of 1892 and the same month saw the new building finished, a marble-fronted structure said to be the handsomest in Canton at the time. Its doors opened for business in January, 1893. The Bank of Canton was the first bank on the line of the Marietta & North Georgia Railroad between Marietta and Knoxville, Tenn.; and was an important addition to North Georgia business. Its capitalization has since been increased to $150,000.

In 1894 Mr. Jones was elected president of this bank, and in this and his other capacities he has played a very large part not only in the development of Canton but of Cherokee County and northern Georgia, having been regarded for many years as one of the state's leading business men. Also in 1894 two new vice-presidents were elected for this bank: B. F. Crisler, who held that

R. T. JONES

position until his death and Col. Sam Tate, who is still serving in that capacity. Among other able officers of the Bank of Canton have been two of Georgia's best-known bankers, the late William Galt, cashier for a long period and also a director in the Canton Cotton Mills; and William S. Elliott, present cashier, who has served as Register of the U. S. Treasury and is now president of the Georgia Bankers' Association.

120

Shortly before the establishment of this bank, Canton succeeded in obtaining its first important industry. For a number of years leading citizens of the town had attempted to bring about such an object, realizing that further growth depended to a large extent on industrial development. After several unsuccessful efforts had been made to bring in manufacturing concerns, Canton was selected for the site of The Georgia Marble Finishing Works by the founder of that company, T. M. Brady. Mr. Perry, through the *Advance,* and other public-spirited citizens were largely instrumental in bringing this industry to Canton, and Mr. Brady's requirement that a suitable location be furnished free was met by public subscription. Thus was started, in 1891, one of Georgia's leading marble factories. Wide attention was focused on Mr. Brady's plant as early as 1894, when he secured the contract for the famous "Lion of the South," a memorial to the Confederate dead which now stands in Grant Park, Atlanta. Mr. Brady executed the design and sculpture himself and carved the memorial from the largest single block of Georgia marble that had ever been quarried. In 1905 Mr. Brady sold his business to R. T. Jones and E. A. McCanless, and the company has since been under their direction.

The contribution of the marble-working industry to the growth of Canton has been important. But the town had not, in 1891, yet acquired an industry that would bring the increase in population and wealth that was sought. During the next few years there was little visible progress in this direction, but in 1899 came Canton's most important advance in industrial development.

For a long time it had been realized that the town offered excellent natural advantages for the establishment of a textile industry. Outside capital had failed to take advantage of the situation. In 1899 a number of local citizens, including R. T. Jones, who became the leading spirit in the movement, succeeded in financing an enterprise which they called the Canton Cotton Mills. It was incorporated for $100,000, and the factory was erected on the Etowah River, commencing operations the following year. The mills were successful from the start (the capitalization has since been tripled) ; and, furnishing employment for a large number of people, were chiefly responsible for Canton's unprecedented in-

HOMES OF E. M. McCANLESS AND E. A. McCANLESS, CANTON

OFFICE OF THE GEORGIA MARBLE FINISHING WORKS, CANTON

crease in population from 1900 to 1910. In 1924 a second unit was added to the Canton Cotton Mills with the organization by Louis L. Jones of Mill No. 2. The new mill employs about 550 of the eleven or twelve hundred workers employed in Canton's cotton-mill industry. It uses from 25,000 to 30,000 bales of cotton a year, has 1,500 looms and 45,000 spindles, and produces "Canton denim," a well-known, standard product.

The present character of Canton has received a good deal of its shaping from the cotton mills. Which is to say that they furnish employment for more than a third of its population (1930: 2,892); that they help to give it prominence outside; and that their coming removed the last traces of drowsiness from what is now a wide-awake and progressive little city. But it is not to say that Canton is the average mill town; its cultural and religious opportunities, its clean and attractive appearance, and its good moral tone are distinctly above the average. In all of which the mill heads have played their part.

Canton Today

The development of Canton has been briefly outlined from settlement days up to the turn of the century. Of what has happened in the last thirty years, the town itself, as it is today, furnishes the best evidence.

The population, including that of North Canton, across the Etowah River, is estimated now at about 4,500. Canton has modern waterworks and sewerage systems, electric light, paved streets, and an efficient fire department. The town contains a large number of attractive homes, some of which are pictured in this book. It has an excellent high school and graded school, and three splendid church buildings: Methodist, Presbyterian, and Baptist.

The business section is filled with modern stores, shops, and offices. There are two banks, Bank of Canton and Etowah Bank (established in 1927), with combined resources of $1,500,000. The Jones Mercantile Company, capitalized at over $1,000,000, has its main store here and also a number of affiliated enterprises, including Canton Wholesale Company, Etowah Manufacturing Company (garments), Cherokee Farm Products Corporation (dairy products), Cherokee Planing & Lumber Company, and the Hotel

CANTON COTTON MILL NO. 2

COKER'S HOSPITAL, CANTON

Canton, a well-known North Georgia hostelry. Still other enterprises are sponsored by the parent company, of which Paul W. Jones, one of Canton's business leaders, is president and general manager.

The principal industry of Canton, besides the cotton mills, is the marble-working business. A number of companies operate in this field, the largest being The Georgia Marble Finishing Works and the Continental Marble & Granite Company. Several hundred men are employed by this industry, and the products of these companies find national use. Other industrial enterprises in Canton include an ice plant, a cotton gin, and a lumber mill.

The *Cherokee Advance,* since 1912 published by J. P. Rudasill, continues to hold its place as one of Georgia's live weeklies and as a stimulating factor in the progress of Canton and Cherokee County.

An active Chamber of Commerce and Woman's Club are among the civic organizations which have played and are playing a large part in the all-round development of Canton. To the efforts of the Woman's Club was largely due the establishment of Brown Park, a historic and beautiful spot made from the old homesite of Joseph E. Brown, Georgia's War Governor.

In the center of Canton stands Cherokee County's magnificent new marble courthouse, and near by is the handsome new government building which houses the second-class postoffice. Coker's Hospital, established in 1923, is one of Canton's important institutions and provides excellent medical and surgical facilities under the supervision of a capable staff.

Canton is easily accessible by railroad or highway. It is situated in an environment of great natural beauty, and is peopled by a high type of citizens, with a background of the Old South and pioneer days. With its many natural advantages, some of them as yet undeveloped, Canton may well be considered as one of the coming cities of Georgia.

CHAPTER XII

OTHER TOWNS OF THE COUNTY .

CONTRIBUTING their own share in the development of Cherokee County are four incorporated towns besides Canton: Ball Ground, Woodstock, Holly Springs, and Waleska. The first three, situated on the line of the Louisville & Nashville Railroad, which runs north and south through the county, and also on the arterial State Highway No. 5, have drawn much of their growth from the presence of excellent transportational facilities. The fourth, Waleska, while off the beaten track, is well known as the seat of Reinhardt College.

All of these towns are peopled with enterprising citizens, and are, if hardly frenzied centers of trade and industry, at least thriving, progressive communities from which trade and industry are by no means lacking. Each has an individual character, drawn from the advantages of its particular environment and from the nature of the part which it plays in the economic life of Cherokee County. And each has its record of participation in the history of the county.

Ball Ground

Ball Ground, the largest of these four places, is a substantial town of eight hundred or more inhabitants, and is situated eleven miles north and slightly east of Canton. It is the northernmost town in Cherokee County, although a small portion of Nelson, three miles farther up the highway, extends from Pickens County into Cherokee.

The name of Ball Ground, as already explained, is a survival of Indian days, when the site of the present town was used by the Cherokees for their national pastime, the ball-play. The several hills on which the town is built sweep up from a broad level space to the south, probably the identical tract on which the Cherokees once won a game of ball from their southern neighbors, the Creeks, for the prize of a thousand square miles of land.

BIRDSEYE VIEW OF BALL GROUND

STREET SCENE, WOODSTOCK

Although its name has always been applied to the immediate locality, Ball Ground did not come into existence as a town until the railroad passed through it in 1882. Its development up to that year consisted mainly of two country stores and half a dozen dwellings. The community was almost purely agricultural.

When the survey of the Marietta & North Georgia line was run through Ball Ground in 1882, the officials of the road decided to put up a depot there and start a town to go along with it. Land for a townsite was contributed to the railroad by landowners of the vicinity, whose deed of transfer stated that "The consideration moving each of us in the establishing of this town is the enhanced value to our lands within and adjacent to the said town, and the general benefit to the country, by which we shall be benefited." Those who donated land were Sarah E. Carpenter, Martha Carpenter, J. W. Byers, P. H. Lyon, F. M. Waldrup, A. M. F. Hawkins, Ancil Bearden, F. M. Waldrup, Ellen Byers, J. C. Carpenter, N. A. Lyon, Hester A. Byers, Berty Carpenter.

The railroad officials laid this land off into town lots and held a sale of them in April, 1882. Nearly all the lots were disposed of at once, and the town immediately began to build up. Within two years Ball Ground had an estimated population of 250, a large number of new buildings, three church organizations, a high school, a charter (from the fall term of the legislature of 1883), and a complete set of municipal officers. The incorporators of the town were W. A. Hayes, W. J. Boling, Captain Patterson H. Lyon, M. G. Bates, and J. A. Byers. The first officers of Ball Ground, elected in January of 1884, were: Captain Patterson H. Lyon, mayor; Dr. A. M. F. Hawkins, W. A. Hayes, R. J. Boling. and J. H. Kilby, councilmen; J. N. Percell, marshal.

A new charter was obtained for Ball Ground in 1911 extending its corporate powers, providing for public schools, and otherwise bringing the town up to date.

Ball Ground has always been considered as one of the best business points on the railroad. In addition to providing a market for nearby agricultural sections it has a number of well-developed industries, such as ginning, saw-milling, and woodworking.

The main industry in Ball Ground for a number of years,

however, and the one for which it is best known, is the marble-working industry. Three sizeable concerns operate in this business, the Consumers Monument Company, the Roberts Marble Company, and the Ball Ground Monument Company. Manufactured from marble quarried at Tate, Ga., the products of these companies are widely known and used.

Ball Ground is a clean and attractive town, and a steadily-growing one. It has an excellent school system and two churches, Methodist and Baptist; supports a number of prosperous commercial establishments, including a bank and a hotel, in addition to its industrial enterprises; and contains many attractive homes. There are no finer people anywhere than its citizens.

Woodstock

Woodstock, in the extreme southern part of the county, has a population of about five hundred and is located twelve miles below Canton, midway to Marietta, on the railroad and the state highway. It is in the heart of one of the finest agricultural belts in North Georgia. The rolling, fertile farm lands around Woodstock have made this town an excellent agricultural market and shipping-point for many years.

It was the southern part of Cherokee that was settled first, on account of its flatter topography and greater accessibility, and Woodstock is one of the oldest towns in the county. The famous old Little River Academy, which was one of the earliest good schools in the section and which educated a large number of students even before the Civil War, was located at Woodstock.

When the railroad came through Woodstock in 1879 on its way from Marietta to Canton, it therefore found a well-established little village, which presently became still more flourishing. It was not until 1897, however, that Woodstock was incorporated by the legislature. It had then nearly three hundred inhabitants.

The incorporating act itself appointed the town's first officers. They were: N. A. Fowler, mayor; W. W. Benson, J. H. Johnston, James M. Latham, Mark S. Paden, and Will L. Dean, councilmen. The act also "forever prohibited" the sale of liquor in the town, as had previously been done by the act of 1875 relating to Canton

BAPTIST CHURCH, WOODSTOCK

HOME OF J. H. JOHNSTON, WOODSTOCK

and Woodstock Academy. The town's charter was revised in 1906 to provide for the inauguration of a public school system.

From almost the beginning of Cherokee County's history the Woodstock section has had industries of various kinds. The first grist-mills in the county were located near by, and later on wool-carding, yarn-spinning, and similar activities were engaged in rather extensively. These early industries were made possible by the abundance of waterpower around Woodstock on Little River, Noonday Creek, and other streams. This waterpower continued to be much utilized throughout the last century, and still runs a few old grist-mills near the town. It constitutes a feature which is likely to aid in the further development of Woodstock.

Located in the Georgia gold belt, Woodstock has in the past been the scene of considerable activity in mineral developments. The old Kellogg gold mine and several others of more or less note are within a few miles of Woodstock, and mica and kaolin developments have been made in the locality.

Woodstock has grown mainly as an agricultural town. Even by the 'nineties it was said to be shipping 2,000 bales of cotton yearly, far in excess of the shipments made by any town of comparable size in the section. The town's developers have nearly all been men with large industrial interests, and a number of them have been influential in introducing into the county new and improved methods of farming.

Woodstock contains a number of thriving commercial establishments, a Methodist and a Baptist Church, and a splendid school building. Its residential section presents an attractive appearance.

Holly Springs

Holly Springs is a thriving little town of some three hundred inhabitants, and is located five miles south of Canton on the L. & N. Railroad. The euphonious name of the place is supposed to have been derived from the presence of several holly trees beside a large spring in the western end of town. One of these trees, an unusually large specimen, is still standing.

Like Woodstock, Holly Springs owes its development mainly to the surrounding agricultural region, but industry is also represented. One of the largest lumber companies in the county is located at Holly Springs, turning out normally several million feet of lumber a year.

Just how old the town is is not certain. It was not incorporated until 1906, but the original settlement dates back to Indian days. Its size in 1884, five years after the railroad passed through, was reported by a correspondent of the *Advance* in that year. "We have," he wrote, "a population of 70, three stores, a cotton gin, sawmill, grist-mill, church, schoolhouse, and blacksmith shop." Obviously the main growth of the town must have taken place since 1884.

Holly Springs is almost in the exact center of the Georgia gold belt, and a number of important mineral developments have taken place in the immediate vicinity of the town. No such operations have been carried on for a number of years, however, except at the famous green marble quarry a mile east of Holly Springs. This quarry, which is one of only two in the United States where green or "verde antique" marble is procurable, is one of the Tate marble properties. Although idle part of the time, it has sent out several large shipments recently.

Holly Springs has a Methodist and a Baptist church and a junior high school. Its business men are of a progressive type, and further development is looked for when the paving of the highway through the town, now in progress, is completed.

Waleska

Waleska is a picturesque little village situated in the foothills of upper Cherokee County, eight miles northwest of Canton. It has a population of around three hundred. The town takes its name from Warluskee, the daughter of an Indian chieftain who lived in the section a century ago. When this Indian maiden was removed with her people to the West, her white settler friends, Mr. and Mrs. Lewis W. Reinhardt, named their settlement in her honor.

In preceding chapters (VI, IX) is told something about the early days of the Waleska section, when the Reinhardts, Sharps, Rhynes, Heards, and a few other families, nearly all of German descent, were pioneers there; and about the beginnings of the town when the three Sharp brothers started a store, a gin, and a tobacco factory at the "cross-roads" in 1856. N. Frank Reinhardt, aforementioned, was a partner of John J. A. Sharp in this early store, and they together obtained permission from the government to open a postoffice. For many years the name of the postoffice was spelled "Walesca," but it was finally changed by the department at Washington to its present form to prevent confusion with some other town.

Waleska was chartered by the legislature in 1889. The bill submitted by the town's incorporators was a long and ambitious document that would have done credit to a medium-sized city; and the story is told of how "Uncle Johnny" Lathem, who lived in the southern part of Cherokee County and who at that time represented the county in the legislature, was asked by his colleagues where this large town, of which they had never heard, was located. When "Uncle Johnny," to the great indignation of the town's citizens, was obliged to confess that he too was entirely ignorant of its whereabouts, the bill was tabled and almost failed to pass. For some time afterwards, "Where is Waleska?" would bring guffaws in the legislature. A few more years, however, and they had all heard of Reinhardt College, by then well-established.

Industry in Waleska has in the past included such enterprises as grist-mills and yarn "factories"—waterpower being derived from a number of streams in the vicinity—lumbering, tobacco manufacturing, and a few more or less productive mineral developments. Lumbering still flourishes; a sizeable amount of trade is carried on; agriculture is active.

The principal "industry" of the town itself, however, since the middle 'eighties has been the education of North Georgia boys and girls in Reinhardt College. A history of this school is given in a later chapter. Waleska furnishes an ideal environment for such an institution and has come to be regarded as almost entirely a "school town." Founded by Waleskans, Reinhardt College has from its earliest days been an important part of the life of the town; and has helped Waleska to produce and send out a number of remarkable men and women.

Unincorporated Communities

The militia districts in which the foregoing towns are located have not been given. Canton, Ball Ground, and Woodstock are respectively in the districts bearing those names; Holly Springs is in Wildcat District; and Waleska is in Harbin's District. The other militia districts of Cherokee County also contain villages, or at least clustered settlements, where trade is carried on and the official business of the district conducted. A number of these places contain substantial business establishments; and practically all of them have developed from settlements made by early pioneers of the county.

Toward the close of the last century, before the introduction of rural free delivery, Cherokee County contained a large number of country post offices. Each of these was located at a place easily accessible to the people of the surrounding countryside, and was a sort of center for their business and social activities. In a few cases the postoffice point was simply the residence of a leading farmer, but usually it was a settlement containing several dwellings, a store or two, perhaps a blacksmith shop, cotton gin, and grist-mill. When rural free delivery went into effect in Cherokee County about 1900 it did away with the need for most of these smaller postoffices, and they were discontinued. Some of the settlements themselves were abandoned after a few years; but others have continued to thrive.

A list of the thirty-two post offices which Cherokee had in 1895 contains a number of names almost forgotten as places, as well as the names of these still-flourishing communities. The list, as of 1895, is as follows:

Payne and Kelpin, in Bell's District; Laughing Gal, Field Brothers, and Sutallee, in Fairplay District; Waleska, in Harbin's District; Salacoa and Greeley, in Salacoa District; Cherokee Mills, in Sixes District; Trucken, Bullock's Barn, and Woodstock, in Woodstock District; Holly Springs, Too Nigh, and Owl Hollow Mills, in Wildcat District; Sharp Top, in Clayton District; Joe, in Little River District; Arnold, in Lickskillet District; Batesville, Hickory Flat, and Watson, in Hickory Flat District; Canton and Keithburg, in Canton District; Orange and Fort Buffington, in Mullins District; Ophir and Boling, in Cross Roads District;

HOME OF L. G. GREENE, BALL GROUND

HOME OF MRS. A. W. ROBERTS, BALL GROUND

Ball Ground, in Ball Ground District; McConnell's, A. C. Conn, Laredo, and Mica, in Conn's Creek District.

There are at present only seven postoffices in Cherokee County. They are at Canton, Ball Ground, Woodstock, Holly Springs, Waleska, Lebanon (Too Nigh), and Orange.

Of the present unincorporated communities in Cherokee County, Lathemtown is probably the largest, while Too Nigh, Hickory Flat, Cherokee Mills, and several other places have populations of some size.

Too Nigh, in Wildcat District, has as its name suggests always suffered the disadvantage of being too "nigh" other places to become a full-fledged town itself. This village bears the distinction of having two names; "Too Nigh" applies to the railroad station while the postoffice is called Lebanon. Too Nigh is an old and time-honored settlement and has always contained a number of substantial citizens, whose interests are mainly agricultural. The village is well served in the matter of transportation, being on a railroad and a state highway. The good residents of Too Nigh, who are by now used to facetiousness, will not object to the following quotation—a description of their village in 1884 written by a carefree correspondent of the *Advance*: "Too Nigh has two stores, two churches, four dwellings, one good schoolhouse, and two old bachelors."

Keithburg, five miles north of Canton on the railroad and highway, is in Canton District. It was established when the railroad passed through on its way to Ball Ground in 1882, and was first given the name of "Mabel." In 1893, when the location of the depot was shifted a hundred yards up the side of a hill so that the engine could get a running start after stopping there, the name of the place also was changed. After the railroad boom was over, Keithburg found itself too near Canton to flourish as a town. The Teasley orchards, largest in the county, are near here.

Hickory Flat is a prosperous farming community six miles southeast of Canton, in Hickory Flat District. It is as old a settlement as Canton, possibly older; and was mentioned in the early days as a possible county seat. The Hickory Flat Academy, incorporated in 1838, was preceded only by Etowah Academy in the County. Several commercial establishments, two churches, and

ONE OF THE G. I. TEASLEY ORCHARDS NEAR KEITHBURG

FIELD OF CORN ON THE W. F. KEITH FARM

an excellent junior high school are supported by the people of Hickory Flat.

Orange, ten miles east of Canton, is in Mullins District. Although still a postoffice, it has decreased in size since the establishment of

Lathemtown, a mile or two distant from Orange. This is a rather thickly-settled community in the midst of a splendid farming region. A mercantile business started here about twenty-five years ago by William A. Lathem now does a larger country trade than any other store in the eastern part of the county. Good church and school advantages are enjoyed by the residents of Lathemtown and Orange.

Cherokee Mills, seven miles southwest of Canton in Sixes District, is the site of a rope factory operated by J. H. Johnston & Sons, prominent Woodstock merchants. This factory, which was established a number of years ago by J. S. Dorn, employs a score or more of men and uses twenty-five or thirty bales of cotton a week. Its product finds wide distribution. This is an attractive little place.

Besides the places mentioned, there are many smaller communities in Cherokee County, containing excellent people and well served by churches and schools, but not particularly significant as towns, which most of them never will be. They are significant, however, as "sub-stations" of the county's greatest industry—agriculture. And they are even notable, when it is considered that their "boy-and-girl crop" has been the source of some of Georgia's best and most useful citizens.

At a number of points in this book reference has been made to the railroad which passed through Cherokee County during the early 'eighties, and to the large part it played in the general development of the section. Because this outlet for the products of the county naturally functioned through the towns and thus contributed importantly to their growth and progress, a chapter on Towns is a logical place for the discussion of this railroad's early history.

It should be borne in mind that the Marietta & North Georgia Railroad (now a part of the L. & N. system) was originally a project of local as well as outside capital and management, and that its establishment was brought about with the active support and encouragement of the county's people. The coming of the railroad was a major event of their times, and of large interest. As such it is an interesting part of the county's history.

Early History of the Railroad

Leading up to the actual establishment of this railroad were several previous attempts to secure such facilities for the county. One of them was made as early as 1846 when the "Etowah Railroad" was chartered by the legislature, but this seems to have been one of the many ill-fated railroad ventures of the last century and the proposed line, which would have crossed Cherokee County somewhere, was never built.

In 1854 the "Ellijay Railroad" obtained a charter. Although this road also failed to get beyond the paper stage, it was the forerunner of something more tangible. Its name was changed by the legislature in 1859 to "Marietta, Canton & Ellijay Railroad"; and in that same year a bill was presented in the legislature asking for state aid in building the line to Canton from Marietta, which was connected with Atlanta by the state's road, the W. & A. This bill had been drawn up in Canton by Judge James R. Brown, Col. William A. Teasley, James Jordan, and others; and was the result of a meeting of citizens held at the courthouse to formulate ways and means of getting a railroad for the county. Prospects looked bright for a time, and the enterprise might have succeeded but for the intervention of the Civil War.

When the war and its aftermath of confusion were over, agitation for a railroad again sprang up in the county, and in 1870 a bill passed in the legislature authorizing the state to lend $15,000 per mile on the Marietta, Canton & Ellijay road when a certain portion of it should have been completed. Pickens County indorsed a part of these bonds. Shortly afterwards the name of the "railroad" was again officially changed, this time to "Marietta & North Georgia."

It now became necessary to raise money locally in order to begin the construction of the railroad, and stock was subscribed in various amounts by a large number of Cherokee Countians and several persons in Marietta. General William Phillips, of Marietta, was the leading promoter of the enterprise and figured prominently in the road's early management. In Canton, Judge James R. Brown took, it is said, some $2,000 worth of stock, Col. William A. Teasley $500 worth, and other citizens varying amounts. Stock was $25 a share. Barbecues and speakings were held, subscriptions were collected, and by small degrees the work of building the railroad got under way.

Construction of the roadbed was started by the firm of Wallace, Haley & Company, which soon gave up and turned the job over to a succession of other local contractors, R. F. Maddox & Company, Fields, McAfee, Tate & Company, and J. M. McAfee & Company. Captain McAfee finished the road to Canton, completing it well before the specified time.

And then, one happy day in November, 1879, "Little Mary" came puffing into the new station at Canton, billowing clouds of black smoke from a huge smokestack and making a noise calculated to wake the dead; and the joy of the populace, which had held its breath during the uncertain stages of the road's construction, was practically unlimited. People from far and near came to attend the ceremonies and look at the train. Presently, the track ending at Canton, the train turned around and headed back for Marietta, while everybody cheered frantically. The railroad was a fact.

The reason the engine was called "Little Mary" is, so far as research discovers, that it ran on a narrow-gauge track. It had to be little. In addition, the whole line was remarkable for the number and suddenness of its curves. The consequence was that "Little Mary" had a habit of jumping the track on an average of about twice a round trip, necessitating the arrival of a "monkey crew" and a delay of several hours. The lost time was not of vital importance, as the train only ran, at first, once in every few days.

Conditions were improved, however, and this schedule was stepped up; and by the latter part of 1881 four trains were running daily. Business in Canton had by then picked up wonderfully, and the entire county was greatly stimulated.

For over two years Canton continued to be the northern terminus of this railroad, while intimations gathered force to the north that it would like to maintain its strategic position. However this might have been, the railroad bridge over the Etowah, three miles east of Canton, was finished in February, 1882, and successfully crossed by an engine, the driver of which was commended in the *Advance* for his ability and courage. The track was soon built through "Mabel" and went on to Ball Ground, where a train arrived on May 20, 1882, to be greeted by another celebration.

In September a similar event took place in Jasper; and by January of 1884 the track was completed to Ellijay. It was five more years before the road was built to Murphy, N. C., the management having become involved in all manner of legal disputes and internal strife. The citizens of Cherokee County had long been out of the enterprise and desired only to see the railroad touch a northern connection.

They were, however, much interested in one improvement which was made at this time, the widening of the track to standard-gauge width. This was done in June, 1889, when, after preliminary work over the entire line, the track was changed to broad or standard gauge in one day, the schedule hardly being disturbed.

After a number of vicissitudes in its management, during which however the track finally reached Knoxville, Tenn., the Marietta & North Georgia was taken over, about 1905, by the Louisville & Nashville system, of which it is still a part.

Other railroads have been proposed for Cherokee County in the past, especially during the last two decades of the preceding century when a railroad fever seemed to hit the entire country. Many citizens of the county will remember the agitation for an east-and-west railroad through the county during that period. Several such projects even reached the incorporation stage, among them the "Kingston, Waleska & Gainesville Railroad" of which Colonel John J. A. Sharp, of Waleska, was an active promoter; though none of these lines were ever built. It is entirely possible that some future mineral or industrial development to take place

141

in the county will revive, and even fulfill, the dream of many an earlier industrialist and promoter, and that an east-and-west railroad through the county will actually come to pass. In the meantime, cross-county traffic will have to confine itself to several well-traveled highways.

CHAPTER XIII

MINERALS AND MINING

SINCE the dawn of time men have delved into the earth in search of mineral treasure; and since DeSoto's march in 1540 Georgia has been one of their important prospecting-grounds. Whether DeSoto passed through what is now Cherokee County on his famous quest for gold, nobody knows; but that he traversed lands which were included in the *original* Cherokee is certain. Thus it can be said that the first recorded event in the history of Cherokee County was the arrival of a group of gold-seekers.

They were not successful, these earliest fortune-hunters from Spain. Was it because the Indians were too crafty to guide them where they might have found gold, or was it because the Indians themselves did not know their hills and valleys contained the precious yellow metal? No one can say. But if the Indians did not have such knowledge then, they came into it some time during the next three hundred years. And they were the first to do so, for the white man's Gold Rush of 1829 was inspired by the sight of gold nuggets and ornaments which the Indians—unfortunately for themselves—had allowed the white man to glimpse.

How the Georgia Gold Rush affected the formation of Cherokee County has already been explained; how gold and other minerals have affected the economic life and activity of the county will be related, in part, in this chapter. The story is, in many respects, a strange one. It seems to raise certain questions to which no entirely satisfactory answer can be supplied. Certain parts of this story come down to us almost as legend. Most of it is, in fact, musty with the odor of time; for today in Cherokee mining is almost a lost art. But despite the haziness, the gaps, and the inconsistencies of the story, it remains one of the most fascinating parts of the history of Cherokee County; and viewed in perspective, suggests not the finished play but only the end of an act, with a new set of events preparing in the wings. . . .

Mineral Resources

Back in 1887 a leading industrial journal heard rumblings of a current mineral excitement in Cherokee County, and sent a man around to investigate. The reporter, himself a mining engineer, visited miners and prospectors and promoters, looked at samples of ore and tested them, and made his report. It read:

"The following minerals abound in Cherokee County: Asbestos, barytes, chert, copper, chromite, feldspar, garnets, gold, gypsum, hornblende, iron, kavanite, limonite, manganese, marble, mica, plumbago, pyrites, soapstone, stealite, and talc."*

This amazing list has since been verified by state geologists. That all these minerals actually "abound," however, is an article of faith that was much more prevalent in 1887 than it is now, as attested by the fact that scarcely half a dozen mineral developments of any kind have been carried on in the county in as many years. The mineral resources of the county are well known, but they are today regarded with calmness, and the desultory attempts at their reclamation with a similar lack of enthusiasm. It was different in the 'thirties, the 'fifties, the 'eighties. The attitudes of the two centuries in this matter are irreducible to a common denominator of facts, suggesting two entirely different sets. Perhaps some commentator will come forward to tell why this should be; it would be preferable, though, to learn for certain which attitude is the better justified.

At any rate, the old enthusiasms produced some notable ventures into the mining field; and actual occurrences are more safely within the historian's province than vain speculations. Much of the color of nineteenth-century life in Cherokee County came from these mining ventures—with a distinct tinge of gold always visible. The fascination that gold has had for the human race since time immemorial, and the adventurous character of the early gold-miners, lend an added interest to accounts of Cherokee County's gold mines; which are first taken up here.

Gold Mines of Cherokee County

The gold belt of Georgia, geologically determined, passes through Cherokee County from northeast to southwest, and is

*Southern Industrial Record, 1887.

about ten miles wide. Cherokee is in the very center of this belt, and shares with Lumpkin and one or two other counties the top honors for (past) gold production in the state. On this belt are located the old gold mines of the county.

Following the height of the Georgia Gold Rush, in the summer of 1830 when 3,000 men were said to be digging gold in the Indian territory, many prospectors remained as more or less permanent settlers to make their living by panning the earth from the hillsides and creek-beds. In some parts of the county where the surface deposits were richest, mining camps were a common sight for many years after the original "rush." One of the largest of these camps was a few miles south of Canton on a small stream known as Blanket Creek.

The customary method for reclaiming free or "placer" gold— ores could not be handled with the crude equipment of these men —was by panning or washing it out of the soil, a few grains at a time, with the aid of a frying-pan filled with a gruel of water and gold-bearing earth, or of a "long-tom" set in a riffle of a stream. This was a long box open at each end, with cleats nailed to the bottom to catch the heavy grains of gold as the stream washed them out of the earth placed in the box.

When the California Gold Rush of 1849 began, most of these men set out for the West and its fabulous gold deposits. The gold-panning business took a slump in North Georgia, but in the meantime several mines had been sunk in Cherokee County, among them the Kellogg, Putnam, Sixes, and Franklin, where crude stamp-mills (a "stamp" was a heavy hammer, driven by water-power and used to crush ore) had been set up. By 1852, it is said, there were several hundred mines in the county—most of them small, of course. These smaller mines were worked with more or less profit until the Civil War, but after the War their owners went back to the raising of foodstuffs. Even then it was said to be a common occurrence for a householder to pick up a nugget in his back yard, or to go out and pan five dollars' worth of gold any time he needed the money.

The industry continued for some years, with a few mines always in operation, until the coming of the railroad to Cherokee County in 1879; and shortly thereafter a fresh boom began, not only in gold-mining but in mineral developments of all kinds. Many old mines were revived and new ones were opened. Mint figures credited Cherokee County with producing $19,500 worth of gold in 1880, $30,271 in 1890. Mines brought fancy prices. Promoters from outside organized stock companies, most of which were based on some poor old run-down mine that had been picked up for a song; and after a few outside investors had lost money in such propositions capital grew wary and honest developers suffered. The eventual decline of gold mining in the county was due in part to this skepticism, in part to the wasteful and inefficient methods used in most of the mines, and in part to the exhaustion of all the large deposits of "free" gold. The end of the century witnessed the decline of nearly all the county's gold mines, and for many years now the activity in this field has been negligible. But it was exciting while it lasted.

Some of the important gold mines operated in Cherokee County during the last century were the Sixes Mine, six miles southwest of Canton, supposedly the oldest in the county and said to have produced half a million dollars' worth of gold between the time when the Indians worked it and the time of the Civil War; the Micou, Putnam, Haynes, Robert, LaBelle, and Old Cherokee, all on Blanket Creek just south of Canton and all extensively worked during the 'eighties and 'nineties; the Georgiana, the Worley, the Kellogg, the Rudasill, the Davis, and others, many of them quite productive in their day.

Most important and most productive of all the gold mines in the county, however, was the Franklin Mine, later called the Creighton, in the northeast corner of the county. Because of the wide interest concerning this old mine a rather full account of it is given here.

The Franklin Gold Mine

Among the gold prospectors attracted in about the year 1833 to the northwestern part of the county was an Englishman named John Pascoe, who had been unsuccessful in the mines of Lumpkin County and arrived in Cherokee almost penniless. He was fortunate enough, however, to obtain a "stake" from Major Wyley Petty, one of the first settlers in that part of the county and by then a well-to-do farmer.

Fitted out with means and provisions by Major Petty, Pascoe leased ten acres of land from the Leonard brothers, who lived near Ophir, and had them run a ditch from a nearby creek to a little five-stamp mill which he erected. Pascoe was successful this time, and from the earnings of his little mill he bought the ten acres and all the lots adjoining, which he left as part of a snug fortune to his brothers and sisters on his death some years later.

A few months before Pascoe came to the county, a poor widow in the southern part of the state, Mrs. Mary G. Franklin, drew a forty-acre lot in the Gold Lottery of 1832. Soon afterwards she was surprised to receive a dozen or so offers in one week for her holding, and becoming excited about the lot herself she mounted her little gray mule and made a trip to Cherokee County to look at her property. When she arrived she found a score of men at work on the lot, shoveling dirt and panning out gold. Mrs. Franklin soon obtained a trusty man to drive away the intruders and take charge of the property until she could return with her family. She then went back after her children in South Georgia, and soon the whole family was panning gold.

Before long Mrs. Franklin was able to build a rude stamp mill, utilizing the waters of the Etowah which flowed through her lot. She proved to be a good business woman, and under her supervision the mill was so productive that she was able eventually to buy the adjoining lots, build a large and beautiful home, own slaves, and give all her children a good education.

Another fortunate drawer in the Gold Lottery had been a young man named McDonald. He married one of Mrs. Franklin's daughters and proceeded to take a fortune in gold from his own lot.

At some time before the Civil War one of these mines, probably that of Mrs. Franklin, is said to have caved in upon and killed a number of slaves working in it.

All of these gold properties and possibly others, amounting in all to some 1,280 acres, were brought together in 1882 under the management of a group of Northern capitalists, who incorporated themselves as the Franklin & McDonald Mining & Manufacturing Company, with a capitalization of $250,000. Colonel A. H.

Moore, the resident manager and a southern mining engineer of note, began to develop the mines in an up-to-date fashion, installing new machinery, throwing up a dam across the Etowah, putting in a tramway system between shafts and mills, and building houses for the hundred or more employes of the mines. Several shafts were put down, one of them with a depth of 500 feet being the deepest in Georgia. When completed about 1890, these improvements had cost about $200,000, and had won the Franklin Mine wide note as a model plant of its kind.

Colonel Moore found that the Franklin properties contained almost every known kind of gold ore, including free deposits, quartz veins, and gold sulphurites. He helped to invent a new chlorination process for the reduction of gold from its sulphurites, and also used the quicksilver or amalgam process as well as the more modern cyanide process. The employment of these methods at the Franklin marked the only scientific approach to large-scale mining that has ever been made in Cherokee County.

In 1883 the vice-president, J. Mc. Creighton, a wealthy railroad official from Philadelphia, bought out the other stockholders, and the property was thereafter called the Creighton Mine. Mr. Creighton died in 1887, and Manager Moore resigned, and the management fell into several different hands before operations were halted shortly after 1900.

Concerning the yield of the Franklin Mine nothing definite can be given. It was said at one time, about 1893, to be producing $1,000 a day, and estimates of its total production after 1880 run as high as $1,000,000. In addition, several hundred thousand dollars' worth of gold is said to have been taken out during the early days of the county. But there is no way to arrive at definite figures.

For nearly thirty years now the Franklin properties have scarcely been touched, except for a few attempts to reclaim free gold by primitive methods. It is claimed, however, that vast quantities of low-grade but profitable ore still exist there. Contributing to the decline of the mines was the system of remote control used by the owners, but a more immediate cause was the breaking through of the river into one of the shafts, flooding the mines and rendering further operations impossible except at great expense for repairs.

Today there is little left to indicate the glory of the gold mine that was, except a hole in the ground and a gaunt and weather-beaten frame structure crumbling into dust on the banks of the Etowah.

Other Minerals

Until 1880 or thereabouts gold was the principal and almost the only mineral to receive attention from developers in Chero-kee County. About that time the extraordinary diversity of the county's mineral resources began to receive attention, and "booms" sprang up, during the rest of the century, in nearly all the other minerals previously listed in this chapter.

During earlier years, however, there were at least one or two mining excitements caused by other minerals than gold. For instance, during the 'fifties a copper-mining fever swept south from Copper Hill, Tenn., and engulfed Cherokee County. One of the developments resulting at this time was the old copper mine near Canton. A corporation was formed by Joseph E. Brown and others to develop what later became famous as "Copper-Mine Hill," and a shaft was sunk from the top of this hill and connected with a lateral shaft opening at the foot. This is said to have been the first shaft sunk for copper in the state. Rather extensive operations were carried on and a good deal of money was invested by various persons, but the mine proved valueless. Only one person profited by the enterprise—Joseph E. Brown, who sold his stock while the excitement was at its height. Tradition has it that he invested $450, all he had, and sold out for $25,000.

The mineral "booms" of the 'eighties and 'nineties produced more excitement than returns, but a few developments, chiefly in mica and asbestos, proved fairly profitable. Attempts to open up a large vein of iron which was supposed to exist in the northern part of the county were unsuccessful, although in Bartow and several other counties to the west iron has been found in paying quantities and developed to some extent. Ford's Furnace, just across the line in Bartow County, turned out quantities of pig iron before the Civil War.

During the present century a number of mica developments have turned out well, in various parts of the county. The old Dean Mica Mine, near Woodstock, and the Cook Mine, near Orange, have been quite productive. There are, however, no mica operations in progress at the present time in Cherokee County.

One of the few mineral developments still active in the county is the green marble quarry near Holly Springs, owned by the Georgia Marble Company; although work there is conducted only at intervals. Discovered some time during the 'eighties, this quarry is unique in the South, and its product, green or "verde antique" marble, is said to be matched by only one other American quarry, in New England.

White, gray, and pink marble deposits are also to be found in Cherokee County, but not, it is said, in profitable quantities.

The future development that may be made of the county's mineral resources does not come under the head of history, but it may be said that there are many persons who confidently believe such developments will play an increasingly large part in the economic scheme of the county. Possibly such activity will take a new line, exploit one of the minerals that have been overlooked heretofore. Or possibly a new and scientific "gold rush" will transpire, with modern and economical methods for the extraction of gold being used on the large quantities of low-grade ore that are known to exist in the county.

At any rate, there are possibilities.

CHAPTER XIV

THE CANTON BAR

I̶T IS TRUE of Cherokee County, as of most other parts of the South, that its ambitious young men in every period have felt a strong attraction to the law as a vocation. The county's lawyers have been numerous and able. A full history of the Canton Bar, giving the names of all the members it has had and relating their more remarkable exploits before the bar and on the "platform," would fill a good-sized book—though one of absorbing interest; and would draw a part of its material from the annals of the state and even the nation.

In the sketch which is all that can be attempted here, the mention accorded to even the most prominent of these men will necessarily be brief; but the names, at least, of a considerable proportion of the members of the Canton Bar—that is, of the lawyers who have both lived and practiced in Cherokee County—are supplied.

Members of the Canton Bar

It is not known who was the first actual resident of what is now Cherokee County to practice law in the county's early courts. Although the names of several lawyers appear on the first court records, none of these are recognizable as having been local men, and it is known that lawyers from outside the county dominated the practice in the Cherokee Superior Court for a number of years. Nor is it known certainly who was the first resident of what is now Cherokee County to be admitted locally to the practice of law. It may have been a young man by the name of Gaston M. Underwood, who was the first person so admitted, but who may have lived anywhere in northwest Georgia since at the time of his admittance—February, 1833—the Cherokee Superior Court was the only court in that part of the state.* So the honor of being the first member of the Canton Bar was probably shared

---

*See p. 43.

by *three* young lawyers, Allen Dyer, Richard W. Jones, and John I. Word, all of whom the records show were admitted to the practice of law at the March term, 1834.

After this, from time to time, other Cherokee Countians were duly constituted by the superior court as full-fledged attorneys, and it was not long before some of them had flourishing practices. Among the recruits to the Canton Bar before the Civil War period were Mortimer G. Donaldson, N. Frank Reinhardt, Augustus M. Reinhardt, General Daniel H. Bird, William A. Teasley, Samuel Weil, James O. Dowda, and James Jordan.

Mortimer G. Donaldson was the son of Judge Joseph Donaldson, Canton pioneer and developer. He made a successful lawyer, served a term as sheriff, and was active in a number of progressive movements.

N. Frank Reinhardt, son of the Waleska settler, read law under Canton's Joseph E. Brown, later attended the University of Virginia, and practiced in Canton several years before the outbreak of the Civil War. He enlisted in the Southern Army and was killed.

Augustus M. Reinhardt, a younger brother, was admitted to the Canton Bar just before the War began, and he also enlisted. He came out of the conflict lame but with the rank of captain, won by his gallantry. Following the War he moved to Atlanta and practiced law there, also becoming, it is said, the founder of Atlanta's street railway. Captain Reinhardt's work in connection with the establishment of Reinhardt College is mentioned later in this book.

James Jordan had a good law business and was also clerk of the superior court continuously from 1838 to 1850.

Samuel Weil, a Hebrew and originally a peddler, came to Canton about 1850 and began reading law. He passed the bar examination, became a lawyer of ability, and gained a lucrative practice. After the War he also moved to Atlanta, where some of his family now live.

Among the early cases pled by Canton lawyers were many of the firm of Bird & Teasley. General Daniel H. Bird was a Mexican War veteran, and a high-grade lawyer. He formed a partnership with William A. Teasley in 1856. Colonel Teasley was also an able attorney and served several terms in the legislature. He was a member of the famous Secessionist Convention which voted for Georgia's withdrawal from the Union; and although he did not favor secession, like the illustrious Lee he cast his lot with the Confederacy out of loyalty to his state. Colonel Teasley was a leading attorney in Canton for more than 40 years.

James O. Dowda, a noted old local (Methodist) preacher, also belonged to the Canton Bar for many years. He was a native of Ireland and came to Cherokee County in 1848. Judge Dowda was a public-spirited man and a great-hearted one, and was much respected.

Another Canton lawyer during this period before the Civil War was one who has not yet been mentioned but who must be considered as the most illustrious member the Canton Bar ever had—Joseph Emerson Brown. An account of the War Governor's life will be found in an earlier chapter.* He was admitted to the bar at Canton in September, 1845, and began his great political career there with his election, in 1849, as state senator.

Cherokee County provides the only instance in the state's history where a father and his son have both occupied the governor's seat. Joseph M. Brown, son of Joseph E. Brown, was never a member of the Canton Bar, but he was born in Canton (1851) and received his preparatory education there. "Little Joe," as he was called, started out in a clerkship of the Western & Atlantic Railway and in 1904 was made state railroad commissioner. Removed from office in 1906 by Governor Hoke Smith, he defeated Smith for the governorship at the next election—only to lose it back to him two years later. When Smith resigned to become a senator, Brown won the office again, over present Chief Justice Richard B. Russell Sr., and three other opponents. Governor Brown was known for his literary as well as his political activities, and was also a successful business man and farmer. He died March 4, 1932, at Marietta.

The remarkable Brown family contributed two other talented members to the Canton Bar, James R. Brown, brother of Joseph E., and *his* son, George R. Brown. Both of them entered on the practice of law in Canton, the former shortly after his brother

*See p. 69.

and the latter about 1885. James R. Brown was assisted to obtain an education at Yale, as his brother had been, by Dr. John W. Lewis, wealthy pioneer physician of Canton, and later married a daughter of Dr. Lewis. Judge Brown became a wealthy farmholder of the county and an influential figure in the political circles of the state. He served several years as judge of the Blue Ridge Circuit. His son, George R. Brown, was one of the most brilliant lawyers the section ever produced. He started his political career at the age of 24 when he was sent to the legislature from Cherokee County, and attained the solicitorship of the Blue Ridge District when little past 30. It is doubtful if any family in the state has ever surpassed the record of these four Browns.

After the Civil War several new names appeared on Canton's roster of lawyers, among them Captain H. W. Newman, a distinguished Confederate officer. Besides legal talent he had a great reputation as a wit, and was famous all over the state for his humorous speeches. Captain Newman practiced in Canton for many years.

Perry Pinkney DuPree, another Confederate veteran, received his education after the War and began the practice of law in Canton during the latter 'seventies. The oldest member of the local bar, he is still active professionally and his large legal knowledge is highly respected by his associates. His brother, Sam DuPree, also practiced law in Canton for a number of years.

Ben F. Payne entered the practice of law in Canton about the same time Colonel DuPree did and was his early partner. Mr. Payne was also a local (Methodist) preacher.

John D. Attaway, law-partner of Captain Newman during the 'eighties, held the office of county school commissioner for a long term of years.

C. D. Maddox was admitted to the Canton Bar during the 'eighties and was for a time the partner of George R. Brown.

George Isham Teasley was admitted to the Canton Bar shortly after 1880 and began his practice in the office of his father, William A. Teasley. He became a successful lawyer, held the office of county school commissioner several years, and acquired important agricultural interests. He is still engaged in the practice of law and is one of Canton's oldest and best-known citizens.

Thomas Hutcherson, of Salacoa, was admitted to the bar at Canton about 1890. A young man of great promise, he defeated the "populist" candidate in 1894 to become Cherokee's representative in the legislature, advanced to the solicitorship of the Blue Ridge Circuit, and was holding that position on his untimely death a few years later.

William Alonzo Covington, of Atlanta, though not a member of the Canton Bar was born and reared in Cherokee County. Judge Covington began the practice of law in Moultrie about 1898, served several terms in the legislature, and has been a prominent figure in state politics.

John H. Smithwick, though likewise not of the Canton Bar, is one of the only two men born in Cherokee County ever to go to Congress. He was elected from a Florida district.

John Stephens Wood, present congressman from the Ninth, is a native of Cherokee County and has been a member of the Canton Bar since 1914. On account of Judge Wood's rapid political advancement he holds the interesting record of having resigned from every public office he held before his present one, including the positions of city attorney, representative from the county, solicitor of the Blue Ridge Circuit, and judge of that circuit. He is one of the ablest statesmen ever produced by the county.

Among the legislators from Cherokee County have been several other present members of the Canton Bar, John Wellborn Collins, Howell Brooke, and Henry Grady Vandiviere—the latter having served both as representative and senator.

The present roster of this bar, besides those members already mentioned, includes W. E. Coleman, Edgar Maxwell McCanless, A. J. Henderson, Elmer Cline, and J. Hines Wood—all of them well-known and capable lawyers. The collective ability and reputation of the Canton Bar are unexcelled in any town of comparable size in the state, and would do credit to many a larger place.

Courthouses of Cherokee County

Through five courthouses in Cherokee County have resounded the forensic duels of the county's "legal lights," past and present.

The first was the building mentioned in the early court records as being "near the house of John Lay," in Canton. At this

"OVER THE HILL"

. . . where Cherokee County provides for its poor, in a manner not only humanitarian but conducive to self-respect. The county farm is located about four miles southeast of Canton.

THE HONOR SYSTEM IS USED

. . . at Cherokee County's convict camp. This system, which is due largely to the present commissioner of roads and revenues, contributes toward the genuine reformation of nearly all the county's prisoners. Cruel treatment is taboo here. The camp is situated near the county farm.

place the second court of the original Cherokee County was held, in September of 1832; and when Canton (then "Etowah") was definitely agreed on as the permanent county seat of the new Cherokee County, this old "courthouse" continued to be the official center for the transaction of legal business in the county. It was not, however, if we may judge from the old court records, a very good courthouse. Recommendations were made regularly by the old grand juries for the replacement, or at least repair, of this courthouse—"if, indeed, we may be said to have any." The location of this old building is not exactly determinable, but is supposed to have been near the present site occupied by the residence of E. A. McCanless, on Cumming Street; and it seems likely that it was a log cabin originally built to be used as somebody's house.

About 1840 the counsel of the grand juries prevailed and a new brick courthouse was erected on the site where the courthouse park is now located in Canton. This building, which is still remembered by several older citizens of the town, was burned by Sherman's raiders in 1865, as previously related. John B. Garrison, noted early settler and at that time clerk of the superior court, succeeded in saving the records and papers in the courthouse by hiding them in his own home; for which service he was voted $50 by the grand jury thirty years later. Among the other buildings destroyed in the general conflagration at that time were the residence and law office of Joseph E. Brown, then governor of the state.

For the next nine years the courts of the county met in the old Presbyterian church, which was located on the site of the present J. J. Groves residence, across the street from the Canton grade school. This old church was also used at one time as a school building.

In 1871 the ordinary was empowered by the legislature to issue $10,000 worth of bonds for the construction of a courthouse, and shortly thereafter the new building was started. By the time it was finished in 1874, an additional $5,000 worth of bonds had been authorized and issued, and the new courthouse was considered a very attractive and expensive building. It was of brick, and stood on the old site of the former courthouse, in the middle of what was then a town square. This building was destroyed by fire in 1928, after standing fifty-four years.

The present courthouse was completed in 1929. Constructed from white Georgia marble, it is one of the most beautiful public buildings in the state, and is thoroughly modern in plan. The county committee which supervised the construction of this build-

PRESENT COURTHOUSE OF CHEROKEE COUNTY

ing was composed of E. A. McCanless (chairman), Carl W. Groover, Dr. R. M. Moore, A. V. Jones, W. D. Latimer, and R. O. Fincher (the latter an ex-officio member as commissioner of roads and revenues); this body having been appointed by the legislature. Bonds in the amount of $150,000, bearing 4½ per cent interest, were voted by the citizens to finance the construction of this courthouse.

CHAPTER XV

EDUCATION

THE "carpetbaggers" who dominated the government of Georgia for several years following the Civil War were, it is agreed, a generally worthless and wild-eyed crew. They perpetrated many outrages. Their name is anathema.

And so it is rather surprising that the carpetbag government should have done a finer thing for the children of Georgia than any previous government, no matter how respectable, had ever done in the history of the state. Such, however, is the case. The new state constitution framed by the carpetbagger-controlled Convention of 1868 was the means of bringing education within reach of children of all classes, by authorizing the first system of public schools that Georgia had ever had.

The Constitution of 1868 was discarded long ago, but the public schools remain. The cause of education has made great progress in Georgia. The state's present public school system, with its many ramifications and refinements, makes the original idea look poor indeed; and owes so little to it that hardly any gratitude at all now seems due from later citizens of Georgia to—of all people!—the carpetbaggers.

Of course, there were many schools in Georgia before 1868. There were no public schools, but there were "poor schools," "tuition schools," and "academies." "Poor schools" were in every sense what the name implies, and were supported by a small appropriation from the state. "Tuition schools" (or "subscription schools") were organized each term by itinerant and usually not very competent teachers, and were supported by the pupils' parents. "Academies" were of a more permanent nature and a higher educational order, sometimes having as many as two and three teachers, but were maintained in the same way.

It was a simple matter to obtain an education under this system, if you were able to pay for it. Theoretically, it was possible to obtain the rudiments of one even if you weren't able to pay for it, by attending a "poor school." But Georgians, and especially mountaineer Georgians, have never relished the idea of accepting charity, in whatever form offered; and poor children stayed away from the "poor schools" in large and impressive droves. "Tuition schools" formed the real backbone of elementary education in the earlier days of the state, and they were well patronized on the whole, though the teacher's ability was in most

FIRST SCHOOL TEACHER and his wife. Joseph Knox, pioneer settler of Sutallee District, was Cherokee County's first school teacher. His picture is shown here together with that of his wife, who was a daughter of John P. Brooke, one of the three founders of Canton.

cases matched by his small income. "Academies" were mostly for the children of the well-to-do, and were usually located in towns of some size.

All three types of schools existed in Cherokee County during the period referred to, and the foregoing explanation of educational conditions in the state as a whole applies also to Cherokee County. There were "academies" in at least three of the towns, and there were "poor schools" and "tuition schools" to take care of the needs of other sections. That they did not fully meet these needs, either in their number or their scope, was characteristic of the era and not a distinction of the county.

Educational conditions in the "Hills" during the last century have already been described in a preceding chapter. It is only fair to say here that those conditions were not matched in the southern and eastern parts of the county, which had been settled earlier and were wealthier and more populous. Particularly around Canton, Woodstock, and Hickory Flat was this true, all three places having "academies" well before the Civil War.

The first school in the county was the Etowah Academy, at Canton (then Etowah). This institution was chartered by the legislature in 1833, and classes were taught there by Joseph Knox in 1834. Mr. Knox, who thus became Cherokee County's first school teacher, was a noted early settler of near Sutallee, and is thought to have been a descendant of the Rev. John Knox of Scotland. His picture is given here, together with that of his wife. Little is known concerning the early teachers of the Etowah Academy, but about 1844 the school obtained a teacher about whom a great deal is known, Joseph E. Brown, who later became governor of Georgia.

What was evidently the second school in the county was an "academy" at Hickory Flat, chartered in 1838. It can not be learned who was the first teacher of this school, but its first trustees, as named in the incorporating act, were George Gunby, Thomas Johnson, John McConnell, John B. Garrison, and George Taylor.

Little River Academy was the school at Woodstock. It is supposed that this institution was founded a number of years before the Civil War, and it played an important part in the educational life of the county for many years after the War.

For children who did not live near any of these "academies" and whose parents could not afford to "board" them away from home, "tuition schools" were available in different parts of the county. As explained, these were organized annually. Parents of the community were solicited by a prospective teacher, and if a sufficient number of them agreed to "send," a school was begun. Sometimes a father, unable to pay tuition for all his children, would agree to sign up for one and "send" every day, thus giving the whole family what was in effect a joint scholarship.

The teacher of a "tuition school" was usually a young man of some education, but not too much, who wanted to go to college or start himself up in business on the proceeds of the term. Sometimes it was a "professional"—man or woman—but even in this event the teacher's qualifications were generally very ordinary. Of course, there were exceptions to this rule, especially where the income was such as to attract competent teachers.

The "tuition-school" idea flourished long after the introduction of public schools. At first the public-school term was only three months, during which "tuition-school" teachers were simply paid so much a month per pupil—$2 it was—by the county; and after that the term could be extended for those pupils whose parents were willing to make such payment themselves. This plan was used at the Etowah Academy, where nine-month terms were held for a number of years before Canton established its own public school system in 1893.

Inauguration of the state system of public education of course increased the number of schools in Cherokee County, and the general awakening after 1880 was another stimulus. More "academies" were built, and "tuition-schools" flourished mightily, what with the assistance of public funds. By 1884 there were 71 public-school teachers in the county, most of them teaching on an average of six months a year altogether. In 1894 the public-school term was increased from three to five months.

In the meantime a movement for public school systems had started in the towns. Waleska was first in line, provision for a school district appearing in the town's charter of 1889. Canton followed in 1893, and the other towns were not long in obtaining systems of their own.

Canton now has an excellent school system, including one of the best high schools in the state. Credit for good work toward this end is due to Prof. J. P. Cash, present superintendent of the Canton schools. Ball Ground and Woodstock also have good high schools. The Holly Springs school is of junior high ranking. Reinhardt Academy offers high school facilities at Waleska.

In addition to the town systems, the county's public schools

GRAMMAR SCHOOL BUILDING, CANTON

ADMINISTRATION BUILDING, REINHARDT COLLEGE

include forty-eight rural grade schools, of which ten are of junior high ranking. Of these ten six have been built during the administration as county superintendent of Prof. R. C. Sharp, who was also instrumental in raising the public-school term in the county to seven months. The forty-eight county schools are listed as follows:

Avery (junior high), Buffington (j. h.), Bascomb, Big Springs (j. h.), Burris, Chalcedonia, Cherry Grove, Conn's Creek, Cokers, Central Heights, Creighton, Dry Branch, Flat Bottom, Free Home (j. h.), Garland, Gravelly Hill, Holbrook (j. h.), Hickory Flat (j. h.), Indian Knoll, Kings, Little River, Liberty, Lays, Modesto (j h.), Macedonia (j. h.), Mayhugh, Midway, Mill Creek, Mica, Mt. Zion, New Hightower, New Bethel, New Home, North Canton, Oakdale, Othello, Oak Grove, Riverdale, Sandy Plains, Oakland, Salacoa (j. h.), Sharptop, Sixes, Too Nigh, Union Hill (j. h.), Waleska, Zion, Zoar. There are also five colored schools in the county system.

Reinhardt Junior College

Few persons in Georgia have not heard of Reinhardt College, and the fame of this school in the obscure little mountain town of Waleska has spread far beyond the limits of the state. Reinhardt is probably unique among junior colleges in the proportion of its student body that have become ministers and teachers of note. But the school's chief claim to distinction is based on its fifty-year record of service among the youth of Mountain Georgia and the consequent enrichment of intellectual life it has helped to bring about in that section.

Reinhardt College was founded in 1883 by Captain Augustus Michael Reinhardt and Colonel John James Augustus Sharp, both veterans of Lee's Army. Captain Reinhardt was a son of Lewis Warlick Reinhardt, pioneer Waleska settler, in whose honor the school was named. Colonel Sharp, who with his two brothers had come to Cherokee about 1855, had married a sister of Captain Reinhardt.

For a number of years these two men had envisioned Waleska as an educational center for the section, and in the fall of 1883 Captain Reinhardt, then a prominent real estate man of Atlanta, outlined the plan to the North Georgia Methodist Conference. At the close of the year the conference sent Rev. J. T. Linn to Waleska as the first teacher of Reinhardt Academy, as it was then called.

Early in January, 1884, Mr. Linn began the school in an old abandoned shop on the south edge of town, with thirty or forty pupils. The character of this early teacher was a factor in the successful establishment of the school. He is described as having

CAPT. AUGUSTUS   COL. JOHN J. A.
M. REINHARDT   SHARP

had a "rarely furnished mind, an eloquent expression, and an optimistic nature;" and his cheerful energy communicated itself to his pupils, with excellent results.

By the time the second term opened, a building of some pretensions had been erected. It was a three-story frame structure, located on the present site of the girls' dormitory. The land and a large part of the $2,500 required for the building were contributed by Captain Reinhardt, and the balance of the money was made up by Colonel Sharp, Mrs. M. A. Sharp, and other Waleskans.

In 1889 the building and grounds were deeded to the North Georgia Conference, which has since owned and supervised the school. In 1893 the legislature granted a charter which gave the school the new name of Reinhardt Normal College. It has been "Reinhardt Junior College" since 1918.

By 1887 the enrollment of the school had increased to over one hundred; and it continued to grow. The extremely low cost of obtaining what was then an excellent education at this school made it very popular. Total expenses for a boarding-student then amounted to about $7 a month. Some time during the 'nineties Captain Reinhardt built a large twenty-room boarding house, known as the Waleska Hotel, and this was kept filled, as well as

PROF. R. C. SHARP

a number of houses erected for the use of families with children in school. This hotel burned down after a few years. It was located just north of the present administration building.

The early presidents of this institution were all preachers, holding the position as a conference charge and staying only a few years at the most. In 1901 Prof. Ramsey Colquitt Sharp, himself a graduate of the school, a teacher of note, and the son of Colonel John J. A. Sharp, began an administration lasting twenty years (1901-16; 1922-27). During this time he brought up the rating of the school, increased the attendance, and grad-

DOBBS VOCATIONAL BUILDING, REINHARDT COLLEGE

NEW GYMNASIUM, REINHARDT COLLEGE

uated some two hundred boys and girls, including about twenty Baptist and forty Methodist preachers.

In 1911 the old college building burned to the ground, and two years later it was replaced with the present administration building—Mary Stuart Witham Hall—contributed by George S. Witham, a prominent banker. Land for the site was donated by the mother of Professor Sharp.

In 1927 the Samuel C. Dobbs Vocational Building, a handsome structure of native stone, was erected to house the science,

PROF. W. M. BRATTON   DR. S. C. DOBBS

vocational agriculture, and domestic science departments. This is said to be one of the best constructed school buildings in the state. Its donor, Dr. Samuel C. Dobbs, of Atlanta, has been foremost among the later patrons of the school. While president of the Coca-Cola Company (1918-20), he became interested in the work of Reinhardt College and has contributed generously of his time and money during the last twelve years in order to promote its efficiency.

The present boys' dormitory, Hawkes Hall, was contributed by A. K. Hawkes, of Atlanta. The girls' dormitory, John W. Heidt Hall, is the gift of the Woman's Home Missionary Society. A five-hundred-acre farm, with modern stock and dairy barns and other buildings, is part of the college property and is worked largely by school boys.

Since May of 1927 Prof. Walter Marvin Bratton has been president of Reinhardt College. An educator of experience and note, Professor Bratton is the current president of the Junior College Division, Southern Methodist Educational Association. Under his supervision the qualifications of Reinhardt were raised by 1931 to meet, for the first time, the standards of the state department of education, by which the school is now accredited. Reinhardt has been a member of the American Association of Junior Colleges since 1927.

Also under this administration a new gymnasium building, erected with contributions from the Canton Chamber of Commerce and Dr. Samuel C. Dobbs and regarded as one of the finest gymnasiums in the state, was built in 1930.

The present enrollment of the school is about 125.

Following is a complete list of the presidents of Reinhardt College, with their terms of service:

Rev. J. T. Linn, 1884-86; Rev. O. C. Simmons, 1886-87; Rev. C. M. Ledbetter, 1887-88; Rev. Hubert M. Smith, 1888-90; Rev. R. F. Eakes, 1890-91; Rev. C. Evans Pattillo, 1891-94; Rev. E. A. Cole, 1894-95; Prof. Richard W. Rogers, 1895-1901; Prof. Ramsey Colquitt Sharp, 1901-1916; Prof. E. P. Clark, 1916-18; Rev. T. M. Sullivan, 1918-1922; Prof. Ramsey Colquitt Sharp, 1922-1927; Prof. Walter Marvin Bratton, 1927-date.

CHAPTER XVI

CHURCHES

SECULAR history is clear on the point that religion has always been an important factor in civilization. The moral and inspirational influence of religion has spurred the human race on to achievement in all ages. It is not surprising that the greatest nation on earth should be a God-fearing nation, or that it should have been founded in the cause of religious liberty. And it is not surprising that the great body of American pioneers should have been devout and God-fearing men and women.

In Georgia, we find Oglethorpe's colonists erecting a board tabernacle for the public worship of God as one of their first acts after landing at Yamacraw Bluff. In Cherokee County, a century later, we find preaching-stations or even churches in all settled parts of the county as evidence of the religious natures of Cherokee County's earliest settlers.

In the years that have followed, the people of the county have not lost sight of the ideals and principles which actuated their forefathers. Churches have been at the center of life in every community, and their influence has been manifest in every department of the county's progress during its hundred years of history.

Religion with the Pioneers

No doubt the racial stock which composes the citizenship has had much to do with this condition. Religious movements in Europe dating as far back as the Reformation figured largely in the racial character of the early immigrants to America; and many persons who had immigrated to this country for religious reasons, or the descendants of such immigrants, settled in the localities from which Cherokee County drew its earliest population. In a number of cases, settlers of the county had themselves come to America from England, Scotland, or Ireland, or from various parts of the Continent, on account of peculiar religious conditions existing in those places late in the eighteenth century, in order to enjoy the privilege of worshiping unmolested according to the dictates of conscience.

With such a background, the pioneers of Cherokee County did not allow themselves to forget their religious instincts in the struggle for existence among new and harsh surroundings; on the contrary, they grew to depend more than ever on spiritual consolations. In each settlement, services were held from time to time by whatever preachers could be secured, and several communities engaged itinerant preachers for regular appointments. It is thought that the first regular preaching-appointment in the county was at Sixes, about 1830. Others were established at Little River, Liberty Hill, Holbrook, Bascomb, Shiloh, Providence, and Canton.

The preachers of this early period were few, and their visits far between, but they did a good work. Some of them were Methodist circuit-riders, some were of other denominations. Also there were missionaries who worked among the Indians, sent out by the Board of Commissioners for Missions. One of these, a Baptist missionary named O'Bryant, is known to have worked among the Indians in what is now Cherokee County as early as 1827. The daughter of Mr. O'Bryant became the wife of R. Frank Daniel, pioneer settler of the county.

In the earliest settlement days, there were no churches; only the rough homes of the pioneers and the open air were available as meeting-places. As various communities grew large enough to support churches, they established them; but this apparently did not happen until after the county was organized. The first church to be established in Canton was a Baptist church, started in 1833, and the following year a Methodist church was founded at Waleska. There are thought to have been one or two earlier churches in the county, but definite information concerning these is lacking.

Separate accounts are now given here of a number of churches which have been influential in the life of the county, and about which it has been possible to obtain the historical facts.

First Baptist Church of Canton

Ten charter members were present at the organization of this church, which now has an enrollment of over 850. The church was constituted on August 23, 1833, with Rev. Jeremiah Reeves and Rev. William Manning in attendance. Mr. Reeves was elected pastor, and served in that capacity until October, 1834. The first clerk was William Grisham, and for a period of ninety-four years, exept for a few months at one time, some member of the Grisham family served as clerk of this church. The ten charter members were: William Grisham, Susan Grisham, Elias Putnam, Faith Putnam, James Wilson, Mary Wilson, Moses Perkins, Elizabeth Perkins, Daniel Butler, and Julia Burns.

A place of worship was erected soon after the church was constituted. In all, four edifices have been used. The present one is a modern brick building of impressive architecture, built at a cost of about $165,000. It was erected in 1925 during the pastorate of Rev. W. H. Moody.

This organization has had a useful and honored history, and has included on its membership roll some of the state's most noted citizens. Able and devout men have served as pastors. The present pastor of this church is T. Baron Gibson, D.D., and the director of religious education is R. B. Simms. Lewis L. Jones is clerk. The Sunday-school, of which R. T. Jones has been superintendent for a number of years, is an efficient one, and the church is so organized as to meet the needs of its constituency in a highly satisfactory manner.

Other Early Baptist Churches

Among the very earliest Baptist churches in the county, besides the one at Canton, were Sharp Mountain, New Bethel, Hightower, and Conn's Creek churches.

Sharp Mountain Baptist Church was organized with six charter members in 1836. This organization is still flourishing, and has a good building near Ball Ground.

New Bethel Baptist Church was organized with seven charter members in 1837. Old records of this church give the following account of its constitution, copied here just as it was written:

"November 8, 1837. We whose names are hear under written,

FIRST BAPTIST CHURCH, CANTON

FIRST METHODIST CHURCH SOUTH, CANTON

holding church letters in full fellowship and at two remote a distance from any church to connect ourselves therewith, conclude as we hope in the presence of the Lord to constitute into a church in gospel order and Baptist principles under the name of the New Bethel Church, have accordingly called on the Brethern Peter Kurkendal and Edwin Dyer, who are now present with us, to witness truth and order. [Signed] I. H. Bell, Martha Bell, Henry G. Ellison, Hannah Ellison, James McNeals, Polly McNeals, Fils Oliver."

New Bethel is located in Sixes District. It is still active.

Hightower Baptist, near Lathemtown, and Conn's Creek Baptist, northeast of Ball Ground, are also very old churches, both having been established during Indian days.

Canton Methodist Church

Canton Methodist had its beginning some time previous to 1842, in which year Rev. Bob Cowart was the pastor. Rev. Smith Crandall, an early Methodist preacher buried in Canton, whose tombstone shows he "labored extensively," may have been a pastor of this church some time prior to 1840, the year of his death.

In 1850 and 1851, during the pastorate of William J. Cotter, a good new brick church was built. Dr. Cotter later wrote an autobiography in which he spoke of the "fine class of people" who had made up the membership of this church, and he also mentioned the interest which Canton showed in education. At this time there was a flourishing school for young women in Canton, in charge of a Dr. DuBose who was also pastor of the Presbyterian Church there. Mrs. Hudson, one of the oldest living residents of Canton, remembers attending Sunday-school at the Methodist Church there as early as 1848, in which year Miss Jane Gramling was her teacher.

Prominent in early Methodism in Canton were the Donaldsons, Fields, Garrisons, Knoxes, and Gramlings.

The present Methodist Church building was completed and dedicated in 1925 by Bishop Warren A. Candler, who stated that it was the first church building of its pretensions he had ever known to be paid for in full before dedication day. Its cost was in the neighborhood of $50,000. This structure was built during the pastorate of Rev. E. C. Wilson.

The present able pastor of this church is Rev. James Oscar Pettis, now serving his sixth consecutive year there. The present Sunday-school superintendent is Alfred W. McClure.

Canton Methodist Church has been and is now a religious organization of remarkable influence and power.

Fairview Methodist Church

Fairview Church, in Salacoa District, was founded with the union of two churches in that section in the year 1857. William

FAIRVIEW METHODIST CHURCH

Mahan and Thomas Roberts deeded the land for so long as it should be used for church purposes. In 1858 a subscription was taken and a house of worship erected. Early members of this church were the Mahans, Jeffersons, Robertses, Hutchersons, Richardsons, Presleys, and others.

In 1890 the church became very active and its enrollment was brought up to 100; but shortly thereafter it began to wane and

was finally disbanded. In the summer of 1910 two young minis-
terial students from Waleska conducted a meeting at Fairview
which resulted in the reorganization of the church and a Sunday-
school besides. The present building was completed and dedicated in October, 1912. Its cost was about $1,000.

This has been one of the most influential country churches
in the county.

Other Churches

Both in the towns and in the rural communities of Cherokee
County are other churches which have played an important part
in the religious life of the county, but space limitations as well
as lack of definite information precludes detailed accounts of
them. A number of the older and the more influential churches
of the county are, however, listed here:

Baptist: Woodstock, Ball Ground, Macedonia, Mount Zion,
Indian Knoll, Hopewell, Sardis, and Shoal Creek. There are in
all about fifty Baptist churches in the county.

Methodist: Woodstock, Ball Ground, Orange, Shiloh, Holly
Springs, Bascomb, Sixes, and Union Hill. There are about twenty
Methodist churches in the county.

Presbyterian: Canton and Woodstock.

Christian: Pleasant Hill and Antioch.

Camp-Meetings

The camp-meeting is a time-honored institution which has
been widely popular in Southern Methodism. Even today camp-
meetings are well attended in various parts of the South, but their
number and influence have decreased to some extent during the
last generation. In Cherokee County only one of the old camp-
grounds, Holbrook, is still used for annual meetings; though Holbrook seems to attract larger crowds every year. But three or
four other camp-meetings, formerly well known and attended
and still remembered by many citizens of the county, have been
discontinued.

Camp-meetings reached the height of their popularity and influence in Cherokee County a generation or two ago, when the
annual meetings at Shiloh (Steerhead), Little River (Trickham),

and Waleska, besides the one at Holbrook, were all attended by large crowds from many miles around.

Affairs of this kind were valuable for the social contacts they made possible as well as for their religious features. Held in the summer or early fall, before crops were ready to be harvested, they offered a brief but pleasurable respite from the routine of everyday life at a time when most farmers and their families could attend; and were high spots in the year.

At each camp-ground there was a large, shingle-roofed shed where services were conducted several times a day, and this shed, or "stand," was surrounded on all four sides by a row of small, roughly-constructed houses called "tents." When camp-meeting time came around, the owners of the "tents" would move in for the period of the meeting, usually a week; bringing with them a supply of bedding and a generous quantity of food, both raw and ready-cooked. Such cooking as was necessary was done in the open air, at the rear of the "tents." Non-tenters by the scores and hundreds came in wagons and buggies, some going back and forth at night and others camping on the grounds, sleeping as best they could.

These old camp-meetings still have pleasant associations for many a citizen of Cherokee County. A former resident of Canton, now living in Atlanta, writes to the author: "My thoughts go back to forty years ago when Mother and Father would load up the two-horse wagon with home-made feather-beds, pots, pans, gourds, plenty of chickens, and last their eight children, and we would tent at old Steerhead for the duration of the camp-meeting."

Holbrook Camp-Meeting, the only one surviving in the county, was established something like a hundred years ago. The land on which the camp-ground is located was donated by a Mr. Wilson, who is said to have shod a mule to obtain it originally. Great interest is shown in the annual meetings here. The attendance has been estimated at as high as 6,000, and about fifty families have tents on the premises.

Shiloh, formerly called Steerhead, was at one time a great camp-meeting. The ridge on which the arbor is located was formerly a station for deer-hunters, who had placed the head of a large steer up in a tree nearby. During the 'eighties many families from Canton tented at Steerhead every year.

Little River, or Trickham, was once a camp-meeting attended by residents of the southeastern part of the county.

Waleska Camp-Meeting probably originated soon after the Methodist church at that place was founded in 1834. All traces of the camp have disappeared.

It is unquestionably true that the religious life of Cherokee County has found a full and normal expression. Good church buildings, well-organized agencies for all phases of religious work, and cultural programs to instill reverence for God and love for man have been provided. Thus has the religious heritage of the county's pioneers been preserved and enriched, for the present generation and for the generations that are to come.

A Look Ahead

The social and economic sides of life in Cherokee County have shown similar development. Good schools, progressive civic and fraternal and patriotic organizations, and a diversified program of economic activity have contributed to all-round progress. The builders of the county have done their work well, and the continued development of its resources—both the natural and the human variety—goes on with undiminished vigor.

At the time this book is being written, the troublous clouds of what has been perhaps the greatest economic depression in history seem to be gradually dissipating in the rays of restored confidence in the nation's resources. No section has escaped the blight of "hard times." But some localities have withstood it better than others on account of saner leadership and a more balanced economic program. Among these is Cherokee County, with a splendid set of business leaders and a practical and efficient ratio between agriculture, trade, and industry. In the transition to normalcy, and in the future progress of the county, these factors are sure to weigh heavily to its advantage. There will be less rebuilding to do, fewer readjustments to make, than in many a less favored section. And there will be a heartier spirit for the attack on new problems that may be encountered on the way.

The soundness of the county's economic program has proved itself, but the full development of its resources has only been well begun. It is not too much to envision for the future large expansion in industrial and commercial activity, successful exploitation of mineral resources, and a fuller realization of the great agricultural possibilities of the county.

The present generation of people will live to see changes take place that can not even be guessed at today. Progress and invention are fast making a new world out of the one we live in; in the next ten years they will alter ways of living more than they have ever been altered in any two decades of the past. What Cherokee County will be like then, what opportunities now existing will have been turned into fortunes, what startling changes will then be regarded matter-of-factly, no one can tell. But one has the feeling that then, as always, Cherokee County will not only be one of the leaders in the Advancement Parade but will still be upholding its reputation of being "a good place to live in."

END OF PART ONE

APPENDIX

I.

POPULATION
OF
CHEROKEE COUNTY AND ITS TOWNS
1840 to 1930
(U. S. Census Figures)

Year	The County	Ball Ground	Canton	Holly Springs	Waleska	Woodstock
1840	5,895	......	....	......	......	......
1850	12,800	......	....	......	......	......
1860	11,291	......	....	......	......	......
1870	10,399	......	214	......	......	......
1880	14,325	......	363	......	......	......
1890	15,412	296	659	......	......	......
1900	15,243	302	847	......	170	276
1910	16,661	448	2,002	251	243	442
1920	18,569	809	2,679	216	308	415
1930	20,003	706	2,892	273	226	421

Note: The 1930 Census shows also 90 residents of Nelson living in Cherokee County; remainder in Pickens County.

POPULATION OF MILITIA DISTRICTS
in 1930

No. 792, Canton	6,301	No. 1010, Hickory Flat	1,176
No. 817, Bells	713	No. 1015, Lickskillet	834
No. 818, Mullins	903	No. 1019, Wildcat	1,086
No. 890, Woodstock	1,501	No. 1028, Fairplay	514
No. 960, Salacoa	495	No. 1031, Conns Creek	484
No. 971, Claytons	576	No. 1032, Ball Ground	1,808
No. 1000, Cross Roads	1,076	No. 1174, Little River	752
No. 1008, Harbins	1,093	No. 1279, Sixes	691

II.

OFFICIAL REGISTER FOR 1932

Cherokee County Officers

Commissioner of Roads and Revenues: James H. Holcomb, Ball Ground.

Ordinary: Jacob Massey, Canton.

Sheriff: J. O. McCollum, Canton.

Tax Receiver: Lee F. Burtz, Canton.

Tax Collector: W. D. Miller, Canton.

Clerk of the Superior Court: Mack Sandow, Canton.

Surveyor: Edward W. Billing, Holly Springs.

Coroner: Claude H. Peacock, Canton.

Superintendent of Schools: Ramsey C. Sharp, Canton.

County Farm Agent: J. A. Maxey, Canton.

Home Demonstration Agent: Elsie Todd, Canton.

County Physician: Dr. James R. Boring, Canton.

Clerk of Commissioner: J. E. B. Lyon, Canton.

Board of Education: Dr. N. J. Coker, Chairman, Canton; W. A. Bearden, Waleska; L. R. Thomason, Ball Ground; L. A. Dean, Woodstock; J. W. Hasty, Canton.

County Officers-Elect

The following have been elected for the term Jan. 1, 1933-Jan. 1, 1937:

Commissioner of Roads and Revenues: James H. Holcomb, Ball Ground.

Ordinary: Jacob Massey, Canton.

Sheriff: Lee Spears, Canton.

Tax Commissioner (consolidates offices of Tax Collector and Tax Receiver): Ras Stephens, Canton.

Clerk of the Superior Court: Lee F. Burtz, Canton.

Surveyor: Edward W. Billing, Holly Springs.

Coroner: Claude H. Peacock, Canton.

Superintendent of Schools: Ramsey C. Sharp.

Members of Legislature

Representative from Cherokee County: Joseph E. Johnston, Woodstock.

Senator from Thirty-Ninth District: Alpha A. Fowler, Douglasville.

(Terms expire January 1, 1933.)

Superior Court Officials

Judge of the Blue Ridge Circuit: John Harold Hawkins, Marietta.

Solicitor-General of the Blue Ridge Circuit: George D. Anderson, Marietta.

(Terms expire January 1, 1933.)

Congressman

Representative from the Ninth Congressional District: John S. Wood, Canton.

III.

CHEROKEE COUNTY OFFICERS

(1832 to 1932)

CLERKS OF THE SUPERIOR COURT

	DATE COMMISSIONED		DATE COMMISSIONED
Oliver Strickland	Feb. 13, 1832	Jabez Galt	Jan. 11, 1881
Reuben F. Daniel	Mar. 20, 1833	Jabez Galt	Jan. 12, 1883
William Grisham	Jan. 10, 1834	James L. Jordan	Jan. 13, 1885
William Grisham	Jan. 16, 1836	James L. Jordan	Jan. 8, 1887
James Jordan	Jan. 18, 1838	James L. Jordan	Jan. 9, 1889
James Jordan	Jan. 10, 1840	James L. Jordan	Jan. 12, 1891
James Jordan	Jan. 10, 1842	William W. Worley	Jan. 6, 1893
James Jordan	Jan. 16, 1844	W. N. Willson	Jan. 8, 1895
James Jordan	Jan. 16, 1846	W. N. Willson	Oct. 14, 1896
James Jordan	Jan. 22, 1848	W. N. Willson	Feb. 14, 1898
James Jordan	Jan. 12, 1850	Jabez Galt	Oct. 19, 1898
Jasper L. Keith	Jan. 10, 1852	Jabez Galt	June 7, 1899
Jasper L. Keith	Jan. 10, 1854	Jabez Galt	Oct. 14, 1902
Jasper L. Keith	Jan. 11, 1856	Jabez Galt	Oct. 17, 1904
Jasper L. Keith	Jan. 11, 1858	Olin Fincher	Nov. 1, 1906
Jasper L. Keith	Jan. 10, 1861	Olin Fincher	Nov. 3, 1908
John B. Garrison	Jan. 23, 1862	Olin Fincher	Nov. 5, 1910
John B. Garrison	Feb. 16, 1864	Olin Fincher	Oct. 15, 1912
Odian W. Putnam	Jan. 22, 1866	Olin Fincher	Nov. 30, 1914
Odian W. Putnam	Sep. 15, 1868	J. Warn Chamlee	Dec. 4, 1916
Odian W. Putnam	Feb. 7, 1871	Mack Sandow	Feb. 12, 1920
Odian W. Putnam	Jan. 9, 1873	Mack Sandow	Dec. 9, 1920
James W. Hudson	Jan. 18, 1875	Mack Sandow	Dec. 20, 1924
James W. Hudson	Jan. 20, 1877	Mack Sandow	Dec. 20, 1929
Jabez Galt	Jan. 10, 1879		

CLERKS OF THE INFERIOR COURT

DATE COMMISSIONED			DATE COMMISSIONED	
William T. Williamson			William A. Williams	
	Feb. 13, 1832			Jan. 22, 1848
William Grisham	Mar. 20, 1833		James M. Daniel	Jan. 12, 1850
Philip Kroft	Jan. 10, 1834		James M. Daniel	Jan. 10, 1852
Benjamin F. Johnson			James M. Daniel	Jan. 10, 1854
	Aug. 20, 1834		James M. Daniel	Jan. 11, 1856
Samuel Thompson	Jan. 16, 1836		Nehemiah J. Garrison	
Posey Maddox	Jan. 18, 1838			Jan. 11, 1858
Posey Maddox	Jan. 10, 1840		Nehemiah J. Garrison	
William T. Hammond				Jan. 10, 1861
	Jan. 10, 1842		J. P. Daniel	Jan. 23, 1862
William A. Williams			J. P. Daniel	Feb. 16, 1864
	Jan. 16, 1844		Joseph B. Barton	Jan. 22, 1866
William A. Williams			(Office discontinued 1868)	
	Jan. 16, 1846			

SHERIFFS

John Jolly	Feb. 13, 1832		Enoch G. Gramling	Jan. 9, 1873
John P. Brooke	Mar. 20, 1833		M. P. Morris	Jan. 18, 1875
Samuel C. Candler	Jan. 10, 1834		H. G. Daniel	Jan. 20, 1877
Marble J. Camden	Jan. 16, 1836		Enoch G. Gramling	Jan. 10, 1879
Randle McDonald	Feb. 27, 1837		Joshua P. Spears	Jan. 11, 1881
John B. Garrison	Jan. 18, 1838		Enoch G. Gramling	Jan. 12, 1883
Langston Worley	Jan. 10, 1840		Enoch G. Gramling	Jan. 20, 1885
James A. Maddox	Jan. 10, 1842		William A. Kitchens	Jan. 8, 1887
Joshua Roberts	Jan. 16, 1844		William A. Kitchens	Jan. 9, 1889
Uriah Stephens	Jan. 16, 1846		William A. Kitchens	
Joshua Roberts	Jan. 22, 1848			Jan. 12, 1891
William H. Evans	Oct. 11, 1849		Augustus L. Coggins	Jan. 6, 1893
Samuel T. Kimbell	Jan. 12, 1850		Joshua P. Spears	Jan. 8, 1895
Reuben F. Daniel	Jan. 10, 1852		Joshua P. Spears	Oct. 14, 1896
Warren R. D. Moss	Jan. 10, 1854		P. S. Bedelle	Oct. 19, 1898
Mortimer G. Donaldson			P. S. Bedelle	June 7, 1899
	Jan. 11, 1856		Silas T. Worley	Oct. 14, 1902
James B. Kelly	Jan. 11, 1858		Silas T. Worley	Oct. 17, 1904
Benjamin Hill	Jan. 10, 1861		Benjamin F. Willingham	
J. A. Fowler	Jan. 23, 1862			Nov. 1, 1906
Benjamin Hill	Feb. 16, 1864		Benjamin F. Willingham	
Ivey A. Finch	Jan. 22, 1866			Nov. 3, 1908
Enoch G. Gramling	Mar. 4, 1867		Joshua P. Spears	Nov. 5, 1910
Enoch G. Gramling	Sep. 15, 1868		Joshua P. Spears	Oct. 15, 1912
Andrew T. Scott	Feb. 7, 1871			

DATE COMMISSIONED		DATE COMMISSIONED	
Joshua P. Spears	Nov. 30, 1914	Lee Spears	Dec. 20, 1924
Joshua P. Spears	Dec. 4, 1916	Lee Spears	Dec. 20, 1929
Floyd M. Blackwell	Dec. 9, 1920	J. O. McCollum	June 26, 1930

SURVEYORS

Jesse Watkins	Feb. 13, 1832	William W. Hawkins	
Roger Green	Mar. 20, 1833		Jan. 10, 1879
Roger Green	Jan. 10, 1834	Fred W. Moore	Jan. 11, 1881
Jipe Leonard	Jan. 10, 1837	Fred W. Moore	Jan. 12, 1883
Andrew Scott	Jan. 18, 1838	William W. Hawkins Jan.	1884
Hartwell Freeman	Jan. 10, 1840	David Rusk	Jan. 13, 1885
John Burns	Jan. 10, 1842	W. P. Taylor	Jan. 8, 1887
William M. Bell	Jan. 16, 1844	Joseph W. Knox	Jan. 9, 1889
Hartwell Freeman	Jan. 16, 1946	Joseph W. Knox	Jan. 12, 1891
Hartwell Freeman	Jan. 22, 1848	James M. Paden	Jan. 6, 1893
Matthew F. Stephenson		Joseph W. Knox	Jan. 8, 1895
	Jan. 12, 1850	Joseph W. Knox	Oct. 14, 1896
James Haley	Jan. 10, 1852	James H. Hendrix	Oct. 19, 1898
Nathaniel F. Reinhardt		W. Virgil Martin	June 7, 1899
	Jan. 10, 1854	J. A. Byers	Oct. 14, 1902
Robert Hawkins	Jan. 11, 1856	Edward W. Billing	May 30, 1903
Robert Hawkins	Jan. 11, 1858	Joseph W. Knox	Oct. 17, 1904
Robert Hawkins	Jan. 10, 1861	B. Frank Coggins	Nov. 1, 1906
Robert Hawkins	Jan. 23, 1862	Joseph W. Knox	Nov. 3, 1908
Robert Hawkins	Feb. 16, 1864	Joseph W. Knox	Nov. 5, 1910
William W. Hawkins		T. A. Lewis	Oct. 15, 1912
	Jan. 22, 1866	Joseph W. Knox	Jan. 20, 1913
William W. Hawkins		Edward W. Billing	May 2, 1913
	Sep. 19, 1868	Benjamin F. Kilby	Nov. 30, 1914
William W. Hawkins	Feb. 7, 1871	J. A. Milford	Dec. 26, 1914
William W. Hawkins	Jan. 9, 1873	S. M. Hillhouse	Dec. 4, 1916
William W. Hawkins		Edward W. Billing	Dec. 9, 1920
	Jan. 18, 1875	Edward W. Billing	Dec. 20, 1924
William W. Hawkins		Edward W. Billing	Dec. 20, 1929
	Jan. 20, 1877		

CORONERS

Asa Keith	Feb. 13, 1832	Samuel M. McCanless	
Lewis S. Langston	Mar. 20, 1833		Jan. 10, 1840
David Dinzemore	Jan. 10, 1834	Samuel M. McCanless	
Samuel M. McCanless			Jan. 10, 1842
	Jan. 16, 1836	Jarrett Chamlee	Jan. 16, 1844
Samuel M. McCanless		Jarrett Chamlee	Jan. 16, 1846
	Jan. 18, 1838	William Wood	Jan. 22, 1848

DATE COMMISSIONED		DATE COMMISSIONED	
William Wood	Jan. 12, 1850	D. C. Roach	Jan. 9, 1889
Paul C. Ingram	Jan. 10, 1852	D. C. Roach	Jan. 12, 1891
William Wood	Jan. 10, 1854	John H. Bell	Jan. 6, 1893
William Wood	Jan. 11, 1856	William T. Kirk	Jan. 8, 1895
William W. Wright	Jan. 11, 1858	Ludlow W. Hodges	Oct. 14, 1896
William W. Wright	Jan. 10, 1861	A. D. Bentley	Oct. 19, 1898
John Wilson	Jan. 23, 1862	A. D. Bentley	June 7, 1899
F. M. Milligan	Feb. 16, 1864	Ludlow W. Hodges	Oct. 14, 1902
Solomon Fuller	Jan. 22, 1866	William T. Kirk	Oct. 17, 1904
William Rampley	Sep. 19, 1868	Clarence A. Perry	Nov. 1, 1906
Solomon Fuller	Feb. 7, 1871	W. H. Lewis	Nov. 3, 1908
William Rampley	Jan. 9, 1873	William T. Kirk	Nov. 5, 1910
William Rampley	Jan. 18, 1875	H. A. Heard	Oct. 15, 1912
William Rampley	Jan. 20, 1877	H. A. Heard	Nov. 30, 1914
William T. Kirk	Jan. 10, 1879	H. A. Heard	Dec. 4, 1916
William T. Kirk	Jan. 11, 1881	H. A. Heard	Dec. 9, 1920
William T. Kirk	Jan. 13, 1885	C. A. Sams	Dec. 20, 1924
William T. Kirk	Jan. 8, 1887	Claude H. Peacock	Dec. 20, 1929

TAX RECEIVERS

Elijah Hillhouse	Jan. 12, 1850	Thomas W. Arwood	Jan. 12, 1883
Littleberry Holcombe		William S. Cobb	Jan. 13, 1885
(T. R. and T. C.)	Mar. 13, 1851	William S. Cobb	Jan. 8, 1887
Littleberry Holcombe		David B. Holbert	Jan. 10, 1889
(T. R. and T. C.)	Jan. 10, 1852	William T. Kirk	Jan. 12, 1891
Warren R. D. Moss	Jan. 17, 1853	H. N. Addington	Jan. 6, 1893
Newton J. Perkins	Jan. 10, 1854	L. J. Doss	Jan. 8, 1895
Mortimer G. Donaldson		G. W. Anderson	Oct. 14, 1896
	Jan. 9, 1855	Lebius B. Hughes	June 21, 1897
William W. Worley	Jan. 11, 1856	Lebius B. Hughes	Feb. 14, 1898
William W. Worley	Jan. 12, 1857	H. N. Addington	Oct. 19, 1898
Newton J. Perkins	Jan. 11, 1858	J. A. Stephens	June 7, 1899
Mark S. Paden	Jan. 10, 1859	Jacob Massey	Oct. 14, 1902
Elijah Hillhouse	Jan. 10, 1861	Robert E. Smith	Oct. 17, 1904
John Guerin		Calvin A. Young	Nov. 1, 1906
(T. R. — T. C.)	Mar. 1, 1862	William W. Worley	Nov. 3, 1908
James Daniel	Feb. 16, 1864	J. M. Smith	Nov. 5, 1910
Miles N. Holden	Mar. 8, 1866	John W. McCollum	Oct. 15, 1912
Miles N. Holden	Sep. 15, 1868	Roscoe Lathem	Nov. 16, 1914
Columbus Archer	Feb. 7, 1871	John M. Holbrook	Dec. 4, 1916
Columbus Archer	Jan. 9, 1873	W. J. White	Dec. 9, 1920
W. N. Willson	Jan. 18, 1875	Mrs. Willie M. White	
James L. Jordan	Jan. 20, 1877		Feb. 18, 1924
James L. Jordan	Jan. 10, 1879	Lewis Poor	Dec. 20, 1924
Thomas W. Arwood	Jan. 11, 1881	Lee F. Burtz	Dec. 20, 1929

TAX COLLECTORS

DATE COMMISSIONED		DATE COMMISSIONED	
Littleberry Holcombe	Apr. 1, 1850	Adolphus L. Kinnett	Jan. 10, 1879
Littleberry Holcombe (T. C. and T. R.)	Mar. 13, 1851	M. C. Coker	Jan. 11, 1881
Littleberry Holcombe (T. C. and T. R.)	Jan. 10, 1852	Daniel W. Ferguson	Jan. 12, 1883
Littleberry Holcombe	Mar. 16, 1853	James H. Kilby	Jan. 13, 1885
Littleberry Holcombe	Mar. 28, 1954	John W. Chapman	Jan. 8, 1887
Isaac Ingram	Jan. 9, 1855	John W. Chapman	Jan. 9, 1889
Joseph W. Pharr	Jan. 11, 1856	John N. Simpson	Jan. 12, 1891
James E. Rusk	Jan. 12, 1857	John N. Simpson	Jan. 6, 1893
William W. Fleming	Jan. 11, 1858	L. M. Ball	Jan. 8, 1895
Craton Archer	Jan. 10, 1859	James M. Paden	Oct. 14, 1896
Thomas H. Hogan	Jan. 10, 1861	James M. Paden	Oct. 19, 1898
John Guerin (T.R.—T.C.)	Mar. 1, 1862	J. W. Edwards	June 7, 1899
J. A. Finch	Feb. 16, 1864	Daniel W. Ferguson	Oct. 14, 1902
J. W. Edwards	Mar. 8, 1866	Levi L. Spence	Oct. 17, 1904
J. W. Edwards	Sep. 17, 1868	Charles F. Weaver	Nov. 1, 1906
Perry Taylor	Feb. 7, 1871	William M. Bishop	Nov. 3, 1908
Cicero Conn	Jan. 9, 1873	William M. Bishop	Nov. 5, 1910
J. Dupree	Jan. 18, 1875	Alfred Edwards	Oct. 15, 1912
L. M. Williams	Jan. 20, 1877	M. J. Wood	Nov. 16, 1914
		W. D. Miller	Dec. 4, 1916
		W. D. Miller	Dec. 9, 1920
		W. D. Miller	Dec. 20, 1924
		W. D. Miller	Dec. 20, 1929

ORDINARIES

John C. Maddox	Jan. 20, 1851	Allen C. Conn	Oct. 14, 1896
James Jordan	Jan. 27, 1852	Allen C. Conn	June 7, 1899
James Jordan	Jan. 11, 1856	W. J. Webb	Oct. 17, 1904
James Jordan	Jan. 10, 1861	W. J. Webb	Nov. 10, 1908
James Jordan	Feb. 16, 1864	W. J. Webb	Oct. 15, 1912
Warren R. D. Moss	Jan. 10, 1866	Joseph M. Satterfield	Aug. 26, 1913
Warren R. D. Moss	Sep. 25, 1868	Joseph M. Satterfield	Dec. 4, 1916
Warren R. D. Moss	Jan. 9, 1873	Jacob Massey	Apr. 24, 1920
Charles M. McClure	July 20, 1874	Jacob Massey	Dec. 9, 1920
Odian W. Putnam	Jan. 20, 1877	Frank P. Burtz	Dec. 20, 1924
Charles M. McClure	Jan. 11, 1881	Jacob Massey	Dec. 20, 1929
Odian W. Putnam	Jan. 13, 1885		
Odian W. Putnam	Jan. 9, 1889		
Allen C. Conn	Jan. 6, 1893		

TREASURERS

Jefferson Barton	Jan. 10, 1861	Isaac Ingram	Feb. 16, 1864
Isaac Ingram	Jan. 23, 1862	Isaac Ingram	Jan. 22, 1866

	DATE COMMISSIONED		DATE COMMISSIONED
H. G. Daniel	Sep. 15, 1868	George W. Evans	Oct. 19, 1898
John W. Chapman	Feb. 7, 1871	J. W. Lovingood	June 7, 1899
John F. Hillhouse	Jan. 9, 1873	William F. Ponder	Oct. 14, 1902
John G. Evans	Jan. 18, 1875	William T. McCollum	
Theodore Turk	Jan. 20, 1877		Oct. 17, 1904
Joseph D. Dobbs	Jan. 10, 1879	Ludlow W. Hodges	Nov. 1, 1906
Jonathan L. Coggins		John A. Scott	Nov. 3, 1908
	Jan. 11, 1881	J. J. Thomas	Nov. 5, 1910
Joseph M. Sharp	Jan. 12, 1883	B. Thomas Bennett	Oct. 15, 1912
James M. Land	Jan. 13, 1885	William J. Huggins	
Andrew T. Scott	Jan. 8, 1887		Nov. 30, 1914
M. S. Findley	Jan. 9, 1889	W. M. Meager	Dec. 4, 1916
M. S. Findley	Jan. 12, 1891	Will C. Fain	Dec. 9, 1920
L. F. Burtz	Jan. 6, 1893	W. E. Hasty	Dec. 20, 1924
E. S. Coker	Jan. 8, 1895	Mrs. W. E. Hasty	Mar. 19, 1926
L. F. Burtz	Oct. 14, 1896		

COMMISSIONERS OF ROADS AND REVENUES

DATE COMMISSIONED

Robert Olin Fincher 1916
William Joseph Satterfield...................................December 9, 1920
Robert Olin Fincher ....December 20, 1924
James H. Holcomb ....December 20, 1928

The office of commissioner of roads and revenues for Cherokee County was created by a legislative act approved August 9, 1915, which also provided for the position of clerk of commissioner.

The duties of the commissioner—including management of the county's property and funds, care of roads and bridges, levying of general taxes, and other important functions—were handled in the early days of the county by the inferior court justices (see list), later principally by the ordinary, and from 1908 to 1910 by a board of commissioners consisting of five members, four of them representing four divisions of the county and the fifth member being the ordinary. The legislature authorized the voters of the county to abolish this board in an act approved July 22, 1910. (Acts, Georgia; 1908, p. 288; 1910, p. 255.)

COUNTY SCHOOL SUPERINTENDENTS

(Formerly called "School Commissioners")

		TERM OF SERVICE*
James Warren Hudson 1872-79	Jabez Galt	1908-12
Chas. Marshall McClure 1879-81	Thomas A. Doss	1912-25
George Isham Teasley 1881-86	Zach Collins	1925-28
John D. Attaway 1886-1907		
Benjamin Franklin	Ramsey Colquitt	
Perry 1907-08	Sharp 1928-date	

*Dates given in this particular list must be regarded as only approximate.

JUSTICES OF THE INFERIOR COURT
(1832 to 1868)

	WHEN COMMISSIONED	WHEN SUCCEEDED
John McConnell	Feb. 13, 1832	Jan. 22, 1833
John Witcher	Feb. 13, 1832	Jan. 22, 1833
Robert Obarr	Feb. 13, 1832	Jan. 22, 1833
Genubath Winn	Feb. 13, 1832	Jan. 22, 1833
Henry Holcombe	Feb. 13, 1832	Jan. 22, 1833
John McConnell	Jan. 22, 1833	1833
Randal McDonald	Jan. 22, 1833	1833
Elias Putnam	Jan. 22, 1833	1833
William Lay	Jan. 22, 1833	1833
William Baker	Jan. 22, 1833	1833
William B. Key	June 14, 1833	Jan. 10, 1834
James Wilson	June 14, 1833	Jan. 10, 1834
Henry Holcombe	July 31, 1833	Jan. 10, 1834
John Waites	July 31, 1833	Jan. 10, 1834
James H. Chambers	July 31, 1833	Jan. 10, 1834
Joseph Donaldson	Jan. 10, 1834	Jan. 10, 1837
John McConnell	Jan. 10, 1834	Jan. 10, 1837
John Sarjeant	Jan. 10, 1834	Aug. 13, 1834
Edward Townsend	Jan. 10, 1834	Jan. 10, 1837
James H. Chambers	Jan. 10, 1834	Jan. 10, 1837
William Lay	Aug. 13, 1834	Jan. 10, 1837
John McConnell	Jan. 10, 1837	Jan. 14, 1841
Joseph Donaldson	Jan. 10, 1837	Jan. 14, 1841
Levi Hoyle	Jan. 10, 1837	Nov. 4, 1839
William Lay	Jan. 10, 1837	Apr. 16, 1838
John Waites	Jan. 10, 1837	Jan. 14, 1841
Reuben F. Daniel	Apr. 16, 1838	May 4, 1840
Elijah Hillhouse	Nov. 4, 1839	Jan. 14, 1841
William Worley	May 4, 1840	Nov. 27, 1840
George B. Quarles	Nov. 27, 1840	Jan. 14, 1841
John McConnell	Jan. 14, 1841	Jan. 15, 1845
Joseph Donaldson	Jan. 14, 1841	Jan. 15, 1845
Jabez Galt	Jan. 14, 1841	Jan. 15, 1845
George S. Hoyle	Jan. 14, 1841	Oct. 31, 1843
Tilman Chamlee	Jan. 14, 1841	Oct. 31, 1843
Daniel Hammond Bird	Oct. 31, 1843	Jan. 15, 1845
John Stephens	Oct. 31, 1843	Jan. 15, 1845
Joseph Donaldson	Jan. 15, 1845	Jan. 6, 1849
John McConnell	Jan. 15, 1845	Apr. 13, 1846
Jabez Galt	Jan. 15, 1845	Jan. 6, 1849

Langston Worley	Jan. 15, 1845	Apr. 13, 1846
Posey Maddox	Jan. 15, 1845	Jan. 6, 1849
Elias E. Field	Apr. 13, 1846	Jan. 6, 1849
George W. Cook	Apr. 13, 1846	Jan. 6, 1849
Joseph Donaldson	Jan. 6, 1849	Jan. 8, 1853
James A. Maddox	Jan. 6, 1849	Jan. 8, 1853
John B. Puckett	Jan. 6, 1849	Jan. 8, 1853
John B. Garrison	Jan. 6, 1849	Jan. 12, 1850
James H. Hardin	Jan. 6, 1849	Jan. 8, 1853
McAnderson Keith	Jan. 12, 1850	Jan. 8, 1853
McAnderson Keith	Jan. 8, 1853	Jan. 24, 1854
James McConnell	Jan. 8, 1853	Jan. 12, 1857
James A. Maddox	Jan. 8, 1853	Mar. 13, 1855
James H. Hardin	Jan. 8, 1853	Mar. 13, 1855
Joseph Donaldson	Jan. 8, 1853	Jan. 12, 1857
Ira Roe Foster	Jan. 24, 1854	Jan. 12, 1857
Benjamin Hill	Mar. 13, 1855	Jan. 12, 1857
Tilman Chamlee	Mar. 13, 1855	Jan. 12, 1857
Joseph Donaldson	Jan. 12, 1857	Jan. 10, 1861
Henry H. Waters	Jan. 12, 1857	Jan. 12, 1858
Tilman Chamlee	Jan. 12, 1857	Jan. 18, 1860
James McConnell	Jan. 12, 1857	Jan. 11, 1859
Andrew H. Shuford	Jan. 12, 1857	Jan. 10, 1861
Joseph Underwood	Jan. 22, 1858	Jan. 18, 1860
William Wise	Jan. 11, 1859	Jan. 10, 1861
Elias E. Field	Jan. 18, 1860	Jan. 10, 1861
Littleberry Holcombe	Jan. 18, 1860	Jan. 10, 1861
William Wise	Jan. 10, 1861	Jan. 23, 1865
Warren R. D. Moss	Jan. 10, 1861	Feb. 1, 1862
Tilman Chamlee	Jan. 10, 1861	Jan. 23, 1865
Andrew H. Shuford	Jan. 10, 1861	May 7, 1864
Littleberry Holcombe	Jan. 10, 1861	Jan. 23, 1865 .
James O. Dowda	Feb. 1, 1862	Jan. 23, 1865
John Robinson	May 7, 1864	Jan. 23, 1865
Enoch G. Gramling	Jan. 23, 1865	1867
Nehemiah J. Garrison	Jan. 23, 1865	1866
William Alfred Teasley	Jan. 23, 1865	1866
J. W. McCollum	Jan. 23, 1865	
G. B. Holbrook	Jan. 23, 1865	
Littleberry Holcombe	Feb. 19, 1866	
Reuben F. Daniel	Feb. 19, 1866	1867
James O. Dowda	July 31, 1866	
James H. Spier	Feb. 10, 1867	1868
A. I. Covington	Mar. 7, 1867	1868

Five justices comprised the inferior court. The foregoing list is arranged to show together the names of justices whose terms ran concurrently. Date of succession is doubtful in a few cases and is not given. This list of inferior court justices of Cherokee County is the compilation of Miss Ruth Blair, State Historian. It is here published for the first time.

The inferior court was dissolved in 1868. In 1850 the court of ordinary had been established by a general act to amend the constitution of Georgia. On the dissolution of the inferior court eighteen years later, its powers and duties were taken over by other county offices, principally that of ordinary.

IV.

MEMBERS OF LEGISLATURE
From Cherokee County, 1832 to 1932
REPRESENTATIVES

1832 William B. Malone	1855/56 Lawson Fields
1833 John W. Leonard	Joshua Roberts
1834 Philip Croft	1857-58 William W. Worley
1835 Samuel C. Candler	Joshua Roberts
1836 Merrick H. Ford	1859-60 William W. Worley
1837 Merrick H. Ford	William W. W. Fleming
1838 Merrick H. Ford	1861-62-63 Ex. W. F. Mullins
1839 Merrick H. Ford	William W. W. Fleming
Joseph C. Hunter	1863-64 Ex.-64-65 Ex.
1840 Merrick H. Ford	William W. Worley
Joseph C. Hunter	P. H. Brewster
1841 Joseph C. Hunter	1865/66-66 E. C. Gardin
John P. Brooke	John J. A. Sharp
1842 Joseph C. Hunter	1868 Ex.-69-70 Ex.
John P. Brooke	Newton J. Perkins
1843 John H. Bibb	1871-72-72 Adj.
Allen Lawhon	John B. Richards
1845 Elijah M. Field	1873-74 William A. Teasley
1847 W. W. Williamson	1875-76 John J. A. Sharp
Lawson Fields	1877 W. B. C. Puckett
1849/50 Lawson Fields	1878-79 Adj.
Joshua Roberts	W. B. C. Puckett
1851/52 L. J. Allred	1880-81 Adj. William C. Dial
Simpson C. Dyer	1882-83 Ex.-83 Ann. Adj.
1853/54 L. J. Allred	William A. Teasley
Lawson Fields	1884-85 Adj. William A. Teasley

1886-87 Adj. George R. Brown
1888-89 Adj. J. H. Lathem
1890-91 Adj. J. B. Hill
1892-93   C. S. Steel
1894-95   Thomas Hutcherson Jr.
1896-97 Adj.-97 William J. Webb
1898-99   Pierce B. Latimer
1900-01   Lee Mullins
1902-03-04   W. D. Mills
1905-06   Russell M. Moore
1907-08-08 Ex. Richard M. Moore
1909-10   John T. Bell
1911-12 Ex.-12   John N. Simpson
1913-14   John N. Simpson

1915-15 Ex.-16-17 Ex.
          John N. Simpson
1917-18   John S. Wood
          (resigned 6-7-18)
1918   John W. Collins
          (July 8———)
1919-20   Howell Brooke
1921-22   John W. Collins
1923-23 Ex.-24 John W. Collins
1925-26 Ex.-26 2d Ex.
          John W. Collins
1927   Henry G. Vandiviere
1929-31 Ex.-31
          Joseph Egleston Johnston
1931   Joseph Egleston Johnston

SENATORS

1. From Cherokee County (1832-1844)

1832   Jacob M. Scudder
1833   Eli McConnell
1834   Eli McConnell
1835   Eli McConnell
1836   Eli McConnell
1837   Marble J. Camden

1838   Marble J. Camden
1839   Marble J. Camden
1840   Eli McConnell
1841   Martin A. Keith
1842   Eli McConnell
1843   Samuel W. Thompson

2. From Forty-first District (1845-1852)

1845   John W. Lewis
1847   William H. Hunt

1849/50   Joseph E. Brown
1851/52   Martin G. Slaughter

3. From Cherokee County (1853-1860)

1853/54   Marble J. Camden
1855/56   Marble J. Camden
1857   Lawson Fields

1858   Littleberry Holcombe
1859-60   T. J. Hightower

4. From Thirty-ninth District (1861-date)

1861   Hiram P. Bell
          (resigned 9/24/62)
1862-63 Ex. James R. Brown
1863-64 Ex.-64-65 Ex.
          J. T. Ezzard
1865/66-66   J. T. Ezzard
1868 Ex.-69-70 Ex.
          Addison W. Holcombe
1871-72-72 Adj. James R. Brown

1873-74   James R. Brown
1875-76   E. C. McAfee
1877   E. C. McAfee
1878-79 Adj.
          Addison W. Holcombe
1880-81 Adj. Benjamin F. Payne
1882-83 Ex.-83 Ann. Adj.
          R. A. Eakes
1884-85 Adj.   Thomas L. Lewis

1886-87 Adj. James E. Rusk	1913-14 W. W. Jones
1888-89 Adj. A. J. Julian	1915-15 Ex.-16-17 Ex.
1890-91 Adj. J. H. Johnston	J. R. Trammell
1892-93 Joseph M. McAfee	1917-18 Floyd M. Blackwell
1894-95 B. H. Brown	1919-20 Charles J. Harben
1896-97 Adj.-97 Jeptha P. Brooke	1921-22 Eugene H. Clay
1898-99 William J. Webb	1923-23 Ex.-24
1900-01 Hiram P. Bell	Pierce B. Latimer
1902-03-04 Thomas L. Lewis	1925-26 Ex.-26 2d Ex.
1905-06 W. D. Mills	James R. Hutcheson
1907-08-08 Ex.	1927 Harold S. Willingham
Lewis A. Henderson	1929-31 Ex. Henry G. Vandiviere
1909-10 J. N. McClure	1931 Alpha A. Fowler
1911-12 Ex.-12 Silas T. Worley	

Explanation of Foregoing List

Until December 23, 1843, each county in Georgia had one state senator. On that date an act was passed by the legislature dividing the state into forty-seven senatorial districts, and providing for one senator from each. Cobb and Cherokee were in the Forty-first. On January 19, 1852, an amendment to the Constitution was adopted, providing for a return to the senator-per-county system. In 1859, however, Gov. Joseph E. Brown urged a reduction in the membership of the state senate—at that time 132—and the legislature subsequently created forty-four districts, with Cherokee in the Thirty-ninth, along with Milton and Forsyth. Cherokee County is still in the Thirty-ninth Senatorial District, but since 1919 Milton and Forsyth have been in the Fifty-first, while Cobb and Douglas have been in the Thirty-ninth with Cherokee.

Ex. (in above list): Extra session.

Adj.: Adjourned session.

1849/50: Designates **one** session, continuous through end of 1849.

1857-58: Designates **two** sessions.

(List of Members of Legislature adapted from compilations of Miss Ruth Blair, State Historian, in Georgia Official Registers of 1925, p. 308; and 1927, pp. 437, 470, 472, and 499.)

Congressional Districts
Cherokee County

In Fifth Congressional District, from December 23, 1843, to March 23, 1861.

In Ninth Congressional District, from March 23, 1861, to October 23, 1865.

In Seventh Congressional District, from October 26, 1865, to August 28, 1883.

In Ninth Congressional District, from August 28, 1883, to date. (Acts 1843, p. 54; Confederate Records Vol. I, p. 732; Code 1860; Confederate Records Vol. IV, p. 146; Acts 1882-83, p. 121.)

Judicial Circuits
Cherokee County

In Western Circuit, from December 26, 1831, to December 3, 1832.

In Cherokee Circuit, from December 3, 1832, to November 24, 1851.

In Blue Ridge Circuit, from November 24, 1851, to date. (Acts 1831, p. 74; Acts 1832, p. 56; Acts 1851-52, p. 219.)

V.

MEXICAN WAR SOLDIERS FROM CHEROKEE COUNTY
"Canton Volunteers"

(A Company of the Georgia Regiment of Volunteers)

Officers:

Gramling, K., Captain
Keith, A., 1st Lieut.
Mullens, W. F., 2d Lieut.
Gramling, W. G., 1st Sgt.
Cook, S. J., 2d Sgt.
Daniel, R. F., 3d Sgt.

Strain, N. F., 4th Sgt.
Rhodes, John G., 1st Corp.
Moody, Allen, 2d Corp.
Knox, Robert S., 3d Corp.
Hughes, Joshua, 4th Corp.

Privates:

Amos, George F.
Archer, William T.
Bird, Daniel H.
Bond, Elijah W.
Bond, John M.
Burns, Alexander F.
Burns, Alfred H.
Camp, William M.
Carpenter, Isaac W.
Carpenter, Lewis A.
Copeland, David P.
Cook, Joseph B.
Cook, William S.
Cook, John B.

Cook, Alfred
Cothren, Ludy
Curtis, Chesley C.
Dean, Benjamin
Delaney, Alexander M.
Delaney, James A.
Dickerson, John T.
Dickerson, Thomas E.
Ellis, Stephen P.
Finchen, John W.
Galt, Henry J.
Garrison, Nehemiah
Gramling, Richard M.
Hatiley, John C.

Harris, Nathaniel M.
Heard, Joseph
Henly, Luther R.
Hillhouse, Elisha
Hillhouse, Samuel W.
Hobson, John O.
Hullett, Christopher
Jordan, Isham
Keith, George W.
Lancaster, Levi
Lawhorne, George W.
Lawhorne, Zimmerman
Lawson, John B.
Long, Henry M.

Long, James M.
Loven, Sanford
Lusk, John
Lusk, William
McConnell, Joshua
McConnell, Samuel
McMahan, James
Machen, Jesse C.
Maddox, John C.
Manning, Ray
Mathis, Samuel G.
Phillips, Christenbury

Phillips, James O.
Rice, Samuel M.
Rich, William W.
Rivers, William A.
Roberts, John A.
Rogers, Albert
Roark, John A.
Scago, Isaac L.
Simeraly, Henderson
Spriggs, Robert
Strain, Benjamin F.
Sutherland, John B.

Thompson, John B.
Thompson, William
Treadway, William H.
Tyler, Isham
Tyler, Jesse
Wadkins, Beverly
White, Samuel L.
Williams, George W.
Wood, John L.
Wood, William S.
Wofford, Benjamin

Musicians:

Anderson W. Turner   Greenbury Brooks

VI.

CONFEDERATE SOLDIERS FROM CHEROKEE COUNTY

1. Companies of the CHEROKEE LEGION, Georgia State Guards Infantry

Company A
"Cherokee Revengers"

Officers:

Perkins, Newton J., Captain
Crowley, George W., 1st Lieut.
Holbrook, James A., 2d Lieut.
Smith, Larkin, 2d Lieut.
Southwick, Tyre H., 1st Sgt.
Hendricks, James H., 2d Sgt.
Waite, Thomas A., 3d Sgt.

Hendricks, William G., 4th Sgt.
Shelley, Thomas P., 5th Sgt.
Hagan, William, 1st Corp.
Law, Robert, 2d Corp.
Tomtlin, John T., 3d Corp.
Smith, James, 4th Corp.

Privates:

Allen, William G.
Bruice, James M.
Boling, William
Barnett, James
Brown, Joshua
Baker, John G.
Butler, William T.
Canon, Silas H.

Cantrell, Joshua A.
Coffee, James C.
Crowley, Seaborn
Compton, Levi
Conrad, Wilson R.
Edwards, William A.
Edwards, Eleazar
Fowler, William

Freeman, George W.
George, Marmaduke
Hemsley, Randall
Houston, Franklin
Harden, Thompson
Hatchers, Josiah G.
Johnson, Alfred R.
Jackson, William

James, Thomas
Jarvis, Samuel
Kimble, Samuel T.
Knox, James
Keown, Thomas R.
Lay, Charles F.
Lawson, Nevelle
Mecraw, George
McClure, Oliver
Martin, William

Nix, Thomas
Nix, Uriah
Nix, Elias
Petty, Wyley
Pool, Marven L.
Price, John B.
Price, Samuel B.
Purcell, Benjamin
Stone, Lewis
Stearnes, Joseph C.

Stephens, John B.
Sands, John
Smallwood, Marcus
Turner, James B.
Thomas, John F.
White, Hugh
Wooten, Lorenzo D.
Williams, Henry B.
Wright, James

Company B
"Canton Infantry"

Officers:

Garrison, John B., Captain
Shuford, A. H., 1st Lieut.
Ingram, Isaac, 2d Lieut.
Harbin, J. L. D., 2d Lieut.
Galt, J. L., 1st Sgt.
Langston, Jesse B., 2d Sgt.
Spear, Hezekiah, 3d Sgt.

Collett, Isaac, 4th Sgt.
Tucker, John S., 5th Sgt.
Hopkins, John B., 1st Corp.
Hutson, Joseph E., 2d Corp.
Whetchel, William, 3d Corp.
Linsey, J. M., 4th Corp.

Privates:

Allen, Hamboldt
Brown, James R.
Brannon, A. G.
Brooke, John P.
Bennett, Richard
Bibb, John H.
Beasley, W. D.
Brown, Jesse
Bass, Redding
Boatman, Robert
Bennett, W. J.
Chapman, Dudley
Carpenter, L. A.
Carpenter, J. W.
Crissenberry, S. G.
Collett, Isaac
Daniel, Edward
Daniel, R. F.
Duke, William
Donaldson, Joseph

Dowda, James O.
Dowda, William A.
Dass, James
Evans, Cane
England, James E.
Finch, Edward R.
Flanigan, Wiley
Garrison, Nehemiah J.
Galt, Edward
Galt, Joel L.
Greer, Joshua
Greer, G. N.
Gay, David
Garmon, William R.
Hammett, D. B.
Holcombe, L.
Harbin, Robert
Hitt, Leonard
Howard, J. M.
Howard, S. S.

Hopkins, John H.
Ingram, Jesse A.
Jackson, Thomas
Jackson, W. H.
Jones, Wiley
King, Jesse
King, Daniel
Keener, J. J.
McCanless, John
McCallum, John
Miller, David
Millwood, Hughey
Moss, Warren R. D.
McCollum, John W.
Mitchell, John
Putnam, David
Pitman, William
Pitman, John
Pool, John S.
Puckett, Wesley

Page, W. D.
Reinhardt, John H.
Reinhardt, Lewis W.
Reinhardt, Adam
Reinhardt, Jacob H.
Rice, William
Riley, W. H.
Rhyne, J. S.
Rhyne, J. P.
Ragsdale, Larkin A.
Ray, W. T.

Redd, Thomas
Say, Martin
Stearnes, Joseph
Smith, M. J.
Smith, William H.
Smith, Robert B.
Simpson, Bayless W.
Sanders, Asberry
Sisk, Bartlett
Stephens, J. M.
Spears, Hezekiah

Thomas, Pinckney
Thomas, Joseph
Turner, B. H.
Timmons, Samuel
Vernon, John G.
Vaughn, William
Wise, William
Wilson, Uriah
Weatherford, John
Whelchel, James D.
Whelchel, William

Company C
"Cherokee Home Guard"
(With Army of Tennessee)

Officers:

Dowda, William T., Captain
Burns, Alfred H., 1st Lieut.
Cobb, John G., 2d Lieut.
Barton, William, 2d Lieut.
Meers, William P., 1st Sgt.
McCollum, John, 2d Sgt.
Boatman, John W., 3d Sgt.

Garmon, Wilson, 4th Sgt.
Jones, J. H., 5th Sgt.
Whelchel, Major, 1st Corp.
Evans, Stanberry B., 2d Corp.
Whitmore, Rolly, 3d Corp.
Holland, John J. C., 4th Corp.

Privates:

Brooks, Elijah
Barnett, Matt
Bass, James
Bass, Redding
Cleghorn, Levi
Cline, John O.
Cline, William M.
Dean, Henry C.
Dean, Zachariah
Dowda, Augustus A.
Finch, Thomas
Farrell, J. C.
Grogan, John
Graham, J. H.
Garmon, James
Garmon, W. R.
Guerin, John
Greer, Joshua
Gunter, John

Hopkins, John H.
Holland, Richard, Sr.
Holland, Richard, Jr.
Hosea, Bennett
Hutson, J. E.
Harris, James
Jarvis, William
Jones, John F.
Keith, Allen
Keeter, James
McCoy, S. P.
Mangum, John T.
Meers, Joseph L.
Morris, John B.
Morris, W. J.
Nicks, F. M.
Nations, Benjamin
Nations, John
Owens, Joseph

Pinson, W.
Robinett, David
Robinett, Allen
Reinhardt, J. M.
Reinhardt, Milton
Reinhardt, George L.
Rampley, James S.
Rampley, William
Say, Patterson
Simms, W. J.
Stroup, Jacob
Scott, Green B.
Smith, William
Smith, Simon
Smith, Henry R.
Shuttleworth, Wiley
Strain, James H.
Simms, A. J.
Tucker, John

Umphreys, Monroe
Whelchel, William

Williams, David N.
Willbanks, Hezekiah
Willbanks, O. P.

Willbanks, W. A.
Wilson, John

Company D
"Cherokee Repellers"
(With Army of Tennessee)

Officers:

Harris, James L., Captain
Hill, John W., 1st Lieut.
Bagwell, William W., 2d Lieut.
Tuell, Nathaniel O., 2d Lieut.
Groover, James P., 1st Sgt.
Moore, John, 2d Sgt.
Cook, J. B. L., 3d Sgt.

Ridings, John C., 4th Sgt.
Spears, William, 5th Sgt.
Youther, Adam, 1st Corp.
Thompson, A. J., 2d Corp.
Porter, Phillip, 3d Corp.
Smith, John, 4th Corp.

Privates:

Covington, John H.
Crenshaw, Henry
Crenshaw, John N.
Dobson, W. P.
Evans, Thomas N.
Fenley, James L.
Fowler, Thomas C.
Fowler, William
Groover, James P.
Groover, Cornelius
Hill, David
Hill, Van Buren
Hill, Reuben
Henderson, Joseph T.
Huff, Simms

Higgins, Charles
Holcombe, N.
Holcombe, Thomas
Ingram, Jefferson
Ingram, Alfred L.
Jackson, Juriah
Kelly, Andrew J.
Leadbetter, George A.
Monroe, Robert S.
Martin, Aaron
Pike, Ransom
Petit, Isaac
Page, James M.
Page, James F.
Qualls, Daniel

Ridings, Rice R.
Simmons, William
Spears, A. L.
Spears, Nicholas
Smith, James
Smith, Moses
Smith, John
Smith, Thomas H.
Sutton, Robert
Saunders, Moses W.
Searcy, William A.
Tanner, James R.
Williams, Augustus
Youther, John
Yarbrough, Thomas

Company E
"Cherokee Volunteers"
(With Army of Tennessee)

Officers:

Covington, A. J., Captain
Covington, John H., 1st Lieut.
Morris, Isaac, 2d Lieut.
Chumley, George W., 2d Lieut.
Minton, John P., 1st Sgt.
Cosmer, David G., 2d Sgt.

Pitman, Zachariah, 3d Sgt.
Pitts, William, 4th Sgt.
Hufstuler, Emanuel, 1st Corp.
Fowler, Jesse, 2d Corp.
Cole, Sandy, 3d Corp.
Gates, William, 4th Corp.

Privates:

Allen, Caleb
Allen, Hollen
Alford, E. E.
Blanton, Daniel
Brown, James
Bennett, Freeman
Cook, Gilford
Castuer, D. G.
Castuer, Thomas
Cook, N. J.
Evans, James M.
Fowler, Jesse
Graham, J. A.

Gay, Albert
Gates, William
Humphreys, Jesse
Head, Doctor E.
Hutson, Thomas
Hyde, Tanty
Huff, John
Kirk, John D.
Kelley, William
King, William
Kinsey, Stephen E.
McCoy, Elijah
Pitts, Henry

Pitts, William
Puckett, John
Puckett, Wesley
Quiller, James
Roberts, Thomas
Redding, James
Roberson, William
Swanson, James M.
Smith, Elijah
Strain, James
Woods, Joseph

Company F
"Salacoa Silver Grays"
(With Army of Tennessee)

Officers:

Fuller, H. P., Captain
Pritchett, J. W., 1st Lieut.
Taylor, Obediah, 2d Lieut.
Hamlett, J. S., 2d Lieut.
Lewis, John B., 1st Sgt.
Collins, T. R., 2d Sgt.
Striplin, Benjamin, 3d Sgt.

Turner, E. S., 4th Sgt.
Young, Thomas, 5th Sgt.
Pritchett, F. A., 1st Corp.
Collins, Jacob R., 2d Corp.
Lewis, W. L., 3d Corp.
Prefley, T. J., 4th Corp.

Privates:

Franklin, J. W.
Fendley, H. G.
Fuller, James H.
Fulton, R. B.
Fulton, S. J.
Fowler, T. H.
Gasaway, T. H.
Hefley, M. L.
Hood, L.
Harmon, H. O.
Hutcherson, Thomas

Ingram, R. W.
Jefferson, George W.
Johnson, W. R.
Johnson, W. M.
Jones, H. L.
Jones, S. J.
Jones, J. J.
Jones, Seaborn
McDow, J. F.
Mahan, J. M.
Mahan, W. F.

Mahan, J. M.
Meadows, J. F.
Pritchett, J. B.
Pritchett, Robert
Price, F. C.
Rice, F. C.
Roberts, William
Spirlin, Stephen
Smith, Micajah
Taylor, J. M.
Worley, John

Company G
"Cherokee Stone Walls"
(With Army of Tennessee)

Officers:

Worley, John L., Captain
Ponder, John T., 1st Lieut.
Cowan, Stephen D., 2d Lieut.
Cook, Samuel C., 2d Lieut.
Stancel, Cader B., 1st Sgt.
Guerin, John, 2d Sgt.
Willbanks, Thomas, 3d Sgt.

Owen, Stewart M., 4th Sgt.
Rea, Stanford V., 5th Sgt.
Archer, Clayton, 1st Corp.
Heflin, Jonathan, 2d Corp.
McCoy, James M., 3d Corp.
Evans, Uriah, 4th Corp.

Privates:

Archer, William B.
Anderson, Bayless
Cook, John
Conner, John
Cagle, J. W.
Duncan, John B.
Evans, William R.

Goss, Sherman
Howell, John
Hitt, Benjamin C.
Little, Henry
Mullins, William F.
Saymore, Allen
Sawyer, William

Timmons, John
Timmons, William J.
Underwood, William
Wyley, G. M.
Wyley, E. H.
Willbanks, Thomas

Company H
(With Army of Tennessee)

Officers:

Edwards, Thomas J., Captain
Wiley, Rufus R., 1st Lieut.
Smith, Anderson D., 2d Lieut.
Holbrook, Green B., 2d Lieut.
Gray, Andrew J., 1st Lieut.
Land, Levi, 2d Sgt.
Carver, Moses, 3d Sgt.

Thaxton, B. B., 4th Sgt.
Ashworth, John, 5th Sgt.
Thomas, Thomas, 1st Corp.
Haygood, John F., 2d Corp.
Westbrook, Stephen B., 3d Corp.
Haygood, David, 4th Corp.

Privates:

Beck, William
Bruce, James N.
Chambers, Martin
Christian, William J.
Day, Reuben
Day, Lewis
Edwards, Edward
Gassett, William J.
Gray, Andrew J.
Harmon, David
Hall, Robert B.

Harless, Andrew
Harless, William
King, James
Kendricks, Julius
Lively, B.
Millen, David
Madders, Gaddeal
McDaniel, William
Nise, Isaac
Nise, John L.
Pace, James

Seagraves, Milzey
Smith, Harvey
Sanders, Ambrose
Thaxton, Charles D.
Treadaway, D. L.
Waites, Asbury L.
Wright, A. J.
Westbrook, Thompson
Westbrook, John
Wood, James
Wiley, James L.

2. Companies of the CHEROKEE LEGION, Georgia State Guards Cavalry

Company A
"Cherokee Rangers"
(With Army of Tennessee)
Officers:

Brewster, P. H., Captain
Strain, B. F., 1st Lieut.
Jordan, James, 2d Lieut.
Payne, S. K., 2d Lieut.
Pearce, G. W., 1st Sgt.
Moss, T. R., 2d Sgt.
Wheeler, N. J., 3d Sgt.

Jordan, S. K., 4th Sgt.
Vernon, F. D., 5th Sgt.
Hughes, James, 1st Corp.
Anderson, James, 2d Corp.
Mitchell, J. E., 3d Corp.
Swansey, E. J., 4th Corp.

Privates:

Bird, J. P. V.
Bryson, Jefferson
Carver, Jefferson
Cagle, Joseph
Chamlee, Tillman
Carn, Elias
Collier, H. W.
Cook, J. B.
Costner, D. G.
Day, James
Daley, James M.
Ellison, E. L.
Ellison, E. G.
Edwards, William A.
Gober, G. B.
Gilchrist, James
Galt, J. R.
Hedgecock, J. C.
Harp, A. C.

Hogan, Thomas
Haynes, Harper
Hames, J. B.
Hamby, M. G.
Huff, John
Hunnicutt, J. W.
Jordan, S. R.
Keeter, Jefferson
Knox, Joseph
Light, P. G.
McKinney, James
Meadford, P. M.
McConnell, James
Mansell, Samuel
Massey, J. W.
Massey, James
Moore, J. K.
Mitchell, J. E.
Pearce, C. A.

Prator, Thomas
Pitman, A. P.
Popham, W. T.
Phillips, R. F.
Pearce, George W.
Payne, Lindsey
Rhyne, James A.
Smith, George
Sullivan, Daniel
Sergeant, W. C.
Strain, J. H.
Sage, P. G.
Stevens, J. A.
Vernon, F. D.
White, J. M.
Wheeler, John
Wayne, J. B.

Company C
"Cherokee Lincoln Killers"
Officers:

Worley, William W., Captain
Underwood, T. G., 1st Lieut.
Fowler, M. W., 2d Lieut.
Wilson, Leroy, 2d Lieut.
Latham, A. P., 2d Lieut.
Morrison, M. T., 1st Sgt.
Latham, John H., 2d Sgt.

Gilstrap, William, 3d Sgt.
Lynch, W. J., 4th Sgt.
Conn, T. M., 1st Corp.
Harbin, Jeptha, 2d Corp.
Carr, W. J., 3d Corp.
Rudicil, L. F., 4th Corp.

Privates:

Avery, A. C.
Bowen, Robert
Bruce, Benton
Bobo, Wiley
Burtz, Jesse
Chamlee, William
Conn, Francis M.
Donald, John A.
Donald, M. M.
Edwards, J. V.
Epperson, W. S.
Fowler, James A.
Fowler, M. W.
Griffin, A. J.
Gilstrap, William
Henson, J. W.

Harbin, Jeptha
Hurt, Robert H.
Johnson, Thomas G.
King, James W.
Lynch, W. J.
Latham, George
Latham, John H.
Leonard, S. D.
Morrow, Daniel A.
Morrison, M. T. C.
Martin, Franklin A.
Messon, S. J.
McCraw, George
Oaks, William
Petty, Isaac
Pascoe, Samuel

Roberson, John
Rudicil, L. F.
Stancil, M.
Stringer, D. M.
Smith, Samuel L.
Tippen, John M.
Tippen, William
Thomas, Jefferson
Wayne, William
Westbrook, J. R.
Wilson, William
Wallis, John W.
Wheeler, C. M.
Wyatt, Abraham
Webster, T. C.
Walker, Henry C.

Company D

Officers:

McConnell, Joseph, Captain
Barnes, George, 1st Lieut.
Hause, J. F., 2d Lieut.
Boring, J. P., 2d Lieut.
Foster, William S., 1st Sgt.
Dupree, W. G., 1st Sgt.
Humphrey, B. M., 2d Sgt.

Dial, Cyrus, 3d Sgt.
McCullom, S. H., 4th Sgt.
Bell, T. R., 5th Sgt.
Spears, Joseph, 1st Corp.
Freeman, D. L., 2d Corp.
Alexander, J. R., 3d Corp.
Evans, A. M., 4th Corp.

Privates:

Barrett, James
Burgess, Gabriel
Burchell, Henry
Barnes, J. T.
Benson, W. B.
Cobb, R. H.
Crow, James M.
Cagle, Henry F.
Deen, Elijah
Duke, Emery
Durham, Levi
Dobbs, Martin W.
Dobbs, Jasper
Dobbs, Marion
Dobbs, George M.
Dobbs, P. C.

Dobbs, Perry
Evans, Thomas D.
Edwards, William A.
Freeman, H. D.
Fleming, N. W. W.
Haley, James
Hancock, Robert
Hames, William
Hames, Coleman
Hughes, John C.
Hughes, L. F.
Herndon, Reuben
Herndon, David
Hook, L. M.
Haney, Jacob
Honea, John L.

Honea, Thomas
Johnson, Lemuel
Johnson, Harmon
Kemp, Alsey
Kemp, Stephen
Kennell, A. L.
Kimberley, J. E.
McCollum, J. W.
McCullom, R. A.
McConnell, H. D.
McConnell, Isaac
McConnell, S. M.
McClure, J. J.
McDaniel, William
McMullen, S. P.
Manning, Ambrose

Mears, Martin G.	Petree, John	Stevens, Jeremiah
Medford, D. B.	Reece, Alfred	Tippens, G. W.
Mitchell, Robert D.	Reece, Aaron	Trout, R. W.
Nuckolls, J. M.	Reece, William	Wise, Henry
Putnam, Daniel	Roach, William	Wiley, A. J.
Page, Robert	Says, William	Word, P. F.

3. Companies of the Georgia Volunteer Infantry

Company F, 2d Regiment
"Cherokee Brown Riflemen"
Officers:

Dickerson, Thomas E., Captain	McCollum, John W., 4th Sgt.
Harris, Skidmore, 1st Lieut.	Langston, Jesse B., 1st Corp.
Donaldson, M. G., 1st Lieut.	Jordon, James L., 2d Corp.
Shuford, Alonzo B., 2d Lieut.	Heard, John G., 3d Corp.
Daniel, Francis M., Jr. 2d Lieut.	Nix, William, 4th Corp.
Dickerson, Nelson L., 1st Sgt.	Downs, John H., Corp.
Daniel, Henry G., 2d Sgt.	Hawkins, Charles A., Musician
Daniel, William, 3d Sgt.	Owens, Thomas C., Musician

Privates:

Baker, Sim	Finch, Thomas E.	Moore, W. J.
Baker, William G.	Fowler, Leonard R.	Morgan, Thomas J.
Barton, Joseph B.	Freeman, Henry F.	Morgan, William N.
Bennett, Samuel K.	Garrison, William E.	Moss, William G.
Black, Moses W.	Gayden, Andrew	Mullins, Henry L.
Bragg, Miles F.	Hampton, George W.	Mullins, John T.
Brand, Joseph M.	Harris, James	McCollum, Benj. F.
Broadwell, James M.	Hatcher, Henry D.	McCrary, Andrew J.
Broadwell, John M.	Heard, Joseph W.	McKinney, J. R.
Bruce, Calton	Hillhouse, William F.	Nix, John
Carpenter, Jasper, W.	Hitchens, John	Padget, Irvin
Coker, Thomas D.	Holland, Oscar A.	Pierce, Clemeth A.
Collum, John	Hood, Humphrey	Pierce, George W.
Copeland, Daniel	Howard, Thomas S.	Pinson, Thomas J.
Couch, John W.	Hutson, L. A.	Putnam, Berry P.
Deaton, John D.	Ingram, William A.	Ragsdale, Allen B.
Dickerson, Israel C.	Jackson, Jasper	Reinhardt, A. M.
Doss, Robert L.	Jones, John T.	Rice, Joseph
Doss, William J.	Kennett, Z. D.	Rice, William
Ellison, Richard	King, Adoniron S.	Richardson, Jasper
Evans, John G.	Loveless, Samuel B.	Richardson, Nathan
Evans, Joseph M.	Manders, James A.	Robertson, Nathaniel
Ferguson, Milligan F.	Millwood, William R.	Seay, Dorsey H.
Finch, Ivy A.	Moore, Edward L.	Smallwood, Allen G.

Smith, Lewis T.	Tidwell, Francis M.	Wheeler, James A.
Staner, Michael	Tierce, William F.	Wheeler, James W.
Starr, John T.	Turner, McCager	Wheeler, William P.
Strickland, Joseph G.	Vernon, Franklin D.	Wilkinson, F. H.
Thomas, Waddie	Watson, Alfred H.	Williams, F. P.
	Watson, Joseph G.	

Company D, 14th Regiment

Officers:

Fielder, James M., Captain	Baker, John V., 3d Sgt.
Hunt, Green B., 1st Lieut.	Sargent, John C., 4th Sgt.
McConnell, John H., 2d Lieut.	Medford, James E., 1st Corp.
Abbott, Armstead T., Jr. 2d Lieut.	Hull, Newton J., 2d Corp.
Putnam, William D., 1st Sgt.	Anderson, George W., 3d Corp.
Tanner, William J., 2d Sgt.	Smith, Stephen D., 4th Corp.

Privates:

Abbott, Theo. F. H.	Dupree, William A.	Morgan, Knellum L.
Adams, Charles G.	Dupree, W. C.	Moss, Edward W.
Adams, James W.	Fountain, L. M.	McCollum, George W.
Adams, J. N.	Fountain, William P.	McCollum, John V.
Adams, R. G.	Fowler, James N.	McCollum, J. W.
Adams, William J.	Gourley, J. A.	McConnell, John A.
Arnold, Clement	Haggerty, John	McGee, William A.
Barnett, H. H.	Hames, John	McGinnis, Martin A.
Barnett, Robert H.	Hames, Thomas	Page, Asbury
Barnett, William F.	Head, H. B.	Page, James D.
Bennett, James A.	Herring, W. J.	Page, M. L.
Blythe, John	Hitt, Jasper	Page, Robert N.
Boyer, Martin E.	Hodgins, John B.	Page, William J.
Brand, J. W.	Holmes, John	Page, W. H.
Brimer, William W.	Hood, James P.	Peterson, William P.
Brown, J. A.	Hull, James A. L.	Poor, Franklin
Bruce, Abraham	Hull, Mark T.	Putnam, Howard B.
Bruce, Martin V.	Jentry, D. M.	Putnam, John B.
Cox, James W. P.	Johnson, Alex. M.	Rainey, James
Davis, William	Latham, David	Reynolds, Andrew J.
Dempsey, Henry D.	Medford, Millford C.	Reynolds, John N.
Dempsey, L. E.	Medford, M. D.	Reynolds, Joseph T.
Dobbs, David	Medford, William L.	Roberts, John M.
Duke, William	Medford, William M.	Ross, Frederick W.
Duke, William A.	Medford, W. M.	Ross, Lemuel E.
Dupree, Daniel L.	Millwood, James S.	Shelly, Benjamin O.
Dupree, Joseph G.	Millwood, Jesse M.	Simpson, Reuben B.
Dupree, Thaddeus M.	Millwood, William R.	Sorrells, George W.

Stancell, William F.
Tanner, Archibald S.
Thurmond, Thomas J.
Turner, George W.
Tyson, Howard R.

Voiles, Nathaniel
White, John M.
White, William F.
Whitlock, James M.
Whitman, W. J.

Wilson, Mathew W.
Wilson, Stephen W.
Wilson, William
Wood, C. W.
Wood, Edmund L.

Company G, 23d Regiment

Officers:

Sharp, John J. A., Captain
Reinhardt, Nat. F., 1st Lieut.
Grist, Benjamin A., 2d Lieut.
Moss, Theodore T., Jr. 2d Lieut.
Moore, W. N., 1st Sgt.
Brooke, W. J., 2d Sgt.

Pinson, A. J., 3d Sgt.
Reinhardt, J. H., 4th Sgt.
Hunnicutt, J. R., 1st Corp.
Greer, John L. E., 2d Corp.
Hawkins, E. S., 3d Corp.
Sharp, C. C., 4th Corp.

Privates:

Anderson, John
Arwood, W. P.
Barrett, John A.
Bates, John C.
Bates, M. S.
Beam, Thomas
Bell, John,
Bird, Thomas M.
Bird, William D.
Bishop, W. M.
Black, Harrison
Brooke, Elijah N.
Brooke, N. C.
Brown, G. W.
Burgess, John
Burrell, S. H.
Cagle, George W.
Cagle, Leonard
Carver, J. T.
Chamblee, James
Chamblee, John
Coker, J. C.
Coker, S. L.
Cole, Landy
Coley, M. P.
Collier, J. C.
Collier, J. L.
Cross, Nathaniel
Cunard, W. H.

Day, Benjamin
Day, Manning A.
Dickson, S. R.
Drew, Willoughby
Echols, W. R.
Edwards, Alfred
Edwards, Henry H.
Edwards, R. S.
Evans, L. M.
Figgins, Francis M.
Figgins, J. M.
Garner, R. E. M.
Garrett, Joseph
Heard, W. T.
Henson, John A.
Henson, J. H.
Henson, W. T.
Hill, T. W.
Hudgins, N. B.
Hudson, J. M.
Huff, W. D.
Humphreys, C. C.
Humphreys, Frank
Humphreys, Jesse
Humphreys, J. M.
Humphreys, L. H.
Humphreys, W. C.
Hunnicutt, G. W.
Huson, J. A.

Jordan, Noah
Keeter, A. N.
Kitchens, James T.
Kitchens, W. T.
Knox, John B.
Knox, W. T.
Lewis, Andrew
Low, James W.
Lowrey, William J.
Massengale, Robert
Massey, J. E.
Morris, W. B.
McClure, James M.
McClure, W. A.
McClure, W. R.
McCollum, J. M.
McKinney, Robert C.
Nations, James
Pharr, A. O.
Pierce, R. S.
Pitman, John D.
Pitman, W. A.
Prater, Thomas F.
Pugh, Isaac G. C.
Pugh, James W.
Pugh, John H.
Reeves, John
Riggins, James M.
Shettleworth, Wiley

Sisk, A. W.
Smith, James W.
Stegall, J. B.
Tesanier, J. G. B.
Tesanier, N.
Thomas, M. H.
Thomas, W. G.
Timmons, James P.

Timmons, William D.
Tolbert, B. J.
Tolbert, E. N.
Tolbert, H. S.
Tolbert, Josiah
Tolbert, J. E. P.
Walker, J. J.
Waters, M. H.

Wheeler, H. J.
Wheeler, W. W.
Whelchel, W. A.
Wiley, Thomas A.
Wilson, Orvin
Wilson, W. B.
Wilson, W. N.
Wilson, W. R.

Company D, 28th Regiment

"McAfee and Donaldson Guards"

Officers:

Garrison, Nehemiah J., Captain
Grambling, Enoch C., 1st Lieut.
Freeman, Hartwell D., 2d Lieut.
Jordan, William J., Jr. 2d Lieut.
Ragsdale, John, 1st Sgt.
Croft, Ira P., 2d Sgt.
Simpson, S. M., 3d Sgt.

Ragsdale, Calvin B., 4th Sgt.
Millican, E. F., 5th Sgt.
Dean, C. T., 1st Corp.
Honea, S. T., 2d Corp.
Roach, Thomas H., 3d Corp.
Cooper, John, 4th Corp.

Privates:

Beavers, John T.
Beavers, William J.
Benson, J. M.
Brand, J. W.
Bryson, John A.
Carmichael, D. C.
Carmichael, J. L.
Cato, W. R.
Chapman, Jacob A.
Chapman, John W.
Christopher, J. S.
Cole, John
Dickerson, John
Dickerson, William
Dupree, Joshua R.
Edwards, Henry H.
Fowler, James N.
Fowler, John C.
Fowler, Thomas T.
Fowler, William L.
Freeman, J. A.
Haines, Simpson

Haines, W. L.
Hillhouse, Elijah
Hillhouse, Robert W.
Hillhouse, Samuel W.
Honea, Albert
Honea, William P.
Huggins, John
Hughes, J. L.
Hughes, L. F.
Hughes, William C.
Johnson, William H.
Johnson, W. J.
Keown, David
Keown, John S.
Keown, Levi
Kimberly, L. C.
King, William
Leslie, Warren D.
Lindsey, James H.
McCollum, James W.
McCoy, J. P.
McWhorter, Irvin

McWhorter, J. A.
Orr, John J.
Pendley, Thomas J.
Phillips, C.
Pittman, William
Ragsdale, John
Ragsdale, Martin
Ragsdale, Richard
Robinett, Elisha
Robinett, William
Smith, L. T.
Stearns, Byers R.
Stone, B. W.
Tapp, T. J.
Teddar, D. W.
Thompson, James
Thompson, M. M.
Watkins, J. B.
Whelchel, R. F.
Wilson, H. P.
Wright, Isaac

Company F, 28th Regiment
"Cherokee Georgia Mountaineers"

Officers:

Burtz, Jesse, Captain
Wade, Lemuel R., 1st Lieut.
McClure, Richard A., 2d Lieut.
Morrison, M. T. C., Jr. 2d Lieut.
Stancell, A. Hamilton, 1st Sgt.
Bowling, H. C., 2d Sgt.
White, James F., 3d Sgt.

Jones, H. C., 4th Sgt.
Warthen, George W., 3d Sgt.
Price, Isaac, 1st Corp.
Smith, W. J., 2d Corp.
Wright, John H., 3d Corp.
Freeman, W. S., 4th Corp.
Tuell, R. A., Corporal

Privates:

Anderson, Isaac
Anderson, John F.
Baber, James
Bearden, William J.
Biddy, L. W.
Boling, Floyd T.
Bone, C. M.
Brown, William J.
Bussell, Hans G.
Causey, C. L.
Colbert, Alfred M.
Coleman, Jeremiah
Conn, Francis M.
Duncan,
Eaton, A. J.
Evans, G. S.
Garrot, A. C.
Gibson, William T.
Gilliland, S. J.
Hall, P. M.
Hawkins, G. W.
Hazelwood, W. H.
Hembree, J. D.
Henderson, F. M.
Henderson, James I.
Hogan, J. C.

Holcombe, Asa
Holcombe, J. J.
Hood, Henry
Hood, Lazarus
Hood, W. C.
Ingram, H.
Kelly, Thomas
King, James W.
Miller, J. T.
Miller, R. F.
Miller, S. G.
Miller, William
Mills, T. G.
Murdock, William G.
McAfee, Alfred A.
McCraw, G. P.
McCraw, John A.
McCraw, W. D.
Nix, Elias
Nix, James E.
Pace, John N.
Pace, J. L.
Padgett, C. S.
Penly, B. A.
Pettet, James H.
Popham, Elijah

Popham, Gideon
Popham, Reuben
Price, A. A.
Price, E. C.
Raines, W. C.
Ramsey, William R.
Richards, A. W.
Richards, John C.
Riggins, A. L.
Russell, Hans G.
Sanders, A. J.
Sharp, William
Simmons, James M.
Simmons, W. H. H.
Smith, J. L.
Smith, S. L.
Smith, S. S.
Smith, T. L.
Thackston, J. H.
Thackston, W. B.
Thomason, G. L.
Williams, Richard
Wilson, J. C.
Wood, J. K.
Wood, J. P.
Woodall, Russell G.

This company was originally known as Co. M. 18th Regt. Ga. Vol. Infantry. It was formed in part by Capt. Jesse Burtz's Independent Company of Ga. Infantry, Nov. 13, 1861. It had on its original roll probably 175 men. It was composed of men from four counties: Cherokee, Pickens, Forsyth and Dawson. Before being mustered into service at Richmond, Va., being too large for one company, it was divided, retaining in the original company, under Capt. Burtz, the men from Cherokee and Pickens Counties, while the men from Forsyth and Dawson Counties were formed into a new company.—From the records of the Georgia Soldier Roster Commission.

Company B, 34th Regiment
(also known as Company K)

Officers:

Daniel, John Posey, Captain
Keith, Amos W., 1st Lieut.
Jordan, James L., 2d Lieut.
Morton, A. B., Jr. 2d Lieut.
Hillhouse, John F., 1st Sgt.
McCollum, Moses D., 2d Sgt.
Hasty, John T., 3d Sgt.

Daniel, John L., 4th Sgt.
Daniel, William F., 5th Sgt.
George, William H., 1st Corp.
Haynes, G. W., 2d Corp.
Hillhouse, Robert W., 3d Corp.
Cochran, Holman, 4th Corp.

Privates:

Barrett, J. S.
Barton, J. J. B.
Brand, Joseph N.
Brand, R. M. C.
Brand, Z. D.
Burriss, J. N.
Cagle, Isaac J.
Cagle, Jacob
Cagle, James
Cagle, James O.
Cline, S. W.
Cornelison, John
Croft, Frederick T.
Dickerson, N. G.
Dilbeck, John J.
Dilbeck, Josiah
Dobbs, Franklin
Doss, J. N.
Duncan, Rufus
Ferguson, C. W.
Fincher, Thomas H.
Flannagan, James M.
Fowler, Coleman S.

Fowler, George D.
Freeman, George W.
Garrison, D. E.
George, V. James
Gramling, Richard G.
Greer, James
Greer, James T.
Grisham, John
Hall, Isaac
Hall, William
Hasty, William P.
Hawkins, Adolphus G.
Jenks, Joseph B.
Kennett, Adolphus L.
Kennett, Nicholas N.
Kennett, R. L.
King, John
Kirk, George W.
Kirk, William A.
Lewis, B. J.
Marlow, G. A.
Martin, Joseph M.
Mitchell, Francis M.

Murphey, W. L.
McRae, John W.
McCanless, W. M.
Nelson, Thomas
Nix, Franklin
Pace, D. C.
Pilgrim, F. Marion
Proctor, James
Randolph, Hezekiah
Rollins, James V.
Rutherford, James
Ryle, Jasper U.
Tolbert, J. M.
Tolbert, Osborn H.
Vaughn, Albert B.
Walters, M. R.
Wheeler, Julius W.
Whelchel, Francis M.
Whelchel, James M.
Wilbanks, W. H.
Wilson, Charles W.
Wilson, Samuel B.
Winn, George W.

Company A, 36th Regiment

Officers:

Glenn, Joseph, Captain
Baker, Samuel H., 1st Lieut.
Connor, Daniel, 2d Lieut.
Sansom, John L., Jr. 2d Lieut.
Hallman, Israel, 1st Sgt.
Kile, G. W., 2d Sgt.
Bence, C. B. W., 3d Sgt.

Mote, Silas T., 4th Sgt.
King, Thomas W., 5th Sgt.
Couch, Jackson, 1st Corp.
North, Alfred, 2d Corp.
Jennings, F. M., 3d Corp.
Laymance, H. D., 4th Corp.

Privates:

Baker, Edmond P.
Barber, Henry C.
Bence, B. F.
Bence, W. T.
Black, Garvin R.
Blackstone, Henry W.
Banks, Joseph
Box, Gilbert L.
Bradley, J. J.
Brown, Lemuel E.
Brown, L. W.
Bryce, Alexander
Carton, Jesse
Christian, J. A.
Clark, George W.
Conner, John C.
Cook, Levi J.
Couch, Jackson
Cox, Phillips E. A.
Cronan, J. N.
Cronan, J. W.
Cruse, T. W.
Currinton, Jesse
Drennan, John C.
Dyer, W. E.
Elrod, Reuben
Etheridge, Bryant
Etheridge, John
Ezzard, George W.
Ezzard, Thomas W.
Fowler, James N.
Frazier, John
George, Jeptha C.

George, Silas
Green, Isaac
Green, Major J.
Hamilton, Andrew L.
Hamilton, A. M.
Hamilton, Joseph M.
Haygood, James L.
Hays, M.
Heerlien, Gustavus
Helton, James
Holcombe, A. G.
Holcombe, P. P.
Huffaker, Ignatius H.
Jennings, F. M.
Johnson, C. M.
Karr, Greenberry
Karr, Jesse W.
Ketchum, James S.
Kinnamon, Aaron
Kinnamon, Leonard S.
Larman, John B.
Laymance, H. D.
Lindsey, Henry
Lindsey, John
Long, John L.
Long, H. W.
Main, H. R.
Mauldin, Cicero H.
Mayfield, George B.
Moon, R. M.
Montgomery, W. H.
Moorehead, F. M.
Morgan, Jacob L.

Morris, Rufus M.
McAfee, Jesse R.
McCraw, Alvin
McCraw, Martin
McCraw, Peter
McKinsey, John A.
Norrell, Robert
Norrell, Samuel A.
Pratt, George
Pugh, John W.
Queen, W. M.
Roberts, Pinckney W.
Rogers, John M.
Rooker, John A.
Roper, J. H.
Roper, Peter H.
Samples, James
Samples, William C.
Sheardon, Thomas C.
Sloan, Green M.
Smalling, William
Smith, James
Smith, John C.
Smith, Wade H.
Sparks, W. R.
Stanley, H.
Stephens, L. H.
Stephenson, W. C.
Stewart, James W.
Stuart, W. A.
Suttle, James L.
Suttle, Thomas K.
Suttle, William A.

Sweatman, John J.
Tankersley, James M.
Tanner, Alfred
Tapp, Alexander
Tapp, Hugh
Tapp, John
Tapp, Leonard

Terry, John W.
Thomas, J. R.
Thomas, O. P.
Turner, Elias L.
Wadkins, W. Lemuel
White, John
Williams, H. P.

Williams, James J.
Williams, S. R.
Winkler, David H.
Wood, Robert
Wood, Robert C.
Yancey, Charles

This company was engaged in the battle of Baker's Creek, Miss., May 16, 1863, and in the bombardment of Vicksburg, Miss., from May 18, 1863, to July 4, 1863.

Company E, 36th Regiment

Officers:

Gilbert, Jesse D., Captain
Jefferson, Thomas E., 1st Lieut.
Richards, William B., 2d Lieut.
Leonard, James L., Jr. 2d Lieut.
Wilkie, H. R., 1st Sgt.
Swinford, John A., 2d Sgt.
Bagwell, Josiah, 3d Sgt.

Tomlin, Winford S., 4th Sgt.
Tomlin, William S., 5th Sgt.
Leonard, Cicero G., 1st Corp.
Beavers, Milton M., 2d Corp.
Wilkie, Francis M., 3d Corp.
Smith, Elisha C., 4th Corp.

Privates:

Anderson, Leroy W.
Andrews, W. J.
Black, C. J.
Bozeman, G. W.
Bozeman, John K.
Bozeman, Samuel A.
Bozeman, S. N.
Bramlett, James A.
Brooks, T. R.
Bruce, Hugh C.
Bruce, James R.
Carter, William
Carvel, P. P.
Chadwick, E. H.
Cochran, Henry L.
Cochran, U. P.
Cochran, William C.
Coffee, James A.
Conn, A. C. D.
Conn, Daniel J.
Conn, Thomas N.
Dooly, J. A.

Findley, James D.
Fisher, Samuel H.
Fowler, Joshua
Gilbert, Sidney H.
Hardin, James M.
Hardin, William R.
Hawkins, William R.
Heath, Francis M.
Hensley, G. W.
Higgins, James A.
Higgins, James M.
Higgins, J. Samuel
Higgins, William
Holbert, A.
Holbrook, Ira R.
Holbrook, James H.
Holbrook, J. L.
Holcombe, H. B.
Howard, J. L.
Hudson, G. W.
Ingram, Joseph
Jones, T. J.

Kinsey, T. A.
Lazenbery, Elias
Lee, William E.
Leonard, J. J.
Leonard, M. F.
Leonard, W. F.
Martin, G. L. J.
Mills, W. J.
Mullinax, R.
Murdock, D. R.
McDaniel, A. T.
Nix, Mathew
Nix, Valentine
Pace, J. H.
Paine, C. H.
Pasco, Jeremiah
Petit, I.
Phillips, J. Crayton
Phillips, Robert
Phillips, William
Price, Alfred
Price, Allen

Purcell, N. J.
Qualls, Luke
Qualls, Samuel
Reaves, J. P.
Redd, James
Redd, James M.
Redd, William B.
Redd, William Perry
Ridins, James O.
Robinson, J. J.
Rogers, J. C.
Scott, Robert
Sewell, Aaron J.
Sewell, Alvin D.
Sewell, C. A.
Sewell, Erwin
Shadwick, E. H.

Shears, R. E.
Simmons, W. R.
Smith, Elisha C.
Smith, N. B.
Southerland, A. J.
Southerland, A. L.
Strayhorn, John P.
Strayhorn, William
Sumner, J. D.
Sumner, S. R.
Swinford, Reuben T.
Thacker, Larkin
Thackston, N. C.
Thomas, Jacob
Tomlin, William S.
Tomlin, Winford S.
Walker, J. W.

Wallace, John J.
Wallace, M. L.
Ward, F. M.
Ward, J. S.
Ward, R. A.
Watson, James P.
Wilkie, Francis M.
Wilkie, George W.
Wilkie, J. C.
Wilkie, Richard
Wilkie, W.
Williams, Aloe
Wood, H. J.
Wood, S.
Wright, Joseph

Company A, 43d Regiment

Officers:

Mullins, William F., Captain
Reinhardt, A. M., 1st Lieut.
Rhyne, James A., 2d Lieut.
Clayton, C. C., Jr. 2d Lieut.
Fowler, James B., 1st Sgt.
Reinhardt, George L., 2d Sgt.
Moore, Michael A. H., 3d Sgt.

Taylor, William, 4th Sgt.
Buford, William M., 5th Sgt.
Pitts, Jesse L., 1st Corp.
Green, Joseph H., 2d Corp.
Stripling, William F., 3d Corp.
Collins, A. G. B., 4th Corp.

Privates:

Agan, William
Agan, W. H.
Archer, Columbus L.
Barrett, F. S.
Beard, James M.
Black, Garrett
Burd, J. M.
Carney, Lott
Carney, William W.
Carpenter, James C.
Carr, O. M.
Carroll, John
Center, William
Childress, William M.
Clayton, James P.

Clayton, John L.
Clayton, Oliver H. P.
Cline, Amos
Cline, J. W.
Compton, Jasper
Cook, Emanuel M.
Couch, Arthur
Covington, John W.
Cox, Samuel
Crow, William
Dill, F. M.
Dill, Jasper N.
Dill, Jefferson
Doss, John L.
Doss, J. M.

Dowda, Allen S.
Dowda, George W.
Duncan, John H.
Eddington, H. A.
Edwards, Sanford
Evans, William
Evett, John R.
Farmer, G. B.
Farmer, Jacob Henry
Farmer, Nathan
Fowler, C. C.
Fowler, George G.
Fowler, J. H.
Gates, William L. R.
Goode, Andrew

Goodno, William
Goss, B. S.
Goss, Henry S.
Goss, William D.
Gravley, Samuel
Harmon, Joshua H.
Harmon, T. W.
Harrell, Amos L.
Harrell, Joseph M.
Harrell, Thomas J.
Heard, B. S.
Heard, C. A. C.
Heard, Irwin
Heard, Joseph O.
Heard, William P.
Heathcock, W. J.
Hitt, D. M.
Hobgood, Francis M.
Hobgood, John W.
Hobgood, Larkin C.
Hobgood, Lewis W.
Hobgood, William H.
Holt, Edley
Hughes, Thomas H.
Hyde, F. Marion
Jarrett, C. K.
Keith, Martin L.
King, J. B.
King, J. V.
King, J. W.

Kirk, John D.
Kirk, William M.
Land, J. J.
Lyon, John B.
Lyon, P. H.
Manley, V. B.
Martin, Joseph M.
Moss, Criswell
Moss, Elihu
Mullins, William M.
McCoy, Elisha
McCoy, Russell
Owen, George W.
Owen, Hiram K.
Owen, John C.
Owen, Josiah
Parker, Thomas
Pearson, H. H.
Pilgrim, F. Marion
Pilgrim, G. M.
Pinson, A. J.
Pinson, James W.
Pinson, Thomas W.
Pitts, Alfred
Pitts, Lawson
Pitts, Simeon
Ponder, George W.
Ponder, William F.
Reaves, James
Redding, T. A.

Redding, William A.
Riell, William
Rhyne, B. B.
Sloan, W. J.
Sluder, Green B.
Smith, Elijah W.
Smith, Henry Jr.
Smith, Henry O.
Smith, Thomas
Spears, John J.
Stephens, W. F.
Stone, William M.
Tanner, Nathan
Tatum, Hugh
Taylor, James W.
Teasley, William
Turner, Henry G. B.
Turner, Martin
Walker, Daniel
Waters, Jesse S.
Waters, J. E.
Weatherby, Joseph A.
Weaverm, David
Whelchel, John A.
Whelchel, John J.
Wiley, William M.
Worley, Langston
Young, James M.

Company B, 43d Regiment

Officers:

Gramtham, M. M., Captain
Boger, Christopher C., 1st Lieut.
Abbott, William R., 2d Lieut.
Harper, Aaron C., Jr. 2d Lieut.
Paden, Mark S., 1st Sgt.
Gober, Green B., 2d Sgt.
Hedgecock, James C., 3d Sgt.

Waldrip, Isaac W., 4th Sgt.
Michael, Evan, 5th Sgt.
Oldham, Isaac, 1st Corp.
Baker, James S., 2d Corp.
Worley, Eli A., 3d Corp.
Hubbard, William M., 4th Corp.
Forester, Alfred K., Musician

Privates:

Abernathy, John F.
Arwood, James C.
Baker, Caleb G.

Baker, Charles J.
Baker, George W.
Beam, Henry M.

Beam, John O.
Bennett, John L.
Britt, Madison R.

Brook, George W.	Hedgecock, F. M.	Payne, John C.
Cain, James A. W.	Hendon, Aaron	Poor, Willis W.
Carro, James	Higgins, Isaiah	Privatt, Pleasant P.
Carson, Nezekiah M.	Hinman, David	Pulliam, George V.
Carter, William P.	Honea, Andrew T.	Pulliam, William H.
Cassidy, James E.	Honea, Chandler	Ragsdale, T. R.
Cloud, Burton	Honea, Charles W.	Reeves, Alonzo P.
Collins, John	Honea, William H.	Reeves, Henry
Cook, Francis	Hubbard, Newton E.	Richardson, Newton
Cook, Jasper M.	Huey, John	Roach, James S.
Corbin, William H.	Hunt, Elijah	Roach, Larkin P.
Cox, Thomas O.	Hunt, Robert M.	Roach, William R.
Croft, Levi	Hunt, Thomas	Robertson, Joseph E.
Crites, William F.	Hunt, Thomas W.	Robison, Joseph E.
Crow, Drury H.	Kearn, Jonas	Roddy, John L.
Dillinger, A. W.	Keeter, Kaniel F.	Sargent, Seaborn H.
Dillinger, Robert W.	Keeter, Thomas J.	Satterfield, Moses C.
Earles, Thomas D.	King, Adoniron S.	Satterfield, S. M.
Edwards, James A.	Leach, Dudley	Sharp, Alexander W.
Edwards, John W.	Leach, Elijah	Sharp, Joseph F. M.
Ellison, Francis D.	Leach, Perry	Sisk, Daniel
Ellison, Vincent J.	Legrand, William M.	Smith, Frederick H.
Eubanks, Lucius D.	Leonard, B. M.	Smith, George E.
Evans, John G.	Leonard, James R.	Smith, John T.
Farmer, Ransom R.	Leonard, Thomas C.	Smith, Jones
Field, Logan	Long, Jackson A.	Snellgrove, Robert H.
Forrester, John J.	Long, Jasper	Sprence, William
Fowler, William A.	Long, John	Strain, William A.
Gentry, William M.	Lowery, James R.	Stroup, Joseph
Gilchrist, George L.	Mahaffey, James B.	Tapp, James
Gravitt, John	Mason, Asa	Tedder, Henry
Gravitt, John P.	Mason, Jackson J.	Tedder, Putman
Green, Joshua	Michael, John J.	Thomas, Allen
Gunter, Andrew E.	Monroe, Daniel G.	Thompson, William C.
Gunter, William	McConnell, William	Tippins, John B.
Hamilton, Joseph J.	McElreath, Aaron	Tyler, William
Hampton, William H.	Page, Franklin	

4. Georgia Cavalry

Company F, 3d Regiment

Officers:

Fowler, James A., Captain
Allen, Frederick L., 2d Lieut.
Brooke, George W., 3d Lieut.
Clark, James S., Sgt. & Lieut.

Privates:

Allen, Leroy P.	Dougherty, Josiah P.	Howell, Thomas
Baker, Thomas S.	Dowda, Columbus A.	Hughes, Andrew W.
Bolins, Reuben J.	Dowda, Julius L.	Johnson, James H.
Carmichael, W. M.	Garrett, Rice O.	King, Thomas W.
Castleberry, W. H.	Hardeman, Thomas D.	Mathews, Joseph A.
Day, James L.	Hood, James	Powell, George W.
Dobbs, Cicero H.	Hood, John	Rudasill, William M.
Dougherty, Charles L.	Howell, Joshua	Smith, M. C. P.

(The roll of this company is incomplete.)

5. Phillips' Legion, Cavalry

Company C
"Cherokee Dragoons"

Officers:

Puckett, W. B. C., Captain	Freeman, J. W., 4th Sgt.
Hardin, E. C., 1st Lieut.	Fowler, T. N., 5th Sgt.
Evans, Phillip J., 2d Lieut.	Brooks, Robert, Quartermaster
Freeman, Benj. F., 3d Lieut.	Hawkins, W. W., 1st Corp.
Brooks, N. H., 1st Sgt.	Foster, Knight, 2d Corp.
Bailey, W. R., 2d Sgt.	Boston, H. F., 3d Corp.
Foster, Robert, 3d Sgt.	Allen, W. K., 4th Corp.

Privates:

Alexander, Dock	Brown, T. W.	Donald, M.
Allen, A. H.	Beck, Samuel H.	Donald, Lewis D.
Brooks, W. A.	Barrett, J. R.	Delaney, T. N.
Brazelton, C. A.	Bozeman, J. W.	Donald, D. F.
Benson, N. H.	Chastain, James	Dyer, Joel H.
Brown, Thomas K.	Chastain, G. B.	Davis, D. O. H.
Brannon, W. E.	Chastain, A. B.	Davis, J. C.
Brannon, George W.	Cole, Francis	Dunn, W. G.
Brooks, Benjamin	Cross, J. W.	Dobbs, W. P.
Brooks, Ed B.	Chamlee, George W.	Dobbs, Parks
Brazelton, R. W.	Craft, James A.	Dobbs, O. T.
Boston, M. J.	Chastain, Joshua	Delaney, J. L.
Burton, R. C.	Cantrell, J. C.	Delaney, W. G.
Bagby, J. R.	Cross, W. H. H.	Eubanks, William
Bagby, A. W.	Cowan, James	Ezzard, Thomas W.
Bagby, Thomas M.	Chambers, W. M.	Emmerson, H. C.
Bailey, J. M.	Chambers, J. T.	Fowler, Elbert
Bennett, E. C.	Chamlee, Enoch	Futrell, W. A.
Bates, Russell J.	Crowley, Seaborn	Fowler, N. A.

Fowler, E. J.	Lattimore, D. F.	Rogers, Henry
Futrell, Joseph B.	Lattimore, J. R.	Revis, Ben
Fowler, W. H.	Low, Alfred	Rusk, W. D.
Fowler, J. B.	Land, W. H.	Rudasil, Jonas
Fitts, J. G.	Latham, A. J.	Roberts, A. M.
Galt, James T.	Long, Joshua	Rumph, J. G.
Gray, J. F.	McConnell, W. D. R.	Reed, J. P.
Graham, H.	McConnell, E. J.	Smithwick, Sam T.
Grimes, J. C.	McConnell, H. D.	Scott, A. T.
Grogan, G. W.	McConnell, Joshua	Smithwick, Sam W.
Harris, W. D.	McAfee, D. R.	Stephenson, A.
Hancock, J. N.	Mullins, J. C.	Scott, John
Haley, D. L.	Mansell, Posey A.	Say, William
Haynes, James	Mansell, Thompson	Smithwick, George
Haynes, S. S.	Mullins, Frank M.	Sargeant, Eph
Haney, J. S.	McCraw, James B.	Tate, John
Hancock, J. C.	Morris, W. H.	Terrell, W. L.
Haynes, Robert	Morris, William A.	Terrell, James A.
Hood, Robert	McCollum, Benj. F.	Tippins, James W.
Hood, Clayton	McCollum, Bob	Trippe, R. H.
Harris, James T.	McNair, L. H.	Trippe, W. M.
Haley, J. C.	Morris, John S.	Terrell, Timothy
Haley, W.	Morris, M. G.	Tippins, John M.
Hawkins, John L.	Merrett, L. F.	Terrell, John D.
Haynes, Z. J.	Merrett, G. W.	Terrell, Henry C.
Howard, W. C.	Merrett, J. A.	Trippe, J. K.
Howell, C. L.	Nix, Charles I.	Trippe, J. H.
Howell, John Dillard	Nix, William	Trippe, J. P.
Howell, A. L.	Oaks, William	Trippe, Coon
Hensley, F. M.	Paden, Mark S.	Underwood, J. W.
Johnson, F. M.	Palmer, James	Underwood, W. B.
Knox, James	Perkins, Moses	Wood, J.
Kemp, H. M.	Petree, L. G.	Westbrooks, J. W.
Kemp, Hausel	Popham, J. T.	Worley, James P.
Lathem, Sam W.	Petree, Charles	Wood, Isham
Latimer, J. R.	Perry, J. L.	Worley, J. W.
Little, J. J.	Rusk, J. E.	Wood, R. G.
Lathem, George W.	Russom, John Price	Wallace, J. M.
Lumas, Ellison	Russom, William A.	Whitten, William
Latimore, H. R.	Russom, Roland	Worley, E. G.

(All Confederate soldiers' names copied from the rolls of the Georgia Soldier Roster Commission. Duplications generally indicate transfers. Service record of each man may be obtained at the office of the Commission.)

VII.

WORLD WAR SOLDIERS FROM CHEROKEE COUNTY

ARMY

Abernathy, Elihue R.　RR, White
Adams, Carl　　　　　　Waleska
Adams, Gus　　　　　　Canton
Adams, Lee R.　　　　　Canton
Addington, James H.　Waleska
Akins, James W.
　　　　　RR, Holly Springs
Akins, James W.　Holly Springs
Akins, John P.　　　　Canton
Akins, Salters　Holly Springs
Alexander (colored)　Canton
Allen, Ernest W.　Ball Ground
Allmon, Roy　RR, Woodstock
Allmon, Jesse B.　Woodstock
Angle, William R. (col.)　Canton
Anderson, Clinton L. Ball Ground
Anderson, James P.　RR, Lyerly
Anderson, Willis W.　Little River
Appleby, Solon (col.)
　　　　　　RR, Woodstock
Armer, Henry W.　　Canton
Armstrong, Charlie F.
　　　　　　RR, Woodstock
Armstrong, Luther　Nelson
Austin, Warren Franklin
　　　　　　Woodstock
Baker, Frank M.　Ball Ground
Barnes, Lester (col.) RR, Canton
Barrett, Fred　RR, Canton
Barrett, Claud L.　RR, Canton
Barton, Joe F.　　Canton
Bates, Albert H.　RR, Alpharetta
Beasley, William J.　Canton
Bell, Homer F.　RR, Woodstock
Bennett, Claude A.
　　　　　RR, Fairmount
Bennett, Jessie A.　Canton
Bennett, William A.　RR, Canton
Benson, Robert M. RR, Woodstock
Biddy, Elsberry G. RR, Woodstock

Bird, Miller (col.)　　Canton
Bishop, James M.　Ball Ground
Bishop, Oscar H.　RR, Canton
Bishop, William A.　Mullens
Bobo, Amos　RR, Canton
Bobo, Louis C.　RR, Canton
Bobo, Luther L.　RR, Canton
Bobo, Scott C.　RR, Canton
Boing, Luther W. RR, Woodstock
Brannon, John R. RR, Woodstock
Brock, Thomas M.　Canton
Bryant, Gordon R.　Canton
Buchanan, Floyd C.　Woodstock
Buffington, Luther H. Ball Ground
Buffington, Raymond L.
　　　　　RR, Ball Ground
Burleson, Herbey L. RR, Acworth
Butterworth, John　Canton
Butterworth, Melvin L.　Canton
Butler, Richard J.　Canton
Byers, Dock　RR, Ball Ground
Byers, Herman　RR, Ball Ground
Byrd, William H. RR, Woodstock
Cagle, Jessie B.　RR, Canton
Cagle, Olin A.　RR, Canton
Cagle, Taylor　　Canton
Caldwell, Ira　　Woodstock
Cantrell, Willie V.　Ball Ground
Carney, Thomas RR, Ball Ground
Carpenter, William (col.) Canton
Casteel, Bill T.　　Canton
Castiel, Henry L.　Canton
Chadwick, John L.
　　　　　RR, Ball Ground
Chadwick, Steve A.
　　　　　RR, Ball Ground
Chambers, James Carl　Canton
Chambers, Marcus T. Ball Ground
Chambers, William E.　Canton

Chumley, Charles T.
RR, Ball Ground
Chumley, James F.   RR, Canton
Cline, Felix C.   Waleska
Cline, Paul A.   RR, Canton
Clontz, Doff   Ball Ground
Cochran, Freeman W.   Ball Ground
Cochran, William P.   RR, Orange
Coggins, Lee R.   Canton
Collins, Milton L.   Fairmount
Colwell, Ira   Woodstock
Cook, Harley Forrest   Woodstock
Cook, Willie   RR, Canton
Covington, Horace J.   Ball Ground
Cowart, Herschel D.
RR, Ball Ground
Cox, Clinton C.   Canton
Cox, William Vaughn   Canton
Croft, Robert L.   RR, Woodstock
Cross, James D.   Canton
Crow, John A.   Orange
Crow, John M. E.   Woodstock
Crow, Millard F.   Canton
Daniel, James C.   RR, Woodstock
Darby, Arthur   Ball Ground
Davis, Benjamin M.   Canton
Davis, George A. F.   Orange
Davis, Leonard   Woodstock
Dean, Thomas S.   Orange
DeLay, Hardy L.   Holly Springs
DeLay, Jason B.   Holly Springs
Dobson, William Ira   Orange
Dobbs, Paul   Woodstock
Dobbs, Samuel M.   Woodstock
Dooley, Marcus H.
RR, Ball Ground
Dorsey, John F.   Canton
Doss, George A.   Canton
Duckett, Henry R.
RR, Ball Ground
Duncan, Henry Samuel   Canton
Duncan, James L.   Lebanon
Duncan, Riley H., Jr.   Canton
Duncan, William F.   Toonigh
DuPre, Robert C.   Canton

Durham, H. W. (col.)   Woodstock
Edwards, David E.   Woodstock
Edwards, Dock L.   Ball Ground
Edwards, Perry N.   Orange
Edwards, Percy M.   Ball Ground
Edwards, Walter Reed
RR, Waleska
Edwards, Winfield S.   Canton
Edwards, William H.   Waleska
Ellenburg, Charlie A. Ball Ground
Ellison, John Virgil
RR, Woodstock
Estes, Eric E.   Canton
Eubanks, Marion   RR, Canton
Evans, Raymond F.   Woodstock
Evans, Wheeler C.   RR, Canton
Evans, James R. RR, Ball Ground
Evans   Canton
Ezell, Ullis   Lebanon
Faulkner, John B.   RR, Canton
Farriha, Arnold RR, Ball Ground
Farriha, Emory RR, Ball Ground
Farmer, Oliver Preston
Ball Ground
Few, Andrew W. (col.)
RR, Ball Ground
Fisher, James J. RR, Ball Ground
Fletcher, Auburn J.
RR, Ball Ground
Floyd, Roy   Canton
Floyd, Samuel W.   Canton
Forrest, James E.   Canton
Fossett, John R.   RR, Orange
Foster, Hal   Woodstock
Foute, Augustus M.   Canton
Fowler, Arthur A.   Holly Springs
Fowler, Harison   Orange
Fowler, John R.   Canton
Fowler, William D.   Lebanon
Freeman, Andrew C.
RR, Woodstock
Freeman, James D.
RR, Woodstock
Freeman, Jeptha S.   Nelson
Forrester, Hoke

Galt, Chet J.	Canton
Garner, John W.	RR, Canton
Garrett, Arie	Woodstock
Garrett, Joseph O.	Ball Ground
Garrett, William A.	
	RR, Woodstock
Gay, Felton	Canton
Gay, Lester Grant	Waleska
Gay, William (col.)	Woodstock
Guerin, John A.	Canton
Gibbs, Harvey Jasper	Canton
Gibbs, Henry G.	Ball Ground
Gibson, Frank M.	Canton
Green, Orestus	Ball Ground
Green, Paul	RR, Ball Ground
Green, Carter L.	RR, Canton
Greene, Oda J.	Canton
Gregory, Everett L. (col.)	
	Woodstock
Gregory, William (col.)	
	Woodstock
Grovely, Jesse L.	RR, Woodstock
Grogan, Mercer H.	Holly Springs
Hadaway, Jodie B.	RR, Canton
Haley, Chester R.	RR, Canton
Hammond, George	Woodstock
Hampton, William R.	
	RR, Ball Ground
Haney, Dock E.	RR, Woodstock
Hanse, Hugh L.	Lebanon
Harbin, Arthur A.	Waleska
Harden, John H. (col.)	Canton
Hardin, John M.	RR, Woodstock
Hardin, Walter C.	Ball Ground
Hasson, Charles B.	Canton
Hasty, Gordon A.	RR, Canton
Hasty, Oscar	Canton
Hasty, Robert K.	RR, Canton
Hathcock, Wallace	Canton
Haygood, James E.	Ball Ground
Heairlston, Charles F.	Canton
Hensley, Cicero P.	Ball Ground
Henderson, George Frank	Canton
Henderson, Oscar A.	Waleska
Hendrix, Carl W.	RR, Ball Ground

Hendrix, Lee A.	RR, Orange
Henley, Carnegie Rockefeller	
	Holly Springs
Henley, Diamond	Holly Springs
Henley, Loomond S.	Holly Springs
Henry, William J.	RR, Woodstock
Hester, Augustus	Orange
Hill, Abbie L.	RR, Canton
Hill, Harvey Ulysses	RR, Canton
Hill, Orin	Ball Ground
Hill, Vivian B.	Canton
Hillhouse, William A.	RR, Canton
Hodges, George J.	RR, Canton
Holbert, Roscoe Jacob	
	RR, Woodstock
Holbert, George W.	Woodstock
Holcomb, Arthur W.	RR, Canton
Holcombe, Earby	
	RR, Ball Ground
Holcomb, Earnest J.	Canton
Holcomb, Joe	Woodstock
Holcombe, William T.	Canton
Holland, Fred W.	RR, Canton
Howard, John H.	RR, Canton
Howard, Kernel	Woodstock
Howard, Major	Woodstock
Howard, William A.	Canton
Howell, John Q.	Ball Ground
Howell, Moses Elijah	Canton
Hubbard, Chester A.	Canton
Hubbard, Emmitt B.	RR, Canton
Hudson, Paul H.	Canton
Huey, Marion E.	RR, Woodstock
Huggins, Rance	RR, Ball Ground
Hughes, Joseph H.	
	RR, Ball Ground
Hughes, Wade	Canton
Ingram, Emmett	RR, Canton
Jarrett, Charlie H. (col.)	
	RR, Canton
Johnson, Sam S.	Canton
Johnson, Seth	Canton
Johnston, Hugh L.	Woodstock
Jones, Grover C.	RR, Ball Ground

Jones, Henry Well
    RR, Ball Ground
Jones, Paul (col.)   Canton
Jordan, Emmett F.   Ball Ground
Kelly, Wade Hampton   Canton
Kelly, William J.   RR, Canton
Killby, Benjamin F.   Canton
Kimbrel, Martin W.   Ball Ground
Kimmons, Bunyan   Woodstock
Kinser, Edgar   Ball Ground
Kinser, Wilbur M.   Ball Ground
Kuykendall, Raymond
    RR, Woodstock
Lance, George F.   RR, Waleska
Lathem, James D.   Woodstock
Lathem, Robert I.   RR, Orange
Lathem, William A.   RR, Orange
Lawson, William J.
    RR, Ball Ground
Ledford, Albert G.   Woodstock
Ledford, James E. RR, Woodstock
Lee, Charles L.   Canton
Leonard, Samuel   RR, Canton
Lott, Dock C. (col.)   Lebanon
Lowe, Garnett E.   Ball Ground
Lyon, Maynard N.   Ball Ground
McAfee, Douglas D.   Canton
McAfee, Miles (col.)
    RR, Woodstock
McBrayer, Lewis S.   RR, Canton
McBrayer, William E. RR, Canton
McClure, Marshall R.   Canton
McCollum, Levi E.   Woodstock
McCoy, Bert   RR, Waleska
McCoy, William M.   RR, Waleska
McElreath, Berley B. RR, Orange
McElreath, Homer N. RR, Orange
McWhirter, Frank Carswell
    Holly Springs
Magnus, Samuel L. Holly Springs
Manous, Clinton J.   RR, Canton
Massey, Alonzo   Holly Springs
Mauldin, Virgil R.   Canton
Maulding, Hoyt S.
    RR, Ball Ground

Millsap, Walter W.
    RR, Ball Ground
Mitchell, George J.   RR, Waleska
Moore, Clifford J.   RR, Silica
Moore, Max S.   Waleska
Moore, Zeddie C.   Waleska
Morris, Fred (col.)   Woodstock
Mullinax, Lemual V.
    RR, Woodstock
Mulkey, Tom W.   Canton
Mulkey, William M.   Canton
Newbury, Cecil E.   Canton
Nix, David N.   RR, Orange
Norton, Harris E.   Canton
Norton, Harris   Canton
Ogles, Dan K.   Canton
Oliver, William   Canton
Padgett, John H. RR, Ball Ground
Page, Ernest E.   Canton
Page, Joe W.   Canton
Parks, Coke B.   Woodstock
Patterson, John   RR, Canton
Payne, Andrew   RR, Canton
Payne, Noel   RR, Canton
Peeler, Florence R.   Canton
Perkinson, Paul   Woodstock
Phillips, Herman G.   Canton
Phillips, James W.
    RR, Ball Ground
Pittman, Elbert   RR, Waleska
Ponder, Horace   Canton
Ponder, John T.   Canton
Ponder, Walter   RR, Woodstock
Ponder, William Joseph   Canton
Pool, Fred   Canton
Poore, Harvey   Woodstock
Porter, Starling W.   Ingram
Powell, Lewis   Ball Ground
Price, James R.   Canton
Price, Lonnie S.   Canton
Purser, Philip J.   RR, Woodstock
Quarles, Robert F.   Ball Ground
Reavis, Harley G.
    RR, Ball Ground
Redd, Asberry   Waleska

Redd, Virgil G. Waleska
Reece, Benjamin Carter
    Ball Ground
Reece, James M. RR, Canton
Reece, Levi P. Woodstock
Reece, Otto C. RR, Holly Springs
Reece, Roy M. Holly Springs
Reece, Seaborn C.
    RR, Holly Springs
Reynolds, Homer L. Ball Ground
Ridings, James G.
    RR, Ball Ground
Ridings, James S.
    RR, Ball Ground
Rice, Fred Canton
Richardson, Thomas
    RR, Woodstock
Richardson; William E. Canton
Roach, James Byron Canton
Roberts, Augustus Canton
Roberts, Delmus C. Ball Ground
Roberts, Dayton W. RR, Canton
Roberts, Griffin L. Canton
Roberts, Loyd B. Canton
Roberts, Martin E.
    RR, Ball Ground
Roberts, Orvel (col.) Toonigh
Roberts, Roy H. Canton
Rogers, Roy (col.) Woodstock
Roper, Marcus B.
    RR, Ball Ground
Rusk, Elbert P. RR, Woodstock
Rusk, Hubert F. RR, Woodstock
Rusk, Paul H. Woodstock
Sandow, Mack Canton
Sam, Charles H. RR, Orange
Saye, George P. Canton
Satterfield, Corbett M.
    RR, Canton
Scott, James W. Orange
Seay, Tom L. Canton
Sewell, Grady G. Canton
Sewell, Mansel A. Canton
Sexton, Jesse L. RR, Ball Ground
Sexton, William McKinley Canton

Sharp, Harold S. Waleska
Sherrill, Henry C. Ball Ground
Shinall, Lawrence A. RR, Canton
Smith, Claud J. M. RR, Canton
Smith, Cliff Canton
Smith, Thomas M. Holly Springs
Smith, Thomas Watson Orange
Smith, Terrell M. Woodbury
Smith, William C. Canton
Sosbee, Allen H. Ball Ground
Sosebee, John H. Waleska
Spears, Lealon Canton
Statham, James E. Waleska
Steele, Joseph M. RR, Canton
Stephens, Edward C. RR, Canton
Stewart, Kimsey L. Waleska
Strickland, John (col.) Canton
Swancey, Andrew J. Canton
Swetmon, Chester W.
    RR, Woodstock
Tanner, Ramsey (col.) Canton
Tate, Oscar H. (col.) Canton
Thomas, Alvin E. (col.)
    Woodstock
Thomas, John C. Canton
Thompson, Carter Tate
    RR, Woodstock
Thompson, James W. D.
    Ball Ground
Thompson, Marvin John Canton
Tilly, Louis F. RR, Woodstock
Tilson, Joe H. RR, Canton
Timmons, Noble S. Waleska
Trout, Elmore (col.) Woodstock
Tyson, Eugene C. RR, Woodstock
Turner, James RR, Canton
Vaughn, Newport Holly Springs
Virden, Judge N. (col.)
    RR, Batesville
Walls, Henry H. (col.) Canton
Waters, John C. Canton
Watkins, Earnest Canton
Watkins, Eugene Canton
Watkins, Herschel J.
    RR, Ball Ground

Watkins, John J.   RR, Orange
Watkins, Joseph E., Jr.
                    Ball Ground
Weahunt, William F.
                    RR, Ball Ground
Weatherby, Marion W.
                    Ball Ground
Weehunt, Charles H.
                    RR, Ball Ground
Welcher, Dave   Canton
West, George E.   Orange
West, Robert E.   RR, Orange
Wheeler, Benjamin F.
                    Ball Ground
Wheeler, Homer RR, Ball Ground
Wheeler, James H.   Ball Ground
Wheeler, Luke M.   Woodstock
White, James L. RR, Ball Ground
White, Walter J.   Waleska
Whitmire, Willie   Canton
Wigley, Henry C. RR, Woodstock
Wigley, Joseph R.   Woodstock
Wilder, Emmett E.   RR, Canton
Wiley, Robert   Orange
Wilkie, Jessie L. RR, Ball Ground
Wilkie, John L.   RR, Orange

Williams, Arthur   Canton
Williams, Roy H.   Canton
Willis, Charles L.   Canton
Willis, George A.   Canton
Wilson, Benjamin T.
                    RR, Fairmount
Wilson, Henry   Canton
Wormley, Chester A. (col.)
                    Woodstock
Wood, Benjamin Riley Cicero
                    RR, Ball Ground
Wood, Ernest S.   Canton
Wood, Harley   Ball Ground
Wood, John S.   Canton
Wood, Mark L.   RR, Ball Ground
Wooten, Elmon R.   RR, Canton
Worley, Henry G.   Canton
Worley, John C.   'Woodstock
Wright, Bonnie   Canton
Wright, Coleman (col.)
                    Woodstock
Wright, Exell A.   Canton
Wright, Harlie W.   Canton
Wright, Robert   Canton
Youngblood, Azy Carl
                    RR, Woodstock

Died in Service

Bell, Vergil T.   Woodstock
Brady, Thomas M.   Canton
Cowart, Grover S.
                    RR, Ball Ground
Elliott, Judge D. RR, Woodstock
Greene, Sidney C.   Canton
Hillhouse, Samuel O. RR, Canton
Holcombe, Herman C.
                    RR, Ball Ground
Honea, John T.   Lickskillet

Hopkins, Fred C.
                    RR, Holly Springs
Kinnett, Zedic Z. RR, Woodstock
Kirby, James E.   Ball Ground
Lawson, Lemmer J.   RR, Orange
Roper, Beura R. RR, Ball Ground
Stewart, Kimsy L.   Waleska
White, Vell   RR, Woodstock
Woodall, Lonnie R.   RR, Canton

Officers

Bradley, John W.   Woodstock
Coker, Newton J.   Canton
Faulkner, Charles J. Ball Ground
Johnston, Joseph E. Woodstock

Lewis, James Bradley   Waleska
Perkinson, Ernest V. Woodstock
Roberts, Martin E.   Ball Ground
Smith, Oscar   Ball Ground

NAVY

Blackstock, William A. Woodstock

Bobo, George Washington Canton

Byrd, John Erwin Orange

Cearley, Edgar Cicero Ball Ground

Cochran, Henry Claud Ball Ground

Colwell, Ira RR, Woodstock

Curry, Peter Colin Canton

Curtis, Guy McRae Canton

Daniel, Alonzo W. RR, Canton

Dickson, Winchester T. Waleska

Dupree, Ralph C. Canton

Edge, Carl Carter Canton

Edge, George Mitchell Canton

Edwards, Harold McKinley Canton

Edwards, John Richard Canton

Fincher, Jesse Waleska

Fletcher, Alfred R. RR, Ball Ground

Fowler, Thomas C. Woodstock

Galt, Odie Putnam Canton

Galt, Thomas H. Canton

Gibbs, Ernest R. Woodstock

Gibbs, John Ernest RR, Canton

Green, Jesse Lewis RR, Canton

Hames, George S. RR, Woodstock

Hasson, John William Canton

Heath, Parks Bell RR, Canton

Holbert, Henry Grady Ball Ground

Jones, Jack Walker Canton

Lovelady, Jack Glenn Ball Ground

Lowe, Vernie T. Ball Ground

McArthur, Leonard S. RR, Orange

McCanless, Edgar M. Canton

Mosteller, Crisp Woodstock

Mullins, Ernest Edgar Canton

Owen, William McK. RR, Waleska

Patterson, Lewis C. Ball Ground

Perry, Herman Ball Ground

Redd, Bryan L. RR, Ball Ground

Roche, William Lloyd Canton

Rollins, Beauron Orange

Roberts, Aaron Webb Ball Ground

Rudasill, Smith J. Canton

Saye, Wilburn Earle Canton

Sherrill, Ernest Hudlow Ball Ground

Spears, Leon B. Woodstock

Taylor, James A. RR, Ball Ground

Teasley, George Isham, Jr. Canton

Teasley, John Robert Canton

Teasley, William Alfred Canton

Timmons, Charles C. Ball Ground

Turner, George Amos RR, Ball Ground

Turner, Paul Jackson RR, Ball Ground

Weaver, William H. Ball Ground

West, Arthur F. Ball Ground

Wheeler, Judson Ball Ground

Wilder, William E. RR, Woodstock

Willingham, William H. Canton

Wood, Enon W. Woodstock

Worley, James Wilburn RR, Canton

Wyatt, Thomas L. Ball Ground

PART TWO

———

PERSONAL SKETCHES AND
FAMILY ACCOUNTS

PERSONAL SKETCHES AND
FAMILY ACCOUNTS

ANDERSON, GEORGE DAVID

Marietta. Born Sept. 2, 1867, near Marietta. Son of William Dickson Anderson (b. June 24, 1839, in Marietta; member, house of representatives from Cobb Co., 1868-75) and Louisa Jane Latimer Anderson (b. Apr. 11, 1845, in Abbeville District, S. C.) Grandson of George David Anderson (b. May 28, 1806; member, house of representatives, DeKalb Co., 1831-33; solicitor-general, Coweta Circuit, 1836-39; member, convention 1839, Cobb Co.; senator, Cobb Co., 1841; judge, Cherokee Circuit, 1842-43) and Jane Holmes Dickson Anderson, and of Harrison and Mary Elvira MaGee Latimer, of Abbeville District, S. C.

Graduated University of Georgia, A. B. Degree, first honor, 1889. Admitted to the bar at Marietta, 1893. Methodist. Democrat. Mason. U. S. referee in bankruptcy, 1898; solicitor-general, Blue Ridge Circuit, June 24, 1926-date.

Married July 12, 1899, in Marietta, Lena Jeannette Sessions (b. Oct. 16, 1875, in Marietta), daughter of William Moultrie Sessions (judge, Brunswick Circuit, 1860-1873) and Melissa Caroline McKenney Sessions. Children: George David Jr., Carolyn Louise, Jeannette, Ruth (Anderson) Northcutt, William Sessions, Harrison Latimer.

BEARDEN, WILLIAM A.

Waleska. Born 1867 in Pickens Co. Son of W. M. Bearden and Elmira Fitzsimmons Bearden. Grandson of Leonard Bearden and Julia Smith Bearden, and of Robert Fitzsimmons.

Married, in 1888, Alice Timmons, b. 1870, daughter of W. J. Timmons and Malinda Taylor Timmons; granddaughter of John Timmons and Polly Timmons and of Solomon Taylor and Sally Taylor; great-granddaughter of Samuel Timmons.

The Bearden and Timmons families have been connected with the development of Cherokee and Pickens Counties for nearly a century. Mr. Bearden's great-grandfather Smith was the director of the old U. S. Mint at Dahlonega and owned a gold mine there; he went West to mine gold and never returned. His sons, whom he left in Lumpkin Co. with their sister Julia, were David (who taught at North Georgia Agricultural College), Collins, Billie, Marion, and Henry. Julia married Leonard Bearden, of Dawson Co. Both Leonard and his son, W. M. Bearden, served in the Confederate Army. W. M. Bearden married Elmira Fitzsimmons, daughter of Robert Fitzsimmons, who had come from Ireland about 1819 and cut the first marble in North Georgia.

Samuel Timmons settled in North Carolina in colonial times. His sons, John and Noble, came from there to Cherokee Co., John arriving about 1820. Noble sat on the first Cherokee Co. jury. Solomon Taylor early in the 1800's settled in Hall Co., from North Carolina and later moved to Pickens Co. His sons Cicero, Gus, and Jasper, went West from Pickens, mined gold in California, and returned with considerable wealth. Jasper was killed in the Civil War, but Gus and Cicero Taylor have a number of descendants in Cherokee Co. and vicinity.

William A. Bearden, subject of this sketch, taught school with Mrs. Bearden after their marriage, near Marble Hill, Pickens Co., in 1889. They came in 1899 to Waleska, where Mr. Bearden opened a store and began farming operations. He has since that time exerted large influence in the development of the Waleska section, and has been a constructive member of the county board of education for more than 20 years. The children of Mr. and Mrs. Bearden are:

Leo (Mrs. J. T. Rawls), of Dunellen, Fla.; Bertha (Mrs. R. W. Wood), of Atlanta; Edna (Mrs. Andrew A. Smith), of Savannah; Aurora (Mrs. G. W. Hock), of Cincinnati; Dewey (graduated Mercer University, A.B., Th.B. degrees; served in Merchant Marine during World War; now in business with his father in Waleska); Lillian (Mrs. Addison Rawls), of Palatka, Fla.; Willard (Mrs. R. W. Flanagan), of Atlanta.

BLANTON, FREDONIA (MISS)

Waleska. Born in Forsyth Co. Daughter of Jason Blanton (moved to Cherokee Co. from Carrollton, N. C., during Miss Fredonia's childhood; was a Confederate soldier) and Martha Reinhardt Blanton (b. July 26, 1838, in Cherokee Co.). Granddaughter of John Blanton (Confederate soldier; died in prison before war ended), and of Lewis Warlick Reinhardt (b. Sep. 2, 1804; came from North Carolina to Cherokee Co. in 1834; established Reinhardt Chapel; friend and adviser of the Indians; helped remove them from Fort Buffington in 1838) and Jane Harbin Reinhardt. Great-granddaughter of John Blanton (immigrated from England in pre-Revolutionary days). Sister of Dr. L. J. Blanton, of Atlanta, and E. J. Blanton, of Florida.

Attended Reinhardt College; was a member of its first graduating class (1888); was a pupil with Judge W. A. Covington, Mrs. R. M. Moore, and Dr. Joseph A. Sharp. Attended Teacher's College, Knoxville, Tenn., and University of Chicago. Has taught at Waleska since 1892; is principal of the grammar school. Active member of the Baptist Church.

BOBO, ALFRED BARNUM

Born June 10, 1887, in Pickens Co. Son of Hiram Benjamin Bobo (b. Oct. 27, 1853, in South Carolina; came at an early age to Cherokee Co.) and Sarah Emmaline Bearden Bobo (b. Feb. 22, 1857, at Sand Mountain, Ala.; also moved to Cherokee Co. in childhood). Grandson of Elijah Bobo (Confederate soldier) and of John Bearden (Confederate soldier; moved from South Carolina to Dawson Co., then to Cherokee; lived in Conn's Creek neighborhood). Mr. Bobo's brother, George W. Bobo, died in Wales during the World War and was cited for courage in the service of the U. S. Navy.

Alfred Barnum Bobo married (1) in 1909, Missouri Martin; (2) in 1923, Ella Doss, b. Aug. 4, 1890, in Cherokee Co., daughter of James Wilburn Doss (b. Jan. 5, 1867) and Mekie Cline (b. Sep. 10, 1871), and granddaughter of James Green Doss and Harriet Green Doss and of Levi Cline and Martha Cagle Cline.

Children of Mr. Bobo's first marriage: Herbert B., b. 1910; Maybess, b. 1912; Leroy, b. 1917. Children of second marriage: Louise, b. 1924; Pauline, b. 1926.

Mr. Bobo came to Cherokee Co. at the age of 15. Moving from near Buffington in 1911, he was employed in Atlanta for several years and then became superintendent of a number of farms in that part of the state. Returning to Cherokee in 1924, he bought a home near Hickory Flat, where he has since been a leading farmer. He is a Mason, a member of Indian Knoll Baptist Church, and active in the affairs of his community and county.

BRADY, GLENN

Ball Ground. Born Aug. 13, 1895. Son of William Simmons Brady (b. 1853 at Villa Rica, Ga.) and Carolyn Elliott Brady (b. 1854) both of pioneer families of North Georgia. Grandson of Rev. John W. Brady, who was a chaplain in the Confederate Army.

Mr. Brady attended the public schools of Pickens Co., Jasper High School, and Young Harris College. Served during the World War in officer work with Headquarters Co. at Camp Gordon. Has been a member of the Methodist Church since boyhood; is a Mason and a member of the American Legion, Thomas M. Brady Post. Is connected with Consumers' Monument Co., at Ball Ground.

Married, in 1925, Imogene Ray, of Colman, Randolph Co., Ga., daughter of Mr. and Mrs. Joe Ray. Mrs. Brady is also an active member of the Methodist Church at Ball Ground.

BURTZ, LEE F.

Canton. Born Jan. 24, 1888, in Cherokee Co. Son of Joseph Madison Burtz (b. Sep. 16, 1854, in Lumpkin Co.; farmer; justice of the peace of Lickskillet District more than 25 years; Methodist; Mason; Odd Fellow) and Henrietta Anderson (b. Mar. 8, 1860, in Milton Co.). Grandson of Levi F. Burtz (b. May 15, 1831, in Pendleton District, S. C.; Confederate soldier from Cherokee Co.; farmer; school teacher; local Methodist preacher; treasurer of Cherokee Co., 1893-95, 1896-98; Mason; d. Jan. 7, 1919) and Hester Ann Dobbs Burtz. Great-grandson of Levi Burtz (of German descent; Methodist; Mason) and Sallie Burtz.

Married, Sep. 12, 1909, Nellie Irene Lathem, of Cherokee Co. Children: Joseph Lee, b. Aug. 22, 1914; Samuel Pierce, b. July 10, 1920; Nellie Ruth, b. Sep. 25, 1922.

Tax receiver of Cherokee Co.; has been elected clerk of the superior court of Cherokee Co. for 1933-37. Served as postoffice clerk and rural carrier for several years; was deputy clerk, superior court, for 7 years; notary public of Canton District for 8 years; city recorder of Canton for 2 years. Methodist. Mason; Odd Fellow; Red Man; W. O. W. Member, Canton Chamber of Commerce.

CAGLE, JAMES WILLARD

Ball Ground. Born Jan. 1, 1894, in Pickens Co. Son of John W. Cagle (b. in Cherokee Co.) and Emma Willard Addington Cagle (b. in Bartow Co.; of a South Carolina family of English descent.) Grandson of John M. Cagle, and of J. T. Addington (civil engineer; teacher; served under Gen. Sherman in Federal Army). Great-grandson of Martin Cagle (b. 1816; came with his brother John to Cherokee Co. from Buncombe Co., N. C.). Great-great-grandson of Peter Cagle, who is buried at Keith Cemetery and whose father came from Germany and fought under Washington in the Revolutionary War.

Married Alma Carney, of Cherokee Co. Children: Arnold, b. 1918; Velma, b. 1920; James Wayne, b. 1924.

Taught school in Pickens Co. Now in business in Ball Ground. Baptist. Mason; Odd Fellow; W. O. W.

CARPENTER, THOMAS J.

Born 1851 in Cherokee Co. Son of Lucien A. Carpenter (who came to Cherokee Co. from North Carolina in 1845; went to Mexican War with Canton Volunteers, 1846). The wife of Lucien A. Carpenter reached the age of 100 years and a few days, and is buried in Reinhardt Chapel Cemetery, Waleska.

Thomas J. Carpenter remembers vividly local events of Sherman's raid, a detachment of soldiers having passed near his boyhood home. Mr. Carpenter owns a fine farm, on the road between Canton and Waleska, which is said to be among the best-tilled and most productive land in Georgia. The Carpenter family has been prominent in the development of the county for many years.

Mr. Carpenter married Artemesia Matthews, daughter of Anderson Matthews of a North Carolina family of English descent. Their children are: Lewis Emmett, b. 1877; Mrs. Nettie Shaw, b. 1879; Jesse, b. 1880; Carl, b. 1882; Mrs. Victoria Galt, b. 1884; Anna Elizabeth, b. 1886; Clifford, b. 1889; Carter Culberson, b. 1895.

CHAPMAN, ARMINIUS ASBURY

Holly Springs. Born Oct. 31, 1851, in Cherokee Co. Son of Dudley Chapman (b. 1816 in Spartanburg District, S. C.) and Margaret Brannon Chapman (b. 1819 in Spartanburg District, S. C.). Grandson of Jacob and Matilda Bishop Chapman.

Jacob Chapman, a veteran of the War of 1812, came from South Carolina to Cherokee Co. in the 1830's and settled near what is now Holly Springs, in the Shiloh Church community. He is thought to have been a grandson of Giles Chapman, who came from England to Virginia, later removing to Newberry, S. C., and who is the original ancestor of a large number of Chapmans in various parts of the U. S. Jacob and Matilda Chapman had eight children: Enoch, Ed, Dudley, Asbury, Caroline, Mary, Tempie, and Winnie. Dudley continued at the Shiloh homestead, and served during the Civil War in Co. B, Cherokee Legion. He married Margaret Brannon. Four of their sons were: Arelius F. (married Susan Haynes), John Wesley (married Sarah Anne McCrae and later Caroline Gibson), Charles Dudley (married Lula Hames); and A. Asbury, subject of this sketch.

A. Asbury Chapman married (1) in 1874, Mary Susan Ragsdale, b. Sep. 18, 1848, at Holly Springs, daughter of Larkin Ragsdale (b. 1800; early surveyor), and (2) in 1885, Mrs. Georgia Bennett Saye. Children by first marriage: Frances

Joan (Mrs. J. V. Lowry), b. 1875; Viola Lugenia (Mrs. J. H. Chalker), b. 1877; Charles Oscar (see account of); Martha Ophelia (Mrs. Luther E. Roberts; see account of); George Allen, b. 1882; Hiram Augustus, b. 1885. Son by second marriage: James Dudley, b. 1886.

Mr. Chapman is a farmer, a leading worker in the Methodist

OLDER MEMBERS OF THE CHAPMAN FAMILY. Upper left, Charles Dudley Chapman; upper right, A. Asbury Chapman; lower left, John Wesley Chapman; lower right, Arelius Folsom Chapman.

Church, in which he has been a steward for 20 years; and a Mason.

A reunion of the Georgia Division Chapman Memorial Assn., which was founded in 1910, has been held annually since that year at Shiloh Campground and is attended usually by 100-200 relatives from several states. A. Asbury Chapman is president of this reunion; other officers are: Arelius F. Chapman, vice-president; Walter F. Chapman, corresponding secretary; Charles O. Chapman, recording secretary.

CHAPMAN, CHARLES OSCAR

Holly Springs. Born 1879 in Cherokee Co. Son of A. Asbury Chapman (see account of) and Mary Susan Ragsdale Chapman. Grandson of Dudley Chapman Sr., who came to Cherokee County from South Carolina, and Margaret Chapman. The Ragsdale family were early settlers of the county, coming originally from North Carolina.

Mr. Chapman attended the public schools of the county and Reinhardt College. He taught school for several years. On Sep. 20, 1905, he married Rosa Bell Barton, daughter of Rev. J. M. Barton, of Pine Log, descendant of a well-known pioneer family.

Mr. Chapman has been a notary public for 25 years, is a justice of the peace, and chairman of the Holly Springs school board. He is a trustee of the Methodist Church at Holly Springs, has been a steward for 30 years, and has served three terms as superintendent of the Sunday school, with several years in each term.

The children of Mr. and Mrs. Chapman: Bertha (Mrs. Cumbee), b. 1906; Ruth, b. 1908; Mary, b. 1909; Lucille (Mrs. Vickery), b. 1911; Willie, b. 1914; Charles B., b. 1916; Rosa, b. 1918. Four of the daughters are teachers.

CHAPMAN, GEORGE MILTON

Holly Springs. Born Oct. 19, 1890, in Cherokee Co. Son of Arelius Folsom Chapman and Susan Haynes Chapman; grandson of Dudley Chapman and Margaret E. Chapman.

Mr. Chapman was educated in the public schools of Cherokee Co. He was engaged in dairying about 7 years; now operates a grocery business in Holly Springs. He is a Mason and an active member of the Methodist Church.

On Nov. 16, 1913, he married Lois Louise Stanley, of Cherokee Co., b. Aug. 8, 1892, daughter of E. N. Stanley, a Baptist preacher formerly of Cobb Co. They have one daughter, Ola Wyolene, b. 1916.

CHAPMAN, JACKSON LEE

Atlanta. Born Aug. 5, 1873, at Hickory Flat, in Cherokee Co. Son of John Wesley Chapman (b. Feb. 1842, at Greenville, S. C.; merchant, farmer, and shoemaker) and of Narcissus Caroline Gibson (b. May 1838 at Spartanburg, S. C.; taught school). Grandson of James Dudley Chapman and Margaret Drucilla Brannon Chapman. (For history of the Chapman family, see account of A. Asbury Chapman.)

Married, in August 1893, at Holly Springs, Beulah Fleming, daughter of William W. W. Fleming. Children: P. A., b. 1894; W. G., b. 1896; A. L., b. 1898; Maggie C., b. 1900; Mary C., b. 1901; Jackson L. Jr., b. 1905; Beulah M., b. 1908.

Mr. Chapman, formerly a salesman, is now in the restaurant business in Atlanta. He belongs to the I. O. O. F. and Junior Order, and he and his family are members of the Methodist Church.

CHAPMAN, MARTIN LUTHER

Woodstock. Born Nov. 29, 1881, in Holly Springs. Son of Arelius Fulton Chapman (b. 1849 in Cherokee Co.; farmer) and Susan Haynes Chapman (b. 1858 at Holly Springs). Grandson of Dudley and Margaret Brannon Chapman. (For family history see account of A. Asbury Chapman.)

Married, in 1904, Arrie Jane Mackey, b. Sep. 19, 1884, daughter of Joseph and Amanda Mackey. Children: Clarence L., b. Apr. 2, 1906; Jessie L., b. Dec. 18, 1907; Willie Mae, b. Mar. 14, 1911; Ora Jane, b. Dec. 1, 1915.

Mr. Chapman is a rural mail carrier. He belongs to the Methodist Church, and is a Mason.

CHAPMAN, WALTER F.

Atlanta. Born Oct. 13, 1893, in Cherokee Co. Son of Arelius F. Chapman and Susan Haynes Chapman. Grandson of Dudley Chapman Sr., and of George Haynes, who lived at Holly Springs and was a Confederate veteran. Corresponding secretary of Georgia Division Chapman Memorial Assn. (see account of A. Asbury Chapman).

Mr. Chapman left his home in Holly Springs at the age of 16 to become an apprentice watchmaker, and is now after 22 years an expert in his profession, holding membership in the Horological Institute of America, a distinction held by only one other person in Georgia; and also the degree of Certified Watchmaker. He is a Mason, a member of the M. W. A. (consul of Atlanta Camp, 1932), and belongs to the First Baptist Church, Atlanta.

In 1919 he married Carrie Allen Fuller, of Atlanta, who was born Mar. 15, 1897, and is the daughter of Gettis Walker Fuller and Alice Tyler Fuller. Mrs. Fuller is a descendant of John Tyler.

Mr. and Mrs. Chapman have one daughter, Miriam Allen, b. June 20, 1925.

Cline, Felix Carter

Born July 8, 1893, in Cherokee Co. Son of John M. and Nancy Heard Cline. Grandson of Michael Cline, and of John M. Heard. Great-grandson of John Cline. Both the Cline and Heard families entered land in Cherokee Co. during Indian days, Michael Cline coming from Swain Co., N. C.

Felix C. Cline attended the public schools of Cherokee Co. and Georgia Institute of Technology, and during the World War served in the A. E. F. and afterward in the Army of Occupation. He is a substantial farmer of the Burris School District, and belongs to Sharp Top Lodge No. 680, F. & A. M.

He married, on Jan. 13, 1924, at Ball Ground, Mittie C. Lindsey, who was born in Gwinnett Co. near Norcross. Their children are: Lida Belle, b. May 10, 1925; and Felix Lindsey, b. Jan. 27, 1928.

Cline, James Luther

Waleska. Born 1889 in Cherokee Co. Son of Elias Franklin Cline and Sarah Hasty Cline. Grandson of Levi Cline and Martha Cagle Cline, and of John Terrell Hasty. Great-grandson of John Cline, and of John Cagle. (See account of John W. Cline.) The Clines and Cagles have been identified with the northern part of Cherokee Co. almost since its origin, and the Hastys were also a pioneer family, living in Keith Settlement.

James Luther Cline married Vista Henderson, daughter of Alex and Callie Henderson, also of an early family. Both Mr. and Mrs. Cline attended Reinhardt College. He began business in Waleska, later taking in his brother, Levi Cline, but is now sole proprietor of a general store there and conducts also a gin and mill. He is a former school trustee, mayor, and councilman of Waleska, and a justice of the peace. Mason. Member, Oak Hill Baptist Church. Mrs. Cline belongs to Sardis Baptist Church. Their children are: Leona, b. 1911; Weldon, b. 1913; Fern, b. 1917; Ruth, b. 1920; Mary Grace, b. 1922; Frances, b. 1924; Margaret, b. 1927; William, b. 1930.

CLINE, JOHN W.

Waleska. Born 1856 in Cherokee Co. Son of Levi Cline (b. in Swain Co., N. C.; came to Cherokee Co. when a young man; of German descent) and Martha Cagle Cline (b. in Buncombe Co., N. C., came to Cherokee Co. at age of 12; d. Jan. 11, 1932, at age of 97). Grandson of John Cline, and of John Cagle, whose grandfather came from Germany and fought under Washington in the Revolutionary War.

Married, in 1879, Lula Sharp, daughter of J. M. Sharp, of the pioneer Sharp family which came from South Carolina to Cherokee Co. in the 1830's; also of German descent.

Children: Ida (Mrs. J. M. Dysart), b. 1883; Virgil, b. 1880; Alma, b. 1885; Earl, b. 1887; Pierce, b. 1890; Ella May (Mrs. J. M. Watkins), b. 1892; Annie Lou (Mrs. F. C. Worley), b. 1894; Esther (Mrs. J. B. Fuller), b. 1896; Mabel (Mrs. W. R. Wilson), b. 1898; Myrtle (Mrs. L. W. McLaurin), b. 1900; Bess (Mrs. J. M. Shields), b. 1902; Fain, b. 1905; Forrest, b. 1907.

Mr. Cline is a substantial farmer of the Waleska section; belongs to the I. O. O. F. Rev. Earl Cline is a member of the North Georgia Conference, M. E. C. S. Prof. Pierce Cline is Professor of History and Economics in Centenary College, Shreveport, La.

COKER, N. J. (DR.)

Canton. Born Mar. 14, 1868, in Cherokee Co. Son of S. L. Coker (Confederate soldier, Co. E, 23d Ga. Reg.; of a pioneer county family) and Elizabeth Perkins Coker, of Cherokee Co. Grandson of Thomas Coker and of Newton J. Perkins, who represented Cherokee Co. in legislature, 1867-68.

Attended public schools, N. G. A. C. at Dahlonega, Young Harris, and State Medical College at Augusta. Practiced in South Carolina 4 years, since then in Cherokee Co. Founded, in 1923 with his son, Dr. G. N. Coker, Coker's Hospital in Canton. Was a captain in the Medical Corps during the World War, stationed with 62d Pioneer Infantry Camp, Wadsworth, S. C. For last 10 years chairman of the county board of education. Deacon in the First Baptist Church of Canton; was a member of the building committee of this church.

Married, in December 1893, Effie Trammell of Milton Co. Children: Dr. Grady N., b. December 1894; Mrs. J. E. Hays, b. October 1896; Mrs. H. G. Phillips, b. March 1900; Bettie, b. September 1903; Shault L., b. June 1906.

COLLINS, DAVID ANDREW

Salacoa. Born 1882 in Cherokee Co. Son of Archibald Grice Collins and Nancy Thompson Collins. Grandson of Thomas Robert Collins. Great-grandson of Jacob Collins. (For family history see account of John W. Collins.)

Married, in 1906, Mary Agnes Hutcherson, b. 1888, daughter of Nat Hutcherson and Margaret Hightower Hutcherson, both of pioneer Cherokee Co. families. Mrs. Collins' grandfather, Thomas Hutcherson, came from Virginia in the '40's to settle on land he had acquired in the Salacoa district, about the same time other Virginians were coming there; and he and his sons, Griff, Nat, and Thomas Jr., became influential in the development of "Little Virginia" colony and the county generally. Col. Thomas Hutcherson Jr., who represented the county in legislature and served as solicitor-general of the Blue Ridge District, was considered one of the ablest legal minds the county ever produced.

Mr. Collins is a substantial farmer of the Salacoa section and has taught school for 18 years in Bartow and Cherokee Counties. He is a Baptist; Mrs. Collins belongs to Fairview Methodist Church. Both attended Reinhardt College. Their children, Thomas, b. 1907, and Susie D., b. 1914, have also attended Reinhardt.

COLLINS, JOHN WELBORN

Canton. Born Nov. 3, 1878, in Cherokee Co. Son of Archibald Grice (Bud) Collins (b. May 3, 1841, in North Carolina) and Nancy Thompson Collins (b. Sep. 12, 1851, in Pickens Co., Ga.). Grandson of Thomas Robert Collins (b. May 3, 1812, in North Carolina) and of Louis Thompson (leading farmer of Pickens Co.; died at the age of 92.)

Archibald G. (Bud) Collins came to Cherokee Co. from North Carolina with his father in 1848, settling in Salacoa District; became a substantial farmer and leading citizen; was justice of the peace for about 40 years; served on county juries for some 50 years. During the Civil War he served gallantly in the 43d Georgia Regiment as a non-commissioned officer.

John W. Collins attended the public schools and Reinhardt College, where he graduated in 1902 and where he was the first to attain the rank of major in the military department. Served in the U. S. Navy, Mar. 27, 1905, to Mar. 27, 1909, obtaining the rank of chief petty officer aboard the U. S. S. Louisiana, one of sixteen battleships completing a world tour in 1908-09. Graduated from the law school of Mercer University, Macon, in June 1910. Practiced law in Canton and was city attorney and recorder for several years. From 1913 to 1917, served as assistant postmaster in the U. S. Senate. During the World War was a member of the legal advisory board of Cherokee Co. Elected in 1918 to serve an unexpired term as representative to the legislature; reelected next three terms, 1921 to 1927.

Married, Aug. 9, 1922, Ora L. Willingham, youngest daughter of Dr. W. M. Willingham, prominent physician and a former mayor of Canton. They have one son, John W. Jr., b. Apr. 19, 1925. Mrs. Collins attended high school at Canton and holds the A. B. degree from Columbia College, Lake City, Fla. She is a member of the First Baptist Church, Canton, the Canton Women's Club, and other religious, social, and civic organizations.

COVINGTON, WILLIAM ALONZO

Atlanta. Born Jan. 19, 1869, in McCoy Settlement near Waleska. Son of Sidney S. Covington (b. in Bartow Co.) and Addie Burns Covington (b. at Waleska). Grandson of A. J. and Olivia Ellis Covington, and of Henry Burns and Ann Rhine Burns. Family traditionally identified with Covingtons who came to England in the Danish Conquest; American line traced back to John Covington, a colonist of Cecil Calvert, who settled in Maryland in 1650. Three of Judge Covington's great-uncles went to the Mexican War from Cherokee Co.; his father and four uncles fought in Lee's army, although they had opposed secession.

Judge Covington ascribes his early education to his mother, who taught him in their lonely log cabin at McCoy Settlement. He attended Reinhardt College as a "charter pupil" and was in its first graduating class (1888). Graduated from Emory College in 1896; no more distinguished record had been made by any student there up to that time.

Admitted to the bar in 1898; began the practice of law in Moultrie, Ga. Was appointed judge of Moultrie city court in 1902; represented Colquitt Co. in legislature, 1905-08, 1919-20, 1923-24. Joint author with Dr. L. G. Hardman of the state prohibition law passed in 1907. Led successful fight in the house against further leasing of convicts, 1908. Sponsored other important measures. Now in private practice in Atlanta, and considered one of the most eloquent members of the Georgia bar.

COX, MARGARET ELIZABETH RUSK (MRS. A. D.)

Woodstock. Born 1871 in Cherokee Co. Daughter of Col. James E. Rusk and Margaret Brooke Rusk. Granddaughter of David Rusk, and of John P. and Esther Bennett Brooke.

James E. Rusk came to Cherokee Co. at an early age with his father, David Rusk, from South Carolina, to which state the family had moved from Ireland shortly before. After serving as an officer in the Confederate Army, Col. Rusk became an extensive farmer, and was elected to the state senate in 1886. He died

Oct. 29, 1893, and was buried in the Rusk Cemetery near the old home. His wife was a member of the noted Cherokee Co. family of Brookes, also of Irish descent. The Bennetts were of English origin.

In 1893, Margaret Rusk married A. D. Cox, whose family had come to Milton Co. from South Carolina about 1850 and had later moved to Cherokee Co. Mr. Cox was an enterprising farmer, for years a member of the county board of education, a trustee, steward and Sunday school superintendent of Mt. Gilead Methodist Church. He died in 1917 and was buried in Mt. Gilead Cemetery.

The children of Mr. and Mrs. Cox: Roy, b. 1894; Nellie (Mrs. C. P. Cowart), b. 1896; Estelle (Mrs. H. F. Cook), b. 1901; all are active in church and school work.

CRISLER, BENJAMIN ROY

Canton. Born Jan. 3, 1884, in Canton. Son of Benjamin Franklin Crisler (b. June 20, 1844) and Emma McClure Crisler (b. 1858). Grandson of Abel and Ann Maxwell Crisler, and of Rev. Charles Marshall McClure (see account of Alfred W. McClure) and Piety Burtz McClure.

Married, Feb. 24, 1904, at Canton, Anne Field McAfee, daughter of Joseph M. and Susan Donaldson McAfee, and granddaughter of Judge Joseph and Malinda Anne Field Donaldson.

Both Mr. and Mrs. Crisler come of prominent families long connected with Cherokee Co. (For Crisler family history see account of Mrs. B. F. Crisler.) Capt. Joseph M. McAfee and Judge Joseph Donaldson were leaders during their respective periods in the commercial and industrial growth of Canton. Judge Donaldson (b. July 12, 1807; d. May 4, 1892) was an early settler; he started a silk business in Canton and soon after helped to have Canton made the county seat. He was noted for his generosity and civic spirit, and during the Civil War contributed largely to the cause of the South. Capt. McAfee (b. Jan. 11, 1833, in Forsyth Co.; d. July 30, 1929) married a daughter of Judge Donaldson. He moved to Canton in 1866. During his 63 years as a merchant he acquired large farming and milling interests; and also pursued a contracting business. He served as mayor of Canton and as state senator; was a leading Methodist and a contributor to many worthy causes.

Benjamin Roy Crisler, who has been in the investment business since retiring in 1929 from B. F. Crisler & Son, is president of Canton Telephone Co.; vice-president and a director, Bank of Canton; director, Canton Cotton Mills; has served as mayor of Canton; is now a member of Canton water and light commission. Mr. and Mrs. Crisler are active Methodists; he has been a steward for many years and she is district secretary of the Women's Missionary Society. They have one son, Benjamin Roy Jr., b. Jan. 22, 1905, who is on the staff of the *Atlanta Constitution;* he was married in 1929 to Marguerite Cobbey, of Seattle, Wash., who comes of distinguished ancestry and is a gifted musician.

CRISLER, EMMA MCCLURE (MRS. BENJAMIN F.)

Canton. Born 1858 at Jasper, Pickens Co. Daughter of Rev. Charles Marshall McClure and Piety Burtz McClure. Granddaughter of William M. and Elizabeth White McClure and of Levi Burtz and Sarah Barrett Burtz.

Charles Marshall McClure (b. July 12, 1827, in Pendleton District, S. C.; d. Sep. 1, 1906, at Canton) was a noted teacher, local Methodist preacher, county officer, and merchant of Cherokee Co., active in religious and civic affairs of his day, and greatly admired and respected. Was said to have married more couples than any other man in the section. Served as chaplain in the Confederate Army. Held office as ordinary and as school commissioner of Cherokee Co. (See also account of Alfred W. McClure.)

The Crislers originally came from Germany, settling at Germantown, Pa., before the Revolutionary War. Later they moved to Virginia, and from there, early in the last century, Abel Crisler came to Georgia and married Ann Maxwell, of Elbert Co. Their son, Benjamin Franklin Crisler (b. June 20, 1844) established in 1870 the present mercantile firm of B. F. Crisler & Son and became one of Canton's most influential business men.

The children of Mr. and Mrs. B. F. Crisler: Roy (see account of); Max, b. 1893. By a former marriage (with Mary

Maxwell Teasley, daughter of W. A. and Jane Baber Teasley, of Canton) B. F. Crisler had two children: Annie Lou (Mrs. De-Witt Jenkins, of Virginia); Daisy (who lives at Canton).

Mrs. Crisler is an active member of the First Methodist Church in Canton.

DAY, CHARLES E.

Canton. Born 1886 in Cobb Co. Son of Carvasso M. Day (b. 1858 in Cobb Co.) and Anna Terry Day (b. 1869 in Cobb Co.). Grandson of Benjamin Day (b. about 1832 in South Carolina; Confederate soldier) and Hester Day (b. about 1836 in South Carolina), and of Alfred Terry (b. 1845 in South Carolina; Confederate soldier) and Lucinda Simpson Terry (b. at McDonough, Ga.).

Mr. Day is connected with the Canton Cotton Mills. He attended the public schools of Cobb Co., and married, on Nov. 13, 1910, Ida Durham of Cobb Co., daughter of N. A. Durham and Mary Alexander Durham. The children of Mr. and Mrs. Day: Emory, b. 1911; Marvin, b. 1919; William Carl, b. 1922; Lewis Clyde, b. 1925. All of the family are members of the First Methodist Church of Canton, in which Mr. Day is a steward and Mrs. Day secretary of the Women's Missionary Society. Mr. Day is also a Mason, an Odd Fellow, and a K. of P.

DEAN, LINTON ALBERT

Woodstock. Born Jan. 15, 1886, in Woodstock. Son of Dr. W. L. Dean (b. in Cherokee Co.; practiced medicine in Woodstock 25 years; first Master of Woodstock Masonic Lodge; prominent in religious and civic affairs; died at the age of 49 from exposure contracted in the line of duty) and Lulu Boring Dean. Grandson of Dr. W. H. Dean (also a practicing physician; Baptist minister; early county settler, and Confederate soldier) and Emily Benson Dean; and of Squire J. P. Boring (Confederate soldier; Mason) and Evie Evans Boring.

Mr. Dean attended the Woodstock public schools, Marietta High School, North Georgia Agricultural College at Dahlonega, and Creighton's Business College at Atlanta. Entered the drug business in Woodstock, 1906, and has owned and operated the Dean

Drug Store there for 25 years. Mason; deacon in the Woodstock Baptist Church; member of the county board of education.

Married, in 1915, Alice Wellons, daughter of Mr. and Mrs. F. B. Wellons, of Marietta, and a niece of the Hon. Robert H. Northcutt and T. M. Brumby Sr. of Marietta. Mrs. Dean was born Aug. 29, 1892; is a Baptist. Children: Elizabeth Wellons, b. Aug. 30, 1916; Alice Northcutt, b. Mar. 19, 1921.

DIAL, EMMETT D.

Woodstock. Born 1877 in Cherokee Co. Son of William S. Dial and Esther F. Rusk Dial. Grandson of Cyrus Dial (one of the earliest settlers of Cherokee Co.; came from South Carolina to Sweats Mtn. section; Confederate soldier) and of Col. and Mrs. J. E. Rusk, of Cherokee Co.

Educated in the public schools of Cherokee Co. Married, in 1915, Mary Claude Simpson, daughter of John N. and Margaret Taylor Simpson, and granddaughter of Dr. John Torrentine, pioneer physician of the Hickory Flat neighborhood and a graduate of the Philadelphia Medical College. Mr. Dial is a member of Sweats Mountain Masonic Lodge and Woodstock Baptist Church. Mrs. Dial is a member of the Hickory Flat Methodist Church. They have one daughter, Sarah Frances, born in 1921.

For 27 years Mr. Dial has been in the government mail service, the last 14 years of which he has been postmaster at Woodstock.

DOBBS, CICERO CHAPPELL, Children of

Born in Cherokee Co. on Jan. 24, 1847, Cicero Chappell Dobbs was the son of Perry Mason Dobbs and Vesta M. Dobbs. The Dobbs family came to Cherokee Co. from South Carolina in the first half of the last century.

Mr. Dobbs was educated at Little River Academy and became a substantial farmer of the Woodstock section. He was a Royal Arch Mason, and for many years both he and his wife were active members of Little River Methodist Church.

On Nov. 16, 1871, he married Sarah DuPree (b. June 24, 1848, in Union Co., S. C.) who had come to Georgia at an early age with her parents, William Griffin DuPree and Miriam Haney DuPree. The DuPrees are of French descent, the Haneys and Dobbses of English.

Mr. Dobbs died Feb. 18, 1912, and Mrs. Dobbs Apr. 1, 1931. Their children were: Willis Dobbs, now of Oakdale Road, Atlanta; Mrs. Henry J. Fullbright, of Alston Drive, Atlanta; Col. Emmett O. Dobbs, of Barnesville; and Miss Iris C. Dobbs, of Woodstock.

Doss, George Alfred

Canton. Born Dec. 13, 1898, in Canton. Son of Lemuel J. Doss (descended from a pioneer family that settled in Cherokee Co. from South Carolina) and Luray Virginia Lowe Doss, of Cherokee Co. Grandson of Alfred Lowe (Confederate soldier; killed on his journey home from the war.) Great-grandson of Solomon Beck, Cherokee Co. pioneer of Indian days.

Attended Canton High School. Served during the World War in Coast Artillery Corps, radio division. Mason; American Legion. Baptist. Is connected with The Georgia Marble Finishing Works, Canton.

Married, in 1921, Irene McAfee White, of Canton, granddaughter of Capt. J. M. McAfee. She was educated at Canton High School and G. S. C. W., Milledgeville. Their children are: George A., Jr., b. 1922; Mary Anne, b. 1925.

Doss, Thomas A.

Canton. Born 1876 in Cherokee Co. Son of George S. Doss and Nancy Green Doss. Father's family came from North Carolina and mother's family from South Carolina, in the early days of Cherokee Co., and settled on the Etowah River. They are of Scotch-Irish descent.

Mr. Doss was educated in the public and high schools of Cherokee Co. and received normal training at Peabody and summer courses in various institutions. Taught school for 13 years; served as county superintendent of schools for 13 years. Is now clerk and treasurer of the town of Canton; has served in this capacity for 15 years. Baptist. Mason; Odd Fellow; Knight of Pythias; Jr. Order; Red Man.

DOWDA, EARL G. (DR.)

Atlanta. Born Mar. 10, 1885, at Canton. Son of Julius L. Dowda (b. Jan. 27, 1838, in Iredell Co., N. C.; served in Confederate Army, Wheeler's Cavalry; Methodist preacher, was pastor at Shiloh in Cherokee Co.) and Lunda A. Reinhardt Dowda (b. 1842 at Canton). Grandson of William Anderson Dowda (b. Aug. 6, 1804, in Halifax Co., Va.) and Mary Jane Slavin Dowda (b. Oct. 27, 1804, in Iredell Co., N. C.) and of John H. Reinhardt (b. Nov. 8, 1808, in South Carolina) and Amy H. Redwine Reinhardt (b. Nov. 11, 1817, in South Carolina). Nephew of Judge James O. Dowda (prominent Cherokee Co. preacher, lawyer, and county officer of the last century; see chapter on Canton Bar).

Earl G. Dowda attended Buford Academy, Buford, Ga., and New Orleans College of Optometry. He has conducted an optical business in Atlanta for a number of years. He is a 32d degree Mason and Shriner, and a member of Grace M. E. Church, South, in Atlanta.

He married, at Fayetteville, Ga., Vivian Barron, daughter of John Barron, a newspaperman of Memphis, Tenn., and Elizabeth Grice Barron; and granddaughter of Judge Grice of Fayette Co., Ga. Children of Dr. and Mrs. Dowda: Elizabeth, b. 1910; Elsie, b. 1912; Dorothy Ann, b. 1922.

DUPREE, PERRY PINKNEY

Canton. Born Jan. 13, 1847, in South Carolina. Son of William Griffin DuPree and Miriam Haney DuPree. The DuPree family came from France and settled in Virginia about 1765, later moving to South Carolina. The Haneys were of English descent. William Griffin DuPree served in the Confederate Army at Atlanta.

Perry Pinkney DuPree is also a Civil War veteran; he was in the 2d Reserves and guarded prisoners at Andersonville, Ga., while General Sherman was at Dalton. After the war he settled at Woodstock, and went to school to Prof. P. D. Wheelan at Little River Academy. Admitted to the bar in Canton during the '80's, he has practiced there since; is a lawyer of note and ability; has been solicitor pro tem. of the Blue Ridge Circuit.

Married, in 1883, Marie Garwood, of Marietta, whose family

settled in Pennsylvania, removed to Athens, Ga., and later to Marietta. Mrs. DuPree is active in church and charity work. Their children: Robert G. (World War veteran); Agnes (Mrs. Thomas Thompson); and Sidney, of Huntington, Ind.

EDWARDS, WILLIAM T.

Canton. Born 1846 in North Carolina. Son of William A. Edwards and Elizabeth Queen Edwards, both of North Carolina. The Edwards family is of English descent. They moved to Cherokee Co. in the early '50's.

William T. Edwards married Frances Sewall, of Milton Co., and later moved from Union Hill, Cherokee Co., to Canton. Children: Margaret (present postmaster at Canton); Effie (Mrs. P. K. Moss); Ada (Mrs. Will Blackwell); Willie (Mrs. Ed Pickett); Bessie; Harold M.; Scott; Joe; Martha (Mrs. N. H. Garrison, deceased).

Mr. Edwards was postmaster at Canton for 16 years. He and his family are all Methodists.

ELLIOTT, WILLIAM S.

Born in Newton Co., Ga. Son of William D. and Sarah P. Jones Elliott. Served in U. S. Treasury Department 20 years, beginning 1899. Was Registrar of the Treasury and Deputy Commissioner of the Public Debt, resigning when President Harding came in. Connected with Bankers Trust Co., New York, for one year. Since 1923 vice-president and cashier, Bank of Canton. Elected vice-president Georgia Bankers Association in 1931; is now president of that association (1932).

Married, in 1900, Martha Boyd, daughter of William Boyd and Frances McCord Boyd, of Newton Co., Ga. Children: Edwin Boyd, William Emmett, John Carl, Charles Francis, Martha Boyd, and Justin McCord, all born in Washington, D. C., or its environs. The home of the Elliott family is at Holly Springs.

EPPERSON, JOHN

Canton. Born Aug. 16, 1883, in Cherokee Co. Son of Green B. Epperson (b. 1859 in Cherokee Co.; farmer; d. 1926) and

Ruth Bice Epperson (married 1880; her father had come to Chero-kee Co. from Spartanburg, S. C., in 1849 at the age of 13). Grand-son of James Epperson (b. 1834 in Cherokee Co.; farmer; Con-federate soldier; d. 1862) and Sarah Griffin (married about 1855). Great-grandson of John Epperson (b. in North Carolina about 1782; came about 1810 to what later became Cherokee Co., where he traded with the Indians and bought land from them; one of the first white men in Cherokee Georgia; helped to organize the old Liberty Grove Methodist Church near Holbrook Campground; d. about 1857).

Mr. Epperson has been agent in Canton for the Mutual Benefit Life Insurance Co. since 1910. He is an active member and a steward of the Canton Methodist Church.

On Nov. 5, 1905, he married Mary Olive Pugh, also of Chero-kee Co. Their children are: Hoyt, b. 1906; Glenn, b. 1908; Maxwell, b. 1916; Lanier, b. 1918; Carolyn, b. 1924.

ERWIN, ROBERT LEWIS

Canton. Born 1899 in Clarksville, Habersham Co. Son of Lee Erwin (of a pioneer family of Habersham Co.; moved from Clarksville to Roswell, Cobb Co., about 1900; engaged in business there with B. C. Ball) and Susan Griffin Erwin (of Habersham Co.).

Mr. Erwin has for the last 3 years been superintendent of Eto-wah Manufacturing Co., Canton. Formerly he occupied other responsible positions with large companies in Atlanta, New Or-leans, and Moultrie, Ga. Member, Junior Order.

Married, in 1919, Bertha Webb, of Alpharetta, Milton Co., daughter of Edgar Webb and Dora Mayfield Webb, and grand-daughter of John Webb, who settled in Milton (now Fulton) Co. in an early day. Mr. and Mrs. Erwin are both members of the First Baptist Church of Canton. They have two children, Charles, b. 1921, and Billy, b. 1919.

FAULKNER, CHARLES JEROME

Ball Ground. Born 1855 near Four-Mile Creek in Pickens Co. Son of James and Lydia A. Gilmer Faulkner. James Faulkner, who was born in 1810 in Ballingarry, Limerick Co., Ireland, left his father's home to come to America at the age of 26. After a perilous voyage across the Atlantic, he settled in Georgia and became naturalized. He married Lydia A. Gilmer, of a pioneer Georgia family, and they had 10 children. Mr. Faulkner died at the age of 79.

The name Faulkner is derived from "falconer," an officer who cared for the falcons of English royalty. The great-uncle of the subject of this sketch was a body-guard of the King of England.

Charles Jerome Faulkner attended the Thalean school near Tate, in Pickens Co., after the Civil War. This school was taught by a noted educator of that day, Prof. John B. Wright. Among Mr. Faulkner's classmates were the Hon. Sam Tate, Dr. Tate, and Dr. McClain. Mr. Faulkner taught school in Pickens Co. for three terms; later studied law and was admitted to the bar, but did not practice. For 6 years he farmed at Waleska while his children were attending Reinhardt College.

His wife is the former Lillie Mae McClure, daughter of Oliver Perry McClure and Catharine Gilleland McClure. Both the McClure and Gilleland families were settlers among the Indians. Mr. and Mrs. Faulkner have resided, since their marriage in 1892, in Pickens and later Cherokee Co. Their children are: Kathryn (Mrs. Alfred W. McClure), b. 1892; Talmadge, b. 1894; James, b. 1897; Joseph, b. 1899; Addie May, b. 1904; Frank, b. 1906; Ethel, b. 1909. All are members of Ball Ground Methodist Church. James was a pioneer in southern aviation and is now chief test pilot for Pitcairn Autogiro Co. Frank is also a licensed air pilot of wide experience.

FIELD, E. EARLE

Born Nov. 18, 1863, in Cherokee Co. Son of Elias Earle Field (b. 1820 in North Carolina) and Susan McKinney Field (b. 1830 in South Carolina). Grandson of Jeremiah Field (b. 1769 in North Carolina).

The Field family, of French descent, trace their ancestry back to the de la Fields of Norman times. Jeremiah Field, a veteran of the Revolutionary War, came with his six children from North Carolina to Cherokee Co. during the Indian days, and settled on the present Field place southwest of Canton, on the Etowah River.

He traded with the Indians at his store and grist mill, and helped them to move in 1838. Field's Chapel was founded by this early settler. Elias E. Field, his son, was an extensive farmer and served in the state legislature. He married Susan McKinney, whose parents had come from South Carolina in her youth and had settled on the Etowah near Canton.

E. Earle Field, their son, also married a Susan McKinney, daughter of Lee W. and Anne Roberts McKinney, of Garden City, Kans., in 1906. Their children are: Jeremiah, b. 1910; Marcus Harvey, b. 1912; James McKinney, b. 1916.

Mr. Field is a noted breeder and distributor of blooded stock, and was the first to introduce Aberdeen-Angus cattle into the state. Stock raised on his large river-bottom farm has been famous for over fifty years.

FINCHER, ANNIE A. (MISS)

Waleska. Born 1872 in Cherokee Co. Daughter of Elias Alexander Fincher (b. 1841 near Hickory Flat; d. 1924) and Emma Jane Atherton Fincher (b. 1852 in Alabama; d. 1926). Granddaughter of Joseph Fincher (b. 1802 in South Carolina; d. 1885) and Lucinda Elliott Fincher (b. 1802 in South Carolina; d. 1896) and of James Atherton (b. 1813 in Manchester, England) and Ann Rathville Atherton (b. 1813 in Manchester, England; d. 1881).

Joseph Fincher came to Cherokee Co. from South Carolina about the middle of the last century, and his son Elias A. was a pioneer in the textile industry of North Georgia. After he married Emma Jane Atherton, whose parents had been married in 1840 by the captain of the ship on which they came from England, Elias A. Fincher built a textile mill at Talking Rock, in Pickens Co. Later he set up a mill on Shoal Creek, near Waleska, where he carded wool, ground corn, and made cotton thread. He established several other mills in Cherokee and Pickens Counties, some of them in association with James Atherton. He served in the Civil War from 1862 until the close, and fought in a number of important battles. In about 1880 he came to the present Fincher home south of Waleska, where three of his daughters now live. He was a Mason, a trustee of Reinhardt College, a Methodist;

and was much esteemed in the county. He died in 1924, and his wife followed in 1926.

The following children were born to Elias A. and Emma Jane Atherton Fincher: Robert Olin (see account of); Annie A., b. 1872; William Wesley (see account of); Atherton A. (see account of); Corean M. (Mrs. Hudson Vernon), b. 1882; Evie O., b. 1884; Jesse D., b. 1887; Mary Wyolene (Mrs. Wallace Matthews), b. 1889; and Emma Elizabeth, b. 1892.

FINCHER, ATHERTON ALEXANDER

Canton. Born 1879 at Fairmount, Ga. Son of Elias A. and Emma Jane Atherton Fincher. (For family history see account of Miss Annie Fincher.)

Married, in 1909 in Bartow Co., Mabel Richardson, daughter of E. B. and Myra Swann Richardson. One son, Arthur Atherton, b. 1910 at Canton.

Mr. Fincher is manager of the Canton Telephone Co. Both he and Mrs. Fincher attended Reinhardt College. The family are all members of the Methodist Church, and Mr. Fincher is also a Royal Arch Mason and an Odd Fellow.

FINCHER, ROBERT OLIN

Canton. Born 1870, at Talking Rock, Ga. Son of Elias A. Fincher and Emma Jane Atherton Fincher. (For family history, see account of Miss Annie Fincher.)

Graduated at Reinhardt College in 1889. Married Rose McIntyre, of a pioneer Murray Co. family. Began business in Waleska; later moved to Canton. Was clerk of the superior court, Cherokee Co., 1906-1916; commissioner of roads and revenue, 1917-1921. With state highway department 4 years. Former mayor of Canton; former member, Canton city council; former secretary and treasurer of Canton; former ordinary, Cherokee Co. Methodist; trustee and steward. Mason; Odd Fellow; W. O. W.; Red Man.

FINCHER, WILLIAM WESLEY

Canton. Born Oct. 26, 1876, at Talking Rock, Ga. Son of Elias A. Fincher and Emma Jane Atherton Fincher. (For family history, see account of Miss Annie Fincher.)

Mr. Fincher is mayor of Canton and is the owner and proprietor of the Canton Drug Co., with which he has been connected for many years. He is a Scottish Rite Mason and a member of the Methodist Church.

On Aug. 16, 1913, he married Mary Chambers Elliott, widow of the Rev. Charles Carson Elliott. Mrs. Fincher is a daughter of John William Chambers (b. Feb. 25, 1855) and Iola Celestia Womack Chambers (b. Aug. 25, 1856, near Covington; m. Dec. 17, 1874), being the eighth of their twelve children. She is a granddaughter of James Absolum Chambers (Confederate soldier) and Mary Anne Dorman Chambers (m. June 17, 1851), and a great-granddaughter of the Rev. Joseph Chambers (Methodist minister; one of five brothers who settled near New Hope Church in Clayton Co., Ga., from South Carolina before the Civil War), and of the Rev. Alfred Dorman (Methodist minister). John W. Chambers, father of Mrs. Fincher, was an active Methodist and a highly respected citizen of Clayton Co.

The children of Mr. and Mrs. W. W. Fincher are: William Wesley Jr., b. May 16, 1914; Jack, b. Nov. 22, 1915; Emily Iola, b. Sep. 22, 1918. A daughter, Sarah Celestia Elliott, was born to Mrs. Fincher's first union.

GALT, JABEZ

Late of Canton. Born May 30, 1851, at Canton; d. Jan. 6, 1916. Son of Joel Lewis Galt and Malinda Caroline Gresham Galt. Grandson of Jabez and Frances Machen Galt and of William and Susan E. Bradford Grisham. (For family history, see account of Mrs. William Galt.)

Jabez Galt was a prominent Cherokee Co. officer (clerk of the superior court, 1879-1885, 1898-1904; superintendent of schools, 1908-11), was a leading merchant in Canton, and owned mining and agricultural interests, being one of the first commercial peach growers in the state. Mr. Galt was an active member of the First Baptist Church of Canton, and helped to organize its first Sunday school, of which he was superintendent for 17 years; succeeded his father as clerk; served for many years as clerk of the Noonday Association; was moderator of this body at the time of his death.

Odd Fellow; Mason; served as worshipful master of Masonic Lodge No. 77.

Married (1) in 1877, Ella Speir, at Barnesville. Son of this marriage: Joel Harrison Galt (Mercer, A.B.; m. Gertrude Mc-Canless, 1908). Married (2) on Dec. 21, 1881, at Canton, Lizzie Teasley (b. Mar. 1861; daughter of William A. Teasley (b. 1833 in Elbert Co.; d. 1908 in Cherokee Co.; see account of George I. Teasley) and Jane Baber Teasley (b. 1837 in Cobb Co.). Lizzie Teasley was born the day the "Brown Riflemen" left Canton for service with the Confederacy. She is a charter member of the Helen Plane Chapter of U. D. C.

Children of Jabez and Lizzie Teasley Galt: Ella Speir (attended Shorter College; m. Monroe Howard of Polk Co., 1906); George Teasley (N. G. A. C., Dahlonega; m. Annie Carpenter of Cherokee Co., 1910); Jabez Leland (N. G. A. C.; in railway service during the World War; m. Maxie Moffett of Cartersville, 1913); Lieut. William A. (Gordon 1908; Mercer, A.B.; enlisted with National Horse Guards and fought on the Mexican border; later served with the 306th Pioneer Infantry, A. E. F., in France; cited for bravery in action, where he was shell-shocked and permanently injured; patient of U. S. Hospital No. 62, Lenwood, Augusta); John Lewis (killed in railway accident 1913, was a sophomore at Mercer); Malinda (attended Bessie Tift and Wesleyan; entered postal department in 1922); Jane (Shorter, A.B. 1915; Columbia, B.S.; m., in 1920, Dr. Edwin M. Bailor, of psychology department, Dartmouth College); Thomas Hutcherson (Gordon 1916; Wofford, A.B. 1923; ensign in U. S. Navy 1916-1920; m. Mrs. Happy Littleton Feamster, 1926); Chester Judson (served in the 16th Cavalry, U. S. A., during the World War, stationed at Brownsville, Tex.; m. Hester Suddeth, 1926); Agnes Fannie (attended Girls' High School, Atlanta, and Damrosch School of Music, New York).

GALT, LECY PUTNAM (MRS. WILLIAM)

Canton. Born Apr. 11, 1869, in Cherokee Co., near Sixes. Daughter of Odian Wilson Putnam and Martha Tate Putnam; granddaughter of David and Lecy Castleberry Putnam and of Daniel and Lena Tate. Attended school in Canton after moving there in 1877 from Sixes; later attended Mary Sharp College,

Winchester, Tenn., where she became an accomplished musician.

Odian Wilson Putnam (b. Mar. 31, 1832; d. Dec. 24, 1913) was the son of David Putnam, prominent slave-holder and farmer who settled on Little River in Cherokee Co. during Indian days after previously moving from Bowling Green, Ky., to Hall Co., Ga.; and the grandson of Thomas and Mary Barton Putnam, of Bowling Green, Ky. He was clerk of the superior court of Cherokee Co., 1856-1875; ordinary, 1885-1893. Lieutenant, 18th Ga. Regiment, Co. E; lost his left arm in the Battle of Gettysburg; was a prisoner on Johnson's Island for almost two years. Three brothers of Mr. Putnam, Thomas W., David L., and Berry P., also saw active service in the Confederate Army, as did two brothers-in-law, Robert H. Tate and Thomas M. Tate. After the War, Mr. Putnam returned to his home on Little River, and in 1877 he moved to Canton. He married, in 1868, Martha Tate, daughter of Daniel Tate who moved to Marion Co., Fla., near Silver Springs. Two daughters survive them: Mrs. William Galt and Mrs. Green B. Johnston.

Lecy Putnam was married on Feb. 6, 1889, to William Galt, son of Joel L. and Malinda Grisham Galt, and grandson of Jabez Galt and of William Grisham. This marriage consolidated two of the first families of Cherokee Co. William Galt (b. Sep. 8, 1861, at Canton; d. Aug. 4, 1931, at Canton) attended the Canton public schools, N. Ga. Agri. College, and the Univ. of Ga., where he graduated with honors and the degree of A.B. in 1882. In 1895 he became connected with the Bank of Canton; in 1900 was promoted to cashier and held this position until 1923 when he retired from active business. Mr. Galt was one of Canton's ablest and most progressive business men, and served a term as mayor and several terms as councilman. Was clerk and treasurer of the Canton Baptist Church for many years. Member, Canton Chamber of Commerce. Served as chairman of Group 3, Ga. Bankers Assn. Life member of this association (an honor conferred on only three others in the state). Member, S. A. E. fraternity. Delegate, National Democratic Convention, 1924.

Joel Lewis Galt (b. June 26, 1817, in Spartanburg Dist., S. C.; d. Mar. 18, 1873, at Canton), the father of William Galt, came with his parents, Jabez Galt (b. Apr. 19, 1789, in Newberry Dist.,

S. C.; d. Oct. 1, 1850, at Canton) and Frances Machen Galt, to Cherokee Co. in the 1830's. Jabez Galt was one of Canton's first merchants and built the town's first brick store building, about 1839, in which four generations of this family have carried on a mercantile business. The children of Jabez Galt were: Margaret Machen, John R., Joel L., Edward B. Machen, Henry, Francis Wilbern, Jabez S., Thomas A., and Leland Landrum. Joel Galt married Malinda Grisham, daughter of William and Susan Bradford Grisham, in 1844 at Canton, and engaged in business at his father's store. Was a member of the Home Guard during the Civil War. Served as clerk of the Canton Baptist Church for many years. His children were: Susan Elizabeth (Mrs. Milton B. Tuggle); Margaret Amanda (Mrs. James H. Speir); Jabez, who served as Cherokee Co. school commissioner and clerk of the superior court, and also as clerk of the Baptist Church, and who married, first, Ella Speir, and second, Elizabeth Anne Teasley; Ada Collins (Mrs. John Prince Lewis); Frances (Mrs. George B. Headden); Mildred (Mrs. Henry L. Roberts; see account of); William; and May (d. in infancy).

William Grisham (b. Mar. 6, 1803, in Pendleton Dist., S. C.; d. May 10, 1876, at Canton), grandfather of William Galt, was the son of John and Martha Halbert Gresham, of Pendleton Dist., S. C., and the grandson of John and Barbara Burdyne Gresham, of Essex Co., Va. He married, in 1825, Susan Bradford, daughter of Philemon and Susan Clopton Bradford, of Granville Co., N. C. They moved to Decatur, Ga., in 1825, thence to Cherokee Co. in 1831. William Grisham's activities in connection with the founding and development of Canton are alluded to earlier in this book. His children were: Elizabeth Sarah (Mrs. John D. Collins); Malinda Caroline (Mrs. Joel L. Galt); and Joseph Lemuel, who married Sarah Cain.

The Galts, Grishams, and Putnams have been among the leading pioneer families of Cherokee Co.

GARRETT, WHITFIELD

Born 1904 in Cherokee Co. Son of James Wiley Garrett (b. 1852) and Jane Pence Garrett (b. 1884). Grandson of William Bluford Garrett (b. in Anderson Dist., S. C.; died in service in the Civil War). Great-grandson of Thomas H. Garrett (b. 1792; came to South Carolina from Ireland). The father of Jane Pence Garrett was William Gibson Pence (b. 1858), whose father moved to Cherokee Co. from Alabama.

Whitfield Garrett attended the public schools of Cherokee Co., and has for some years been a substantial and progressive farmer of the Mill Creek section. His father, James Wiley Garrett, was chief engineer for the Atlantic Ice Co., in Atlanta, for 20 years.

In 1926 Whitfield Garrett married Myrtle Lee Turner, whose mother came to Cherokee from Union Co., Ga., about 32 years ago, and whose father was born and reared in Cherokee Co.

GRAMLING, GEORGE R.

Born May 4, 1871, in Cherokee Co. Son of James Matthew Gramling (b. in Cherokee Co.; farmer; Confederate soldier) and Sarah Brand Gramling. Grandson of Enoch George Gramling (Mexican War soldier; sheriff of Cherokee Co., 1867-70, 1873-74, 1879-80, 1883-86; brother of Kennedy Gramling, the captain of Cherokee Co.'s Mexican War company). Great-grandson of William Andrew Gramling (early Methodist minister of Cherokee Co.; one of five brothers who were preachers). Great-great-grandson of H. F. Gramling, who emigrated from Germany to South Carolina.

Mr. Gramling is a progressive farmer of the Canton section, and is also a notary public. He has for many years been a steward in the Methodist Church, and is superintendent of the Sunday School at Field's Chapel.

Mrs. Gramling, the former Lena Knox, is a daughter of Willis Truman Knox, who was a Confederate soldier and the son of Joseph Knox, noted pioneer of Cherokee Co. The children of Mr. and Mrs. Gramling: Elsie (Mrs. Ernest Stone); Mrs. Grace Ragsdale; Byron; Alfred; Miriam; and Milan.

GROOVER, CARL WESLEY

Ball Ground. Born Jan. 30, 1884, in Cherokee Co. Son of Joel C. Groover and Donie Hill Groover, both of pioneer families of the county. Grandson of Andrew H. Hill.

Educated in the public schools of Cherokee Co. United

with Methodist Church at an early age; is a steward and active in church work. Mason; has filled all offices in Ball Ground Lodge. Member, Ball Ground city council; school board; county courthouse committee of 1929. Has been in the marble business for 25 years; is president of the Consumers' Monument Co., Ball Ground, which position he has held for 15 years.

Married, in 1915, Jewell West, daughter of Dr. Tarpley W. West, who was for many years a practicing physician of Cherokee Co., and Mary West. Children: Carl Wesley Jr., b. 1917; Marshall E., b. 1919; William A., b. 1921; Mary Hill, b. 1923.

GROVES, JAMES JEFFERSON

Canton. Born in Murray Co., Ga., 1881. Son of James J. Groves and Caroline Brown Groves, both of White Co., Ga. Educated in Dalton, Ga., public schools. Moved to Canton, 1900. Married, in 1905, Sallie Lockhart, of Canton, daughter of L. P. Lockhart and Evelyn McAfee Lockhart; granddaughter of Capt. J. M. McAfee (Canton developer; Civil War veteran); educated in Canton public schools and Reinhardt College. Children: James LeRoy, b. 1906; Ruth, b. 1909; Sarah, b. 1912.

Master mechanic, Canton Cotton Mills. Mason; Red Man; Jr. Order. Baptist. Member Canton city council, three terms.

HARBIN, SAMUEL RICHARD

Late of Canton. Born 1873 in Cherokee Co.; d. Jan. 26, 1932. Son of Jephthah Harbin (b. 1838 in Cherokee Co.; served in the Confederate Navy aboard a sailing-ship for 26 months; a prominent farmer of Cherokee Co.; d. Oct. 3, 1910) and Mary Jane Freeze (b. 1852 in North Carolina; m. 1867 in Cherokee Co.). Grandson of Abram Harbin and Mary Champion Harbin. Brother of William F., Gibson Nathaniel, Sherman LaFayette, James Abram, Jephthah Alonzo, and Mary Jane Harbin.

Samuel Richard Harbin attended Atlanta Eclectic Medical College and practiced medicine for many years in Cherokee Co.;

for the last 20 years before his death was a leading physician of Canton. He was a member of the First Baptist Church of Canton and of the I. O. O. F. In 1895 he married Montaree Bell, who was born in 1877 near Ball Ground and was the daughter of Jefferson and Frances Robinson Bell; and they had six children: Ethel, b. 1895; Stella, b. 1897; Otis, b. 1900; Tillman, b. 1902; Wallace, b. 1905; and Jeffie, b. 1918.

HARMON, EMALINE COOK (MRS. GEORGE)

Waleska. Born 1856 in Cherokee Co., near Sharptop. Daughter of Lemuel and Rebecca Cook, old residents of the county. Married in 1875 George M. Harmon, who farmed and operated a tobacco factory near Waleska.

Mr. Harmon was the son of Joshua and Rebecca Harmon. He served as county commissioner and game warden. Deeply interested in education and churches, he was a strong supporter of Reinhardt College, where he helped a number of boys and girls to obtain an education. He was a member of the A. F. & A. M. at Waleska, and both he and Mrs. Harmon joined the Methodist Church many years ago. They lived together happily for 56 years. Mr. Harmon died Apr. 22, 1931.

Their children are: Mrs. Arilla Elrod, b. 1876; Mrs. Florrie Anderson, b. 1878; Fred, b. 1881; Mrs. Agnes Smith, b. 1883; Ethel, b. 1891; Mrs. Bessie Guyton, b. 1888; Samuel G., b. 1893; Mrs. Daisy Bell Thompson, b. 1900; and Frank, b. 1902.

HILLHOUSE, SAMUEL MCKAY

Holly Springs. Born June 2, 1868, in Cherokee Co. Son of Samuel Wilson Hillhouse Jr. who was a son of Samuel W. Hillhouse Sr., who was a son of Abraham Hillhouse, of Sussex, England.

Samuel W. Hillhouse Jr. came with his parents to Spartanburg, S. C., about 1830, and in the same year John Cole, of Scottish descent, came to that place. In 1836 Samuel W. Hillhouse Sr. and John Cole moved to Cherokee Co. and settled near the present Holly Springs. In the '40's Samuel W. Hillhouse Jr. and Augusta Ann Cole, daughter of John Cole, were married by William W. Fleming, Esq. Samuel W.

Hillhouse Jr. was a Mexican War soldier; he also served in the Confederate Army for four years.

Samuel McKay Hillhouse is a justice of the peace and was county surveyor in 1916-20. He married, on Dec. 21, 1891, Mary Elizabeth Howard, daughter of Oliver Howard and granddaughter of Jesse McCollum, an old settler of near Univeter. Children: Samuel Oliver Hillhouse (died Sep. 24, 1918, in England, while serving in the A. E. F.; buried in the Hillhouse family cemetery at Holly Springs); Mary (Mrs. N. J. Maddox); William A. (Rev.); Coleman F.; Jessie M.; Alice (Mrs. Boyd Chumley); Sarah (Mrs. Otis Chumley); Minnie (Mrs. Lee Taylor); Alma (Mrs. Reynold Phillips); Adah (Mrs. Vincie Jackson); Frank; Howard Lee.

HOGAN, ALTON PAUL

Canton. Son of Paul and Alice Heard Hogan, both of old Cherokee Co. families. Grandson of Dr. T. W. Hogan, Canton's first dentist.

Attended Canton High School and Mercer University. On graduation took position as overseer in Canton Cotton Mills, which position he now holds. Mason; Red Man.

Married, Sep. 3, 1931, Helen Wilkins, b. Nov. 5, 1905, daughter of Mr. and Mrs. W. G. Wilkins, of Forsyth Co. Mrs. Hogan attended the Fayetteville schools, G. S. T. C. at Athens, and University of Georgia (degree of B.S. in home economics). She taught school in Mansfield, Ga.; was later home demonstration agent in White Co. for 3 years; then home demonstration agent for Cherokee Co. 2 years, being the first to hold that position in Cherokee Co.

Mr. and Mrs. Hogan are both members of the First Baptist Church of Canton and take a prominent part in civic affairs.

HOLCOMB, JAMES H.

Ball Ground. Born 1876 in Conn's Creek District, Cherokee Co. Son of B. F. Holcomb and Elsie Conn Holcomb; grandson of Thomas H. Holcomb and of Samuel Conn; great-grandson of Henry Holcomb.

Henry and Thomas H. Holcomb came from North Carolina during Indian days and settled on Conn's Creek. B. F. Holcomb fought in the Confederate Army; he is still living at the age of 84; has reared nineteen children, producing nearly all they used; remembers a trade between his early neighbors, the Hendrixes and the Tates, for much of the land now comprising the Tate marble quarries.

Samuel Conn also came to Cherokee Co. from North Carolina during the early '30's, and Conn's Creek, Conn's District, a church and a schoolhouse were later named for him. He obtained a large tract of land on the upper Etowah from the Indians, trading them a pony for it. Several of the Conns had Civil War records.

James H. Holcomb was educated in the public schools of the county, farmed in early life, was in business with A. W. Roberts in Ball Ground for 12 years. He is now county commissioner of roads and revenues, and has been reelected for 1932-36. He is a Mason and an active member of the Baptist Church.

In 1895 he married Caroline Donald, daughter of Malcom Donald, and five children were born to them: Edgar, Greely, Glenn, Clifton, and James H. Jr. After her death he married Alva Wheeler, daughter of Francis Wheeler; and after her death he married Asalie Godfrey, daughter of Elbert Godfrey, and they have four children: Hulon, Roy, Elsie, and Grady.

HUGHES, ELLIS M.

Canton. Born Mar. 25, 1880, in Forsyth Co. Son of Lebius B. Hughes (Methodist local preacher of Cherokee Co.; founded Hughes Schoolhouse near Sutallee; held several county offices), and Florenda Knox Hughes, of a pioneer family.

Married, in November 1916, Rose Garrison, a descendant of the noted Cherokee Co. Garrison family, and the granddaughter of Capt. Nehemiah J. Garrison. The old Garrison home in Canton was rebuilt from the old Methodist Church. During the Civil War Federal soldiers attempted to burn this home but were persuaded by the entreaties of Mrs. Barbara Jamison Garrison to let it stand.

Mr. and Mrs. Hughes are active members of the Methodist Church. He is a member of the A. F. & A. M. in Canton, and is employed in the government mail service. Their children are: James, b. 1919; Rosemary, b. 1922; and Robert, b. 1925.

JOHNSON, ELIZABETH CARMICHAEL (MRS. WILLIAM J.)

Lebanon. Born 1869 in Cherokee Co. Daughter of Joseph L. Carmichael (b. 1832 in Cherokee Co.; farmer; Confederate soldier) and Mary Spears Carmichael (b. 1834 in South Carolina; sister of Joshua Spears, former sheriff of Cherokee Co.). Granddaughter of William C. Carmichael (b. 1802; d. 1887) and Nancy Carmichael (b. 1803). The Carmichaels moved from South Carolina to Cherokee Co. in the '40's and the Spears family came from that state shortly before the Civil War.

Elizabeth Carmichael was married in 1888 to William Jefferson Johnson, who was the son of James H. Johnson (b. 1830; Confederate soldier from Cherokee Co.; d. 1887) and Lavinia Berry Johnson (b. 1840); the grandson of James Jordan (who came from England to South Carolina in an early day) and of James Berry (former judge of the Blue Ridge Circuit); and a cousin of Rev. R. I. Johnson (noted Methodist preacher). Mr. Johnson died in 1913.

The children of Mr. and Mrs. William Jefferson Johnson: Mattie (Mrs. J. F. Grisham, married 1910); Annie (Mrs. J. F. Childers, married 1914); Carl Butler (married Beulah Bell Green in 1931); Madie (Mrs. E. M. Barrett, married 1921); (Miss) Mamie, of Lebanon; Floyd (married May Kitchens in 1931). There are thirteen grandchildren. All the family are members of Lebanon Methodist Church.

JOHNSTON, ELIZABETH HASTINGS BROOKE (MRS. JOSEPH E.)

Canton. Born Dec. 31, 1869. Daughter of George Washington Brooke (b. 1829 in Hall County; enlisted in Co. G, 3d Ga. Reg. of cavalry; was taken prisoner at Dalton, Ga., and held till the close of the Civil War; was a deacon in the Baptist Church; d. November 1912) and Mary Dial Brooke (of

Cherokee Co.). Granddaughter of John Prescott Brooke (b. Feb. 26, 1795, on the Atlantic Ocean while his parents were sailing to American from Knox County, Ireland; moved from South Carolina to Hall Co., Ga., thence to Cherokee Co.; twice in legislature from Hall Co.; militia colonel; inspector-general, Hall, Habersham and Rabun Counties; helped to establish Canton; second sheriff of Cherokee Co., 1833; d. 1880, buried at Sixes Cemetery), and Hester Bennett (of South Carolina; mar-

ONE OF CHEROKEE'S OLDEST CITIZENS. Mrs. George W. Brooke, of Canton, at the age of 95. Mrs. Brooke and her husband both came from settler families of Cherokee County.

ried 1812), and of Joseph L. Dial (early Cherokee Co. settler from South Carolina) and Aralinta Dial.

Married, in 1891, to Joseph E. Johnston, son of J. W. Johnston (moved from South Carolina to Milton Co. in the early '60's; served during the Civil War as enlisting first lieutenant, Ga. Hdqrs., 6th Enrollment), and Mary Yancey (of South Carolina); is vice-president of Jones Mercantile Co., Canton.

Mr. and Mrs. Johnston are members of the First Baptist Church of Canton. They have five children: George Edwin, Tully Joe, J. Brooke, Myrtle, and Bess.

JOHNSTON, JOHN H.

Woodstock. Born Apr. 24, 1855. Son of D. M. Johnston and Elizabeth Sledge Johnston. Grandson of James Johnston.

D. M. Johnston came to Cherokee Co. from Warren County, N. C., in 1836, bringing his family and thirteen slaves in wagons and settled near Hickory Flat. His sons were Alfred, Jack, William, James, and John H.; the first four served in the Civil War, Jack dying while in service. After the war, the family suffered reverses, the father died.

John H. Johnston came to Woodstock in 1887 and opened a general mercantile store, now an extensive business and one of the oldest in the county. Mr. Johnston is president of the Bank of Woodstock, a director in the Bank of Canton, president of Cherokee Cotton Rope Mill, founder and president of J. H. Johnston Co., chairman of the board of stewards of Woodstock Methodist Church (which he helped to organize in 1889), chairman of the Ninth Congressional District Democratic Committee.

Married, in February 1877, Sarah Avis Benson, descendant of a pioneer family of Cherokee Co. Their children are: W. A., of California; J. W., of Chattanooga, Tenn.; Smith L., of Woodstock; Joseph E., of Woodstock; Ava Elizabeth (Mrs. J. W. Bradley), of Chattanooga; Hugh Lee, of Woodstock; and Jack H., of Chattanooga. There were three other children, Connie and Albert Sidney, who died when children, and Luther, who died in 1917 at the age of 35.

JOHNSTON, SMITH L.

Woodstock. Born 1887 in Cobb Co. Son of J. H. Johnston (see account of) and Avis Benson Johnston, who was born near Woodstock. Parents moved to Cherokee Co. in the same year he was born.

Married, in 1917, Florine Dial, of a pioneer Cherokee Co. family. Children: Smith L. Jr. b. 1918; Harold Sledge, b. 1920; Richard, b. 1923.

Mr. Johnston attended the public schools of the county

and Young Harris College; Mrs. Johnston is a graduate of G. S. C. W., at Milledgeville. They are both Methodists. Mr. Johnston is a former mayor of Woodstock, a member of the Woodstock school board, a member of the firm of J. H. Johnston Co., vice-president of Bank of Woodstock, and district lay leader, Marietta District, M. E. C. S.

JONES, ALBERT VAUGHAN

Canton. Born Aug. 7, 1886, in Canton. Son of Robert Tyre Jones Sr. and Susie Walker Jones. (For family history, see account of Robert Tyre Jones Sr.)

Attended Canton public schools and Georgia School of Technology. Is president, Continental Marble & Granite Co. Member, First Baptist Church of Canton; president, R. T. Jones Bible Class. Mason, 32d degree; Shriner. President, Canton board of education. President, Canton Chamber of Commerce. Chairman Cherokee Co. jury revising committee. Chairman, Canton democratic committee.

Married, Jan. 8, 1907, in Atlanta, Ella Grady Perry, daughter of Benjamin Franklin Perry Sr. and Addie Blanche Upshaw Perry. (For family history, see account of Ben F. Perry.)

The children of Mr. and Mrs. A. V. Jones are: Albert V. Jr., Blanche, Robert, and Ben.

JONES, BAKER ROGERS

Ball Ground. Born Nov. 15, 1889, in Terrell Co. Son of John S. Jones (b. in Webster Co.; moved early to Terrell Co., where he held county office and was a much esteemed citizen) and Anna Jones.

Educated in the public schools of Terrell Co. and at Norman Institute, a junior college at Norman Park. Has held positions with various banks; is now cashier of Citizens Bank of Ball Ground. During the World War, was prominently identified with local war work committees. Has been a member of the Baptist Church for 26 years; is a deacon and Sunday School teacher in Ball Ground Baptist Church. Scoutmaster. Treasurer, Ball Ground city council. Mason; secretary of Ball Ground Lodge No. 261.

Married, Feb. 19, 1914, Mae Cunningham, daughter of R. L. and Susan E. Cunningham. Mr. and Mrs. Jones have one daughter, Catharine, b. 1917.

JONES, LOUIS L.

Canton. Born Mar. 24, 1890, in Canton. Son of Robert Tyre Jones (see account of) and Susie Walker Jones. Attended Canton High School; graduated Virginia Military Institute, Lexington, Va., 1909. Married, Nov. 28, 1912, Jesse Pearl Turner of Dawson, Ga. (related to the Baldwin family of Terrell Co.) Children: Louis L. Jr. b. 1913; Sarah, b. 1916; Turner, b. 1918; Peggy, b. 1920.

Has been connected with Canton Cotton Mills since 1909; now vice-president and general manager. Organized new mill, 1924. Director, Bank of Canton, Jones Mercantile Co., Canton Cotton Mills. Member, Canton city council, city water and light commission. York and Scottish Rite Mason; Shriner; Odd Fellow; Red Man; Jr. Order. Deacon, clerk and treasurer of First Baptist Church, Canton, of which his family also are members. Has been the teacher of R. T. Jones Bible Class for 14 years.

JONES, PAUL WALKER

Canton. Born July 14, 1881, at Canton. Son of Robert Tyre Jones Sr. and Susie Walker Jones. (For family history see account of Robert Tyre Jones Sr.)

Attended the public schools of Canton. Married, Feb. 14, 1907, at Cartersville, Mary Foute, daughter of Judge A. M. and Mrs. Laura Foute, of Cartersville.

President, Jones Mercantile Co. Scottish Rite Mason; Shriner. Member, First Baptist Church of Canton.

Children of Mr. and Mrs. P. W. Jones: Sue, b. November 1907; Paul Walker Jr., b. November 1909; Augustus Foute, b. December 1911; Thomas, b. March 1914; Mary, b. July 1915.

JONES, ROBERT TYRE (SR.)

Canton. Born Oct. 27, 1849, in Newton Co. Son of William Green Jones (b. Dec. 13, 1822, in Newton Co.) and Emily Frances

Chaffin Jones (b. Feb. 6, 1825, in Newton Co.). Grandson of Micajah Jones and of Tyre Chaffin.

Mr. Jones attended the public schools of Newton Co. and Moore's Business College in Atlanta. He came to Canton in 1879 and started a mercantile business, which has grown into the present Jones Mercantile Co., the largest business of its kind in North Georgia. Mr. Jones was instrumental in organizing the Bank of Canton in 1893 and the Canton Cotton Mills in 1899, and is president of both. In addition to being one of the state's best known business men, he is active in religious affairs. He has been a member of the Baptist Church since 1873, a deacon in the First Baptist Church of Canton since December, 1881, and superintendent of the Sunday-school of that church since January, 1888. Mr. Jones has also been a Mason since 1883.

In 1878 he married Susie Walker and eleven children were born to this union: Robert P., of Atlanta; Paul W. (see account of); Emily Foster (Mrs. G. W. Brooke); May Reynolds; Albert Vaughan (see account of); William Green (decd.); Louis Lindley (see account of); Susie Walker (decd.); Jack Walker; Horace Edwin; and Ruth (decd.).

On April 18, 1901, Mr. Jones married Lillie Coggins Cross, who came from a pioneer family of Cherokee Co. Their children are: Eleanor Frances (Mrs. A. C. Reed); Rube Coggins (see account of); Louise Coggins (Mrs. John S. Wood); and Robert Tyre Jr.

JONES, RUBE C.

Canton. Born Aug. 31, 1903, in Canton. Son of R. T. Jones (see account of) and Lillie Coggins Jones. Attended Canton High School, G. M. A., and Georgia Tech. Married, in 1924, Nina Thompson, of Madison, Fla. Children: Jane, b. July 1926; Anne, b. April 1931.

Mr. Jones is an official of the Canton Cotton Mills. He is a Mason; a Knight Templar, Constantine Commandery; and a member of the Baptist Church. Mrs. Jones is a Methodist.

KNOX, JOSEPH W.

Born Feb. 9, 1846, in Cherokee Co. Son of Joseph Knox (b. Aug. 14, 1812, in Pendleton District, S. C.; d. Mar. 3, 1886, in Cherokee Co., Ga.) and Malissa Brooke (b. June 28, 1815,; m. Apr. 3, 1836; d. Aug. 8, 1885). Grandson of James and Mary Ann Abbott Knox.

The Knox family and descendants have long been prominently identified with Cherokee Co. James Knox, who is said to have been related to the Rev. John Knox of Scotland, came from that country about 1800 and settled in South Carolina, first in Pendleton and later in Pickens District. His wife, Mary Ann, was the daughter of Jackson Abbott. To this union were born ten children: William, James, Matthew, John, Robert, Joseph, Drewery, Benson, Polly, and Sallie Ann.

Joseph Knox, one of the sons, came to Cherokee Co. in 1834 and became Canton's first school teacher. There on Apr. 3, 1836, he was married to Malissa Brooke, of another very early family of the county, the ceremony being performed by Judge Joseph Donaldson. Joseph Knox settled near Sutallee, where there has been a Knox cemetery since 1850, and where a reunion of the numerous Knox descendants is held each August. The children of Joseph and Malissa Brooke Knox were: Frances, John B., Mary Ann, Willis Truman, Sarah Malissa, Joseph W., Buena Vista, Montery, Evalen Florida, William George, Jefferson D., and Esther.

Joseph W. Knox, one of these sons and subject of this sketch, was for 29 years county surveyor of Cherokee Co. He is now 86 years old and lives in Sutallee District on the land where he was born and reared. He married, on Jan. 2, 1868, Eugenia Stone, of Cherokee Co., who was born Feb. 4, 1851. Their children: Ida Ann, b. 1869; Sallie, b. 1872; James Marshal, b. 1874; Osie B., b. 1877; Mary Eva, b. 1881; Joseph Chester, b. 1883; Naomi Eugenia, b. 1886; Hubert and Robert, b. 1890; George, b. 1893.

Mr. Knox, two brothers (Benson and Willis Truman), and their father all served in the Confederate Army, and all returned safely from the war.

LANDRUM, EMILY BELLE (MISS)

Waleska. Daughter of Rev. Larkin LaFayette Landrum and Minnie Q. Wilson Landrum. Granddaughter of Larkin LaFayette Landrum Sr. and Lucinda Isabella Brown Landrum.

Rev. L. L. Landrum was born at Alexander, Morgan Co., on Sep. 27, 1868, the first of seven children. His parents were loyal members of the Methodist Church. He was called to preach in early manhood. First an exhorter for 4 years, he was licensed a Methodist preacher in 1898, and served as supply for Lumpkin Mission and later Rabun Gap. Admitted to the itinerancy in 1901, he served the following appointments from that time on: Rabun Gap, 1902; North Coweta Mission, 1903-04; Ellijay, 1905-06; Glenn, 1907; Turin, 1908-09; West Point Circuit, 1910-12; Locust Grove, 1913-14; Dacula, 1915-16; Homer, 1917-18; Chickamauga, 1919. His ordinations were: deacon, by Bishop Candler, Nov. 23, 1902; elder, by Bishop Ward, Nov. 24, 1907.

His health failing in August, 1919, Rev. Mr. Landrum was superannuated at the following annual conference, after a ministry of splendid usefulness and power. He retired to his little farm in Fayette Co., where he died on July 18, 1926.

He was survived by Mrs. Landrum, the former Minnie Quintilla Wilson, of Madras, Ga., whom he married Jan. 17, 1901, and by their six children: Emily Belle, Quintilla Ruth, Mary Grace, Berta Eula, Seth Wilson, and Pierce LaFayette.

LATHEM, E. M.

Orange, Ga. Born Feb. 10, 1883, at Orange. Son of William A. Lathem (b. Sep. 28, 1857, at Orange) and Arazona Davis (b. June 25, 1858, at Orange). Grandson of Andrew J. (Bud) Lathem and Louisa Lathem, and of Frank Davis and Obediance Davis; all the grandparents were born in South Carolina.

The Lathems, one of the oldest and largest families in Cherokee Co., trace their ancestry back to Sam Lathem, who came from England to South Carolina shortly before 1800. One of his sons, Jack, came to Georgia in 1834 and settled in the eastern part of Cherokee Co., with his wife and eight children—John, George, Martha, Perry, Richard, Sam, Andrew, and Jane. All the children were members of the church and became useful citizens. John and Bud became preachers—Baptist and Methodist, respectively. William A. Lathem, son of Andrew (Bud), established at Orange over 25 years ago the mercantile firm of W. A. Lathem & Sons, which now serves a large country trade.

E. M. Lathem is manager and part owner of this firm. He is also a steward in Orange Methodist Church and chairman of the board of trustees of Free Home High School. He married, in December, 1906, at Buffington, Ga., Georgia Bell, daughter of Robert G. Bell, of Buffington. They have six children, Grace, Ruth, George, Francis, Katie, and Loyce.

LEWIS, HENRY WARREN

Canton. Born Mar. 8, 1876, in Bartow Co. Son of John W. Lewis (b. 1848 in Bartow Co.; farmer) and Nancy Thomas Lewis (m. 1869). Grandson of Thomas Alfred Lewis, a well-known early Methodist minister, and Lucy Duncan of South Carolina; and of Alfred and Nancy Thomas, who came from South Carolina to Bartow Co.

Mr. Lewis is engaged in the mercantile business at Canton. He is an active Methodist, and superintendent of the Sunday-school at Sixes.

On Dec. 26, 1901, in Cherokee Co., he married Ada A. Wiley, daughter of Orsborne Reece Wiley and Lavonia Mullins Wiley. Mrs. Lewis' grandfather, William F. Mullins, was a captain in the Confederate Army and also spent two years in California during the Gold Rush of 1849. He married Elizabeth Taylor.

The children of Mr. and Mrs. Henry W. Lewis: Myrtle (Mrs. Charles Fowler); Roger (married Ella Holcombe); Mabel; Florine (Mrs. Elbert Keeter); Reba (Mrs. Howard Sams).

McCANLESS, EDGAR MAXWELL

Canton. Born 1898 in Cherokee Co. Son of Eugene Augustus McCanless (see account of) and Henrietta Kitchens McCanless. Attended Canton High School, Georgia Military College, and University of Georgia (degree of LL.B., 1921). Admitted to bar, 1921. Served in U. S. Navy, World War. Mayor of Canton, 1927. Past commander, Thomas M. Brady

Post, American Legion; Service Officer, same. Scottish Rite Mason; Shriner. Deacon in the Baptist Church. Now practicing law in Canton.

Married Ruth Pund, of Augusta, Ga. Children: Edgar and Charles.

McCANLESS, EUGENE AUGUSTUS

Canton. Born 1877 in Cherokee Co. Son of Jesse Andrew McCanless (b. in Cherokee Co.; millwright, built many mills in North Georgia; served 4 years in the Confederate Army; was wounded three times), and Sarah Barton McCanless (of a pioneer Bartow Co. family). Grandson of William K. McCanless (also a pioneer millwright; helped to organize Bascomb Methodist Church in his home, where early services were held).

Attended Reinhardt College. Married, in 1898, Henrietta Kitchen, of Cherokee Co. Children: Edgar Maxwell, b. 1898; William Jesse; b. 1903; Katherine, b. 1900, d. 1920.

President and general manager, The Georgia Marble Finishing Works, Canton; has been connected with this company for 32 years. Former member, Canton city council; commissioner of water and lights, Canton; chairman, committee on building new courthouse; former mayor of Canton (four terms); vice-president, Bank of Canton. Scottish Rite Mason; Knight Commander, Court of Honor; Shriner; Odd Fellow; Red Man; Junior Order; K. of P. Deacon in the Baptist Church.

McCANLESS, LEE

Canton. Born Feb. 20, 1887, in Cherokee Co., two miles south of Waleska. Son of Jesse Andrew McCanless and Sarah Barton McCanless. Grandson of William K. McCanless. (See account of E. A. McCanless.)

Attended Reinhardt College. Married, in 1910, Pearl Doss, daughter of L. J. Doss, of Cherokee Co. Children: Jesse Luke, Lemuel Lee, Virginia Jean, James Thomas. Married, in 1927, Kathleen Thomas, daughter of William M. Thomas, of Cherokee Co.

Mr. McCanless is secretary of The Georgia Marble Finishing Works at Canton. He is a Scottish Rite Mason and a member of the Baptist Church.

McCLURE, ALFRED W.

Canton. Born Aug. 11, 1884, in Canton. Son of Adolphus N. McClure (b. June 20, 1851, in Cherokee Co.) and Mary Wright McClure (b. Feb. 5, 1852, in Gordon Co., Ga.). Grandson of Rev. Charles Marshall McClure and Piety Burtz McClure, and of Alfred Wright and Polly Poole Wright.

Rev. Charles M. McClure, who was born in Pickens Co., S. C., and came at an early age to that part of Cherokee Co., Ga., which was later cut off to form Pickens, was the first ordinary of Pickens and later served two terms as ordinary of Cherokee. He was also a local Methodist preacher, a leading educator of his day, and a merchant in Canton. During the Civil War he served in the Home Guards under Major Evans. He was survived by five children, one of whom, Adolphus, was the father of the subject of this sketch.

Alfred W. McClure married, on June 15, 1921, Kate Faulkner, of Ball Ground, daughter of Charles J. Faulkner (see account of) and May McClure Faulkner; and granddaughter of James Faulkner, who came to the U. S. in 1837 from Ireland. Mr. and Mrs. McClure have three children: Charles Alfred, b. Mar. 21, 1923; Joseph Adolphus, b. Apr. 3, 1928; Cleomae, b. Apr. 19, 1930.

Mr. McClure is a Methodist; a Mason, Odd Fellow, and W. O. W.; and is engaged in the mercantile business in Canton.

McCLURE, LAURA VIRGINIA HOLLEN (MRS. L. A.)

Canton. Born Aug. 1868, in Kingston, Gordon Co. Daughter of Peter M. Hollen (b. 1838 in Rockingham Co., Va.) and Emma Speck Hollen (b. 1840 in the same county). Granddaughter of Eli Hollen and Catherine Shinkle Hollen, and of Barnett Rader Speck and Elizabeth Koogler Speck, all natives of Virginia.

Peter M. Hollen served under "Stonewall" Jackson in Co. D, 10th Reg., Va. Inf. Shortly after the Civil War he moved to Cherokee Co., Ga., where he pursued a contracting business, building houses and fine furniture. Mr. and Mrs. Hollen had three daughters and one son.

Laura Virginia Hollen was married, June 26, 1890, at Canton, to Levi Alonzo McClure, b. Feb. 10, 1861, in Pickens Co., son of Rev. Charles Marshall McClure (see account of Alfred W. McClure) and Piety Burtz McClure. Mr. McClure was a general merchant at Ball Ground and later became connected with the Bank of Canton. He united in early youth with the Methodist Church and was officially connected with it during the rest of his life, serving as superintendent of the Ball Ground, Waleska, and Canton Sunday schools. Mrs. McClure also is a Methodist.

The children of Mr. and Mrs. L. A. McClure: Ouida (Mrs. Edward Yonkman, of Detroit, Mich.); Rochelle (clerk, Canton postoffice); Rhodes (served in A. E. F., Co. B, 106th F. S. Battalion; married Miss Johnye Steed of Etowah, Tenn.); Emma Dale (teacher, Canton public schools).

McWHORTER, C. T.

Ball Ground. Born 1894 at Mannsville, Ky. Son of J. D. McWhorter and Emma Mann McWhorter, both of whom came from pioneer families of Kentucky and Virginia. The McWhorters are of Scotch descent; the Manns of English.

In 1923 C. T. McWhorter married Lucile Kilby, of Cherokee Co., who is also of distinguished ancestry, being descended from the pioneer Barton and Daniel families of North Georgia.

Mr. McWhorter attended the public schools of Kentucky; began a railroad career in 1912; has been employed since then by the L. & N. R. R., for which railroad he is agent at Ball Ground. World War veteran; served in U. S. Navy. Commander, Thomas M. Brady Post, American Legion. Local chairman, Agents & Operators Union. Former mayor of Ball Ground. Methodist; steward and assistant superintendent of the Sunday School at Ball Ground.

MAHAN, SIDNEY DAVID

Salacoa. Born 1862 in Cherokee Co. Son of William T. Mahan (b. Oct. 10, 1822, in Pittsylvania Co., Va.) and Jenetta Reynolds Mahan (married July 24, 1845). Grandson of W. S.

Mahan (b. 1793, of English and Irish descent) and Peggy Wright Mahan (b. 1792 of an old Virginia family of Irish ancestry; d. 1862). Great-grandson of Thomas Wright, who was a Revolutionary soldier.

William T. Mahan came from Virginia to Cherokee Co. in 1850 and settled in the Salacoa Valley, along with other Virginia families who moved there about the same time. His brother, Tom Mahan, served in the Mexican War, and three other brothers, Calvin, Joe, and Coleman, fought in the Civil War. William T. Mahan was a miller and a justice of the peace; was widely known for charity and benevolence; was a Mason and a member of Fairview Methodist Church.

Sidney D. Mahan married, in 1890, Cleo Boston, who was born in 1874 and is the daughter of Jerome and Elizabeth Wilson Boston. Jerome Boston, born in North Carolina of Dutch descent, came in his youth to Cherokee Co., where he lived to the age of 75. His brother John married a sister of Gov. Joseph E. Brown.

The children of Mr. and Mrs. Mahan: Thomas, Y. O., Clyde, Gladys, Joe, David, Julius, Cleo. The family are all members of Fairview Methodist Church. Mr. Mahan is a substantial farmer, and Mrs. Mahan is an active church worker of wide influence.

MOORE, RUSSELL MALACHI (DR.)

Waleska. Born 1863 in Cherokee Co. Son of John K. Moore (b. 1815 in Hall Co.; moved to Cherokee Co. about 1835; taught school; farmed; founded Moore's Mill and the old postoffice of that name where he was for many years postmaster; deacon in Shoal Creek Baptist Church; Confederate soldier) and Frances Independence Garrison Moore (b. July 4, 1826, in South Carolina). Grandson of Moren Moore (noted layman and writer of Baptist literature), and of Capt. Nehemiah Garrison (b. 1776 on Dan River in Virginia; moved with father to Greenville District, S. C.; moved to Hall Co., Ga., as one of first settlers there; served as captain in the War of 1812; represented Hall Co. in legislature; moved to Cherokee Co. near Fort Buffington; helped remove Indians in 1838), and Sallie Evans Garrison (b. 1774; daughter of Judge Evans of South Carolina; married 1799).

Nephew of John B. Garrison (b. 1807; sheriff of Cherokee Co., 1838-40; son of Nehemiah Garrison) and of Judge Garrison (Mexican War soldier; Methodist minister; Confederate soldier; son of Nehemiah Garrison).

Attended public schools of Cherokee Co.; graduated at Georgia Eclectic Medical College, Atlanta, in 1885; has practiced in Cherokee Co. ever since. Represented the county in legislature, 1905-08. Member of commission to build present courthouse, 1929. Member, county board of education. Secretary, board of trustees of Reinhardt College; has been officially connected with this school since its origin. Former mayor of Waleska. Deacon in Shoal Creek Baptist Church.

Married, in 1890, Lucy Sharp, of Cherokee Co., daughter of White Sharp and a descendant of the pioneer Sharp and Reinhardt families. Children: Juanita, Max, Claire, and Wilton.

MOORE, THOMPSON, Children of

Born in 1829 in Gwinnett Co., Thompson Moore was the son of Abram Moore and Rebecca Haley; his father had come from South Carolina and his mother from Franklin Co. In 1851 Thompson Moore married Amanda King (b. 1833; daughter of John and Kezia King, who had come from Virginia and South Carolina) and the following year he moved to Cherokee Co., where he acquired land and became a successful planter. Mr. Moore joined the 56th Ga. Reg., Confederate Army, in 1863, enlisting at Big Shanty; after serving honorably until the close of the war he was discharged at Kingston, in 1865. He finished out his long and useful life in 1905, and Mrs. Moore followed him in 1926.

The children of Mr. and Mrs. Thompson Moore: John T. Moore, b. 1852, d. 1930; Mrs. Julia Thomas, b. 1854, d. 1924; James L. Moore, b. 1856, d. 1926; Mrs. Mary Jameson, b. 1858; William A. Moore, b. 1861, d. 1878; Miss Savila Moore, b. 1870; Mrs. Lillie Forrester, b. 1872.

All the children joined the Methodist Church in early youth, except James L. who became a Presbyterian. In the J. L. Moore family are four grandchildren; in the Thomas family, nine. The present Moore home is located two miles from Hickory Flat, and is one of the most beautiful country homes in the county.

JOHN T. MOORE RESIDENCE, NEAR HICKORY FLAT

Moss, Theodore P.

Waleska. Born Sep. 15, 1877, in Cherokee Co. Son of John B. Moss, who came to Cherokee Co. from South Carolina about 1840, and Volumnia Moore Moss, who descended from the prominent Cherokee Co. Garrison family.

Married, in 1909, Eltha Stone, b. 1889 in Cherokee Co., daughter of Augustus Stone, originally of Bartow Co., and Esther Knox Stone; and granddaughter of Joseph Knox, early settler, and Malissa Brooke Knox. Mrs. Moss is also the great-granddaughter of John P. and Hester Bennett Brooke and of James and Mary Ann Abbott Knox. (For Brooke family history, see account

of Mrs. Joseph E. Johnston; for Knox history, account of Joseph
W. Knox.)

Mr. Moss is a member of Shoal Creek Baptist Church; Mrs.
Moss belongs to Waleska Methodist Church. Their children are:
Elizabeth (b. 1910; graduated at Reinhardt College in 1928, at
LaGrange College in 1930; teacher) and Rachel (b. 1916).

PERRY, BEN F.

Ball Ground. Born June 14, 1883, in Canton. Son of Benjamin Franklin Perry Sr. (b. July 27, 1859, in Marietta), and
Addie Blanche Upshaw Perry (b. in Alabama; married June
24, 1880). Grandson of Anselum Roe Perry (b. Mar. 30, 1826,
in South Carolina; d. 1872) and Parthenia Adeline Gault Perry,
and of John R. Upshaw, of Alabama. Great-grandson of
Joseph Gault, of Marietta.

Ben F. Perry Sr. was perhaps most widely known through
his editorship of the *Cherokee Advance*, which he founded in
1880, at the age of twenty, in Canton. With a limited education, he made the *Advance* one of Georgia's leading country
weeklies and earned high rank in journalism and the esteem of
everyone who knew him. Helped to organize Bank of Canton,
of which he later became cashier. Appointed postmaster at
Canton, 1893. Made assistant state treasurer at Atlanta, 1908;
served under Capt. R. E. Park, Capt. Speirs, and J. Polk
Brown; was later appointed state bank examiner; afterwards
formed the Realty Trust Company with J. Polk Brown. Mr.
Perry was a Mason, an Odd Fellow, and a leader in the Methodist Church, being superintendent of Canton Sunday School
and a steward for many years. He died in 1916 and was buried
in Canton.

Ben F. Perry Jr. was educated in the public schools of Canton and a business college in Atlanta. At an early age, became secretary to Hon. Carter Tate, then in Congress from the
Ninth District. Later edited the *Cherokee Advance* for several
years. Was stationed at Newport News, Va., during the World
War, as chief voucher clerk on projects for which expendi-
tures totaled $22,000,000 in two years. Detailed to Washing-

ton, D. C., at the close of the war; came from there to Ball Ground and organized the Atlas Marble Co., of which he is president and general manager. Mason; Odd Fellow; K. of P.; W. O. W.; Elk; Maccabee. Methodist since youth; steward and Sunday School superintendent. Has served on Democratic senatorial committee for several years and as mayor and councilman of Ball Ground.

Married, in 1911, Grady Whitley, of Douglasville, daughter of Dr. T. R. Whitley, Douglasville physician and legislator. Mrs. Perry is also an active Methodist and is president of the Woman's Missionary Society at Ball Ground.

PETTIS, JAMES OSCAR (REV.)

Canton. Born in Twiggs Co., Ga., 1875. Son of Elijah F. Pettis (pioneer sheriff of Twiggs Co.; Confederate soldier), and Joannah Pettis. Married Sarah Munro of Columbus, Ga., daughter of C. Warn Munro and Georgia Bilbro Munro, pioneer family of Muscogee Co.

Graduated at University of Georgia, A.B. degree; took graduate work at Columbia University. Taught 14 years in Georgia public schools, one year at LaGrange College. Member of North Georgia Conference, M. E. C. S., for last 19 years; charges include Adairsville, East Rome, Greenville, Palmetto, Senoia, Canton. Now serving fifth year as beloved pastor of Canton Methodist Church.

PONDER, THOMAS J.

Canton. Born Sept. 6, 1868, in Cherokee Co. Son of William Franklin Ponder (b. Feb. 1836; of English descent; Confederate soldier; returned from War in safety) and Mary Jane Weaver Ponder (b. Apr. 29, 1844). Grandson of Ransom Ponder (b. 1799; lived in North Carolina) and of David Weaver (Confederate soldier; killed in action; settled in Cherokee Co. during Indian days; also of English descent). Mr. Ponder's great-grandfather of the same surname immigrated to America from England in colonial days.

Mr. Ponder married, in 1891, Elizabeth James, of Forsyth Co., daughter of William T. and Mary Fowler James, a pioneer family of Forsyth Co.

He is superintendent of The Georgia Marble Finishing Works, and has been with that company since Mar. 18, 1895. Was a member of Canton city council for 8 years. Odd Fellow; Red Man. Deacon, First Baptist Church, Canton. Mrs. Ponder is a member of the same church.

POWER, WALTER DEAN

Woodstock. Born July 4, 1889, in Cobb Co. Son of Lawrence Monroe Power (b. July 8, 1848; in Cobb Co.; of a pioneer family of that county; farmer) and Elizabeth Wing Power (b. Dec. 6, 1856, at Roswell, Ga.). Grandson of Joseph Pinkney Power and Letha Manning Power, and of Jehu Wing and Mary Johnson Wing.

Mr. Power graduated from Reinhardt College in 1906 and later from the Atlanta College of Pharmacy, after which he engaged in the drug business. He is also a rural mail carrier at Woodstock. Mr. Power belongs to the Masonic fraternity and is a member of the Presbyterian Church.

On November 30, 1910, at Blackwells, Ga., he married Nellie Pearl Dobbs, daughter of John McCutcheon Dobbs and Florence Dawson Dobbs, and granddaughter of David W. Dobbs and Cynthia McCutcheon Dobbs and of William Pinkney Dawson and Jane McCleskey Dawson.

Mr. and Mrs. Power have three children: Nellie Marian, b. Mar. 29, 1913; Walter Dean Jr., b. July 30, 1917; and Irma Jeanne, b. May 22, 1924.

REDD, JOHN L.

Late of Waleska. Born Nov. 22, 1859, in Forsyth Co.; d. Nov. 17, 1931, at Waleska. Son of G. W. Redd (b. in Forsyth Co.; Civil War veteran; of a pioneer family from South Carolina) and Harriet Wingo Redd.

John L. Redd married Phœnicia Holbrook in 1880 in Forsyth Co., and later moved to Bartow Co., where he farmed on a large scale for several years, and then to Orange in Cherokee Co., where he entered the mercantile business. Five years later he removed to

Waleska to put his children in Reinhardt College. He served as mayor of Waleska for a time and was regarded as one of the town's most substantial citizens. Mr. Redd joined the Friendship Baptist Church, near Cumming, in early boyhood, and continued as an active church worker up to the time of his death in 1931. He was buried in Friendship Cemetery, in Forsyth Co.

The children of Mr. and Mrs. Redd are: E. P.; E. M.; Mittie (Mrs. Striplin); A. M.; J. C.; V. G.; and Maggie (Mrs. Brooks). There are several grandchildren. Mrs. Redd died August 27, 1927.

RICHARDSON, JOSEPH BASCOMB

Fairmount. Born Dec. 11, 1880, at Salacoa. Son of Eli B. Richardson and Agnes Elmyra Swann Richardson (b. May 21, 1855; m. Jan. 20, 1876; d. Sep. 15, 1931). Grandson of John Richardson (b. 1816) and Elizabeth Sphinx Richardson (b. 1822); and of Meredith and Jane Swann.

John Richardson, of Scotch Presbyterian stock, came from North Carolina to Cherokee Co. as a pioneer of the '40's, and the Richardson family has since been influential in the development of the Salacoa section. Eli B. Richardson was an officer of Fairview Methodist Church for many years.

Joseph Bascomb Richardson married, in 1900, Rachel Claribel Davidson, who was born in 1878 at Cassville, near Cartersville. She is the daughter of William D. Davidson, who immigrated from Scotland when a young man, and Rachel Posey Davidson; and the granddaughter of William and Agnes Mien Davidson. The Davidsons have long been identified with northwestern Bartow Co.

The children of Mr. and Mrs. Richardson are: Agnes Mabel (Mrs. David N. Vaughan), b. 1907 at Salacoa, A. B. LaGrange College; Hubert Andrew, b. 1913 at Salacoa, B. S. Georgia Tech; and Rachel Elizabeth, b. 1919 at Salacoa.

ROBERTS, ALTHEA GEORGIA ANN COGGINS (MRS. ALFRED W.)

Ball Ground. Born Mar. 28, 1861. Daughter of Alfred Burton Coggins (b. Oct. 22, 1838, in Gilmer Co.; merchant in Canton 16 years; Confederate soldier, Co. D, 6th Ga. Cavalry) and Mary Louise Smith Coggins (b. Mar. 11, 1844, at Morganton, Fannin Co.). Granddaughter of Jonathan Lilly Coggins (b. 1815 in Tennessee; early Gilmer Co. settler; d. 1890) and Mary Elizabeth King Coggins (b. 1808; d. 1874), and of John Balus Smith (b. 1814; d. 1857) and Rachel Mathilde Addington Smith (b. 1820; d. 1858). William Addington (b. 1759; d. 1846), Mrs. Roberts' great-great-grandfather, served in the Revolutionary War from Union District, S. C.

Althea Georgia Ann Coggins was married, Dec. 22, 1879, to Alfred Webb Roberts, by Rev. Alfred Webb. Mr. Roberts, a Confederate veteran, had come to Cherokee Co. with his father, Martin Roberts, from North Carolina, home of the Roberts family since colonial times. He engaged in the mercantile and real estate businesses in Ball Ground. He was a Mason and a member of the Baptist Church. Mr. Roberts died July 27, 1918.

The children of Mr. and Mrs. A. W. Roberts: Martin Clyde, b. 1880; Judson Brown, b. 1882; Alfred Roy, b. 1885; Augustus Paul, b. 1887; Carl Weldon, b. 1890; Lou Bernice, b. 1896; Aaron Webb, b. 1898. Mrs. Roberts is a Baptist, as are all her children except one. All the sons are interested in the Roberts Marble Co., Ball Ground, except Aaron W., who has a marble business in Dallas, Tex., Roberts Memorials, Inc.

ROBERTS, MARTHA OPHELIA CHAPMAN (MRS. LUTHER E.)

Marietta. Born Mar. 11, 1881, at Holly Springs. Daughter of A. Asbury Chapman (see account of) and Mary Susan Ragsdale Chapman. Granddaughter of Dudley and Margaret Chapman.

Married, Jan. 6, 1901, at Holly Springs, to Luther Edgar Roberts. The children of Mr. and Mrs. Roberts are: Lois, b. Nov. 11, 1902; Gladys, b. Mar. 7, 1904; Frances, b. Oct. 31, 1905; Martin Luther, b. Sep. 18, 1913; Thelma, b. May 1, 1915; Inez, b. Aug. 8, 1919.

The family are Methodists.

ROBERTS, MILDRED GALT (MRS. HENRY L.)

Canton. Born 1858 in Cherokee County. Daughter of Joel Lewis Galt and Malinda Grisham Galt; granddaughter of Jabez Galt and Frances Machen Galt, and of William Grisham and Susan Bradford Grisham.

The Galt family is of Scotch-Irish descent. They have been identified with Canton and vicinity for the last one hundred years. Jabez Galt came to Cherokee Co. from Spartanburg, S. C., in the early 1830's. Joel Galt served during the Civil War in the Cherokee Legion and was for many years a leading merchant in Canton.

The Grishams, of an old English family, came to Cherokee Co. from Decatur, Ga., to which they had immigrated from South Carolina before 1830. William Grisham started one of the silk industries from which Canton received its name, held county office several times, and helped to organize the Baptist Church in Canton, Aug. 20, 1833. For 94 years, except 3 months, some member of the Grisham family was clerk of this church. (See also account of Mrs. William Galt.)

Mildred Galt was married to Henry Lamar Roberts, a well-known and prosperous merchant of Cherokee Co., on Jan. 26, 1892, at Canton. Mr. Roberts was born at Stylesboro, Paulding Co., Ga., Oct. 7, 1853. He came to Cherokee Co. in 1882 and entered the mercantile business; and continued successfully in this business, locating in Canton, till his death on Nov. 26, 1919. He was also a large landowner and farmer. He was a Baptist, an active Mason and Shriner, and interested in educational work. On his father's side he was descended from the Roberts and Lamar families, prominent in the history of Georgia and other states; on his maternal side, from the Rogerses, Clarks, Glenns, and Samuels, many of whom were pioneers of the West.

The children of Mr. and Mrs. Roberts are Mary Glenn, Malinda, Adelaide, and Griffin Lamar, who is a prominent business man of Canton, having owned and operated an automobile business there for several years.

There are two grandchildren, Lamar Hudson and Sarah Joyce Roberts, children of Griffin L. and Sarah Hudson Roberts.

RUDASILL, JOHNNIE P.

Canton. Born Nov. 16, 1890, in Canton. Son of J. E. and Frances Rudasill. Grandson of Major Wesley B. C. Puckett, of Hickory Flat (who organized a Confederate company of cavalry in 1861, which later formed a part of Phillips Legion; was promoted to major and later to colonel; served with distinction until the surrender in 1865).

Married, at Opelika, Ala., Irene Puckett, daughter of Mr. and Mrs. S. M. Puckett.

Mr. Rudasill has been editor of the *Cherokee Advance* for 20 years, having purchased the paper in 1912 from the late Ben F. Perry. He is a Mason, Odd Fellow, and Red Man, and a member of the Baptist Church.

SHARP, RAMSEY COLQUITT

Canton. Born Nov. 9, 1870, in Waleska. Son of John James Augustus Sharp (b. 1828, in Pickens District, S. C.) and Mary Jane Reinhardt (b. June 17, 1840, in Cherokee Co.). Grandson of John Sharp (b. 1805 in North Carolina) and Catharine White Sharp (b. in South Carolina), and of Lewis Warlick Reinhardt (b. Sep. 2, 1804, in Lincoln Co., N. C.) and Jane Harbin Reinhardt (b. 1810 in South Carolina; married 1831 in Hall Co., Ga.). Great-grandson of John Sharp (immigrated from Germany following Revolutionary War), of Alexander White (b. in South Carolina), of Daniel Reinhardt (b. 1779 in North Carolina) and Fanny Hoyle (b. 1783 in North Carolina), and of Jesse Harbin (b. 1771, in South Carolina) and Sarah Boone (b. 1786 in South Carolina).

Col. John J. A. Sharp came from South Carolina to Waleska in 1856; taught school, ran a store until the Civil War opened; joined the 23d Georgia Infantry Regiment and served four years. As lieutenant-colonel, was wounded leading his regiment at Bentonville, N. C., Mar. 28, 1865. Reorganized his mercantile business after the war; represented Cherokee Co. in legislature, 1865-66, 1875-76; fought the carpet-baggers. Helped to establish Reinhardt College, 1883-84; was president of its board of trustees till his death in 1896. Married, in 1868, Mary Jane Reinhardt, daughter of Lewis W. Reinhardt, who had settled in Waleska in 1834 and founded there the first Methodist Church in the northern part of Cherokee Co.

Ramsey Colquitt Sharp graduated at Reinhardt College, 1891; at Emory University, 1894. Taught school in Pickens and Cobb Counties, 1895-1901. President of Reinhardt College, 1901-1918, 1922-1927 (see chapter on Education, Reinhardt College). Elected superintendent of schools, Cherokee Co., 1928. Reelected for 1932-1936, 1932 primary.

Married, in May 1897, Mary Jane Sewell, of Cobb Co. Children: Colleen (Mrs. M. H. Davis); Mary (Mrs. P. M. Boyd); and Harold (graduated at Emory University; now with Coca-Cola Co. in New Orleans).

SIMPSON, EDWARD CHESTER

Ball Ground. Born 1872 in Charlotte, N. C. Son of Dr. Isaiah Simpson and Sallie Patton Simpson. The family is of Scotch and Irish descent. Dr. Isaiah Simpson was a dentist of extensive practice in Charlotte, N. C. One of his sons is a Presbyterian minister.

E. C. Simpson has held the positions of agent, operator, and traveling auditor with the L. & N. R. R. For 17 years he has been operator at Ball Ground, where he is prominent in civic life. He joined the Methodist Church in South Carolina, under the ministry of Bishop J. C. Kilgo. He is a Mason and a member of the Order of Railway Telegraphers.

Mrs. Simpson is the former Hattie Ferguson, of Rock Hill, S. C., and comes from a well-known family of that section. The children of Mr. and Mrs. Simpson are: Margaret, b. 1896; Elizabeth, b. 1898; Rachel, b. 1900; Edward (died in youth).

SPEARS, LEE

Canton. Born 1895 in Cherokee Co. Son of Joshua P. Spears (sheriff of Cherokee Co. for 28 years; justice of the peace, 20 years) and Mollie Dean Spears (of a South Carolina family which settled near Hickory Flat). Grandson of Josiah Spears (who moved to Cherokee Co. from South Carolina following the Civil War).

Mr. Spears is sheriff-elect of Cherokee Co. for 1933-37, and has also filled this position previously. He was chief of police of Canton for 4 years and a prohibition enforcement officer for about the same length of time. During the World War he served in the Quartermaster Corps. He is a member of the American Legion and also belongs to the Masonic fraternity.

In 1921 he married Ruth Hillhouse, of Toonigh, and their children are: Jack Caldwell, b. 1922; Lee Jr., b. 1926.

STONE, ERNEST L.

Canton. Born June 19, 1896, in Cherokee Co. Son of Augustus Stone, originally of Bartow Co., and Esther Knox Stone. Grandson of Joseph Knox, pioneer settler of Cherokee Co., and Malissa Brooke. Great-grandson of John P. and Hester Bennett Brooke, and of James and Mary Ann Abbott Knox. (For Brooke family history, see account of Mrs. J. E. Johnston; for Knox history, see

ERNEST L. STONE, PRESIDENT OF THE KNOX RE-
UNION, AND YOUNG SON

account of Joseph W. Knox.) Mr. Stone is president of the Knox family reunion.

In 1919 he married Elsie Gramling, descendant of an old and respected Cherokee Co. family; and they are both members of Field's Chapel (Methodist). They have one son, Ernest L. Jr., b. 1920. Mr. Stone served during the World War in the Third Infantry Replacement Regiment, A. E. F. For several years he was connected with the Chevrolet agency in Canton; is now employed by Standard Oil Co.

TATE, EDNA FERGUSON (MRS. PHILIP M.)

Fairmount. Daughter of Daniel Wyatt Ferguson and Sarah Jefferson Ferguson.

The mother of Mrs. Tate was the daughter of George Washington Jefferson, who was born in Pittsylvania Co., Va., of Welch lineage, and Mary Dent Jefferson, born at Port Tobacco, on the Potomac River in Maryland, of English lineage. Mr. Jefferson emigrated from Virginia to Heard Co., Ga., in 1839, and came the following year to Cherokee Co. where he located in the Salacoa

SARAH J. (JEFFERSON) FERGUSON

Valley on lands purchased from Ephraim Dent of Heard Co., who had obtained them in the 1838 lottery.

The daughter of George W. and Mary Dent Jefferson, Sarah Jefferson, was born in "Little Virginia" colony, Salacoa, Cherokee Co., on Jan. 28, 1846. At the age of 8 she joined Fairview Methodist Church, where she remained a loyal and useful member for 77 years. In 1872 she received the A. B. degree from Asheville

(N. C.) Female College, and in the same year she married Daniel Wyatt Ferguson, of Evergreen, Va. (a village near Appomattox Courthouse). Mr. Ferguson served as a Confederate soldier during the entire course of the war and was in Pickett's Charge at Gettysburg.

The children of Daniel Wyatt Ferguson and Sarah Jefferson Ferguson were: Edna (b. 1873; married Philip M. Tate of Pickens Co. in 1901); Wade Dent (b. 1875; married Elizabeth Mercier of Maryland in 1910); Charlie P. (b. 1878); Virgil W. (b. 1884; married Lucy Bradford of Bartow Co. in 1919; d. 1928); Mary (b. 1886; d. 1887).

TEASLEY, GEORGE ISHAM

Canton. Born 1859 in Cherokee Co. Son of William Alfred and Jane Baber Teasley. Grandson of Isham and Mary Maxwell Teasley, and of George and Ann Baber.

Isham Teasley left Elbert Co. about 1840 and settled in Cherokee Co. His wife came from what was later Milton Co. William A. Teasley, his son, became one of the leading members of the Canton bar, where he practiced for many years, beginning about 1856. The Babers were very early settlers of the county. The children of William A. and Jane Baber Teasley, besides the subject of this sketch, were Mary Maxwell (Mrs. B. F. Crisler); Lizzie (Mrs. Jabez Galt); Agnes (Mrs. J. J. Coggins); Fannie (Mrs. Thomas Hutcherson); William A. Jr.; and Chester Baber.

George I. Teasley was admitted to the Canton bar in 1881, and arose to eminence as a lawyer. He has served as county school commissioner and as mayor and councilman of Canton. He is the largest orchardist in the county, owning the Cherokee Heights orchard which contains about 30,000 peach and apple trees.

In 1884 Col. Teasley married Jeffie Fain, of a prominent Gordon Co. family. Their children are: Ann, William Alfred, George Isham Jr., Martha Edwina (Mrs. H. R. Thomas), and John R.

THOMAS, HOMER OSCAR

Born June 7, 1875, in Cherokee Co. Son of Lorenzo Thomas (b. 1849 in Cherokee Co.) and Julia Moore Thomas (b. 1854 in Cherokee Co.). Grandson of Jefferson Thomas (who moved to

Cherokee Co. from Arkansas; of English descent) and of Thompson Moore (Confederate soldier; old settler of Cherokee Co.; see account of) and Amanda King Moore.

Mr. Thomas attended Avery school and has since been engaged in farming in the Hickory Flat section, except for one year spent in California. He is a progressive and influential farmer of the Hickory Flat neighborhood, and active in the affairs of his community and county.

He married, on Mar. 6, 1901, Lilla Carmichael, daughter of A. W. Carmichael and Laura Day Carmichael. Mrs. Thomas was born June 28, 1881, in Cherokee Co. They have the following children: Vera, b. 1902; Myrtie, b. 1909; Wesley, b. 1918.

THOMASON, LUTHER R.

Ball Ground. Born 1879 in Union Co. Son of Young J. Thomason and Maranda Williams Thomason. Grandson of Simeon Thomason (killed in action at the Civil War battle of Seven Pines; had settled early in Gaddistown, Ga., and married there), and of Capt. F. M. Williams (also served with distinction in the Confederate Army; later was ordinary of Lumpkin Co. for 20 years or more).

Married, in 1901, Amanda Mauldin, of Milton Co., who comes of an old family of Milton and Forsyth Counties which moved in the early days from South Carolina.

Mr. Thomason is an insurance agent and real estate broker at Ball Ground; was formerly manager of the Roberts Power Co. there. He has been mayor of Ball Ground for three successive terms; is a member of the county board of education; member, Democratic senatorial committee; local chairman, district committee; jury commissioner, Cherokee Co. Active member of Ball Ground Methodist Church; steward and trustee.

TIMMONS, MARY ELIZABETH KING (MRS. JOHN C.)

Waleska. Born Jan. 7, 1867. Daughter of A. S. and Martha Matilda Evans King. The family is of English and Irish descent. Mrs. Timmons' grandfather, a Baptist preacher, was a slaveholder and owner of a large plantation on the Etowah River below Canton. He served in the Civil War. A. S. King left medical school to join the Confederate Army before he was of age and served as a drillmaster during the war. He was wounded twice, but lived to the age of more than 70 before succumbing to his injuries.

John Cobb Timmons, who married Mary Elizabeth King May 20, 1877, was born July 4, 1861, and was the son of William and Sarah Ann Hubbard Timmons. His grandfather, Noble Timmons, was an early settler and traded with the Indians before their removal from Cherokee Co., and also served on the first grand jury of Cherokee Co. William Timmons lived on Shoal Creek and was a farmer, Confederate soldier, Mason, Baptist. John Cobb Timmons was a farmer of the Waleska section and belonged to the Baptist Church and the I. O. O. F. He died Nov. 7, 1926.

The children of Mr. and Mrs. John Cobb Timmons: Emmie Timmons Mackey; Noble, Cordelia; Christena; King; and Mary Timmons Barksdale.

VANDIVIERE, HENRY GRADY

Canton. Born July 27, 1894, in Dawsonville, Dawson Co., Ga. Son of Almarine Washington Vandiviere (b. Apr. 12, 1859, in Dawson Co.; superintendent of schools, Dawson Co., for 35 years; lawyer) and Rachel Catherine Wood Vandiviere (b. Aug. 9, 1868, in Cherokee Co.). Grandson of E. C. Vandiviere, of Dawson Co., and of Jesse and Sarah Holcomb Wood, of Cherokee Co.

Graduated at N. G. A. C., Dahlonega, with A.B. degree, 1915; Atlanta Law School, LL.B. degree, 1917. Began the practice of law in Canton, 1921, with Judge John S. Wood. Married, Sep. 19, 1919, in Lancaster, S. C., Helen Lathan, daughter of J. B. Lathan and Elizabeth Wise Lathan. Methodist. Democrat. Mason; Junior Order; Red Man; W. O. W.

Col. Vandiviere served the county as representative to the legislature in 1927-28 and as state senator in 1929-30 and the extra session of 1931.

WOOD, J. HINES

Canton. Born Sep. 3, 1887, in Washington Co. Son of Mizell G. Wood (b. 1851 in Washington Co.; farmer; d. Nov. 8, 1899) and Margaret E. Stubbs Wood (b. 1851 in Washington Co.; d. June 13, 1924). Grandson of Henry Wood and Polly Gilbert Wood, and of Gabriel Stubbs and Gracie Collins Stubbs, all of Washington Co.

Attended public schools of Sandersville, Ga.; Mercer University, degree of B.L., 1910. Served as first lieutenant, 18th M. G. Battalion, 6th Division, Regulars, U. S. Army, throughout World War and overseas. Is a practicing lawyer of Canton; a Mason and Shriner; a Methodist.

Married, Sep. 12, 1923, at Sandersville, Lida Jones, daughter of N. H. Jones and Mahala Gambill Jones, of Allegheny Co., N. C. One child, J. Hines, Jr., b. Oct. 8, 1924.

WOOD, JOHN STEPHENS

Canton. Born Feb. 8, 1885, near Ball Ground. Son of Jesse L. and Sarah Holcomb Wood, of Cherokee Co.; grandson of Solomon and Jane Tarbotton Wood, who lived near Ball Ground, and of Thomas and Rachel Gurley Holcomb, also from near Ball Ground.

Attended North Georgia Agricultural College; graduated Mercer University, LL.B., June 8, 1910. Began practice of law at Jasper, Ga., June 1910; moved to Canton, October 1914. Served in World War, air service. Baptist. Democrat. Mason; Shriner; Odd Fellow; Red Man.

Married: (1) Sep. 3, 1913, in Cherokee Co., Margurete May Roberts, daughter of Dr. J. M. and Saphronia McClure Roberts, of Ball Ground. One daughter, Margaret, b. Dec. 19, 1918. Married: (2) May 23, 1926, in Canton, Louise Jones, daughter of Robert Tyre Jones Sr. and Lillie Coggins Jones, of Canton. Daughters of second marriage: Patsy, b. Mar. 17, 1927, and Bobby, b. Aug. 21, 1928.

Judge Wood's notable political record includes the following offices and distinctions: delegate, National Democratic Convention, Baltimore, 1912; city attorney, Canton, 1915-16; representative from Cherokee Co., 1917 (resigned to enter army); solicitor-general, Blue Ridge Circuit, Jan. 1, 1921-June 24, 1926; judge, Blue Ridge Circuit, June 24, 1926-Mar. 1931, resigned; congressman from Ninth District, Mar. 4, 1931-date.

WOOD, RALPH W. (REV.)

Atlanta. Born 1895 in Scotland, Ga. Son of R. Newton Wood, who is a farmer and merchant of Wheeler Co., and Addie Martin Wood. Grandson of William Wood, a Confederate soldier, and G. N. Martin, son of a Confederate soldier.

Married, in 1921, Bertha Bearden, daughter of Mr. and Mrs. W. A. Bearden, of Waleska. (See account of W. A. Bearden.)

Attended South Georgia College, at McRae, and Emory University, where he received the degrees of A. B. (1920) and M. A. (1928). Taught in Reinhardt College 3 years; was afterward president of South Georgia College; later became connected with the Atlanta public school system. Is an ordained elder in the North Georgia Conference, M. E. C. S., and now assistant pastor of St. John's Methodist Church, in Atlanta. Holds membership in Alee Shrine Temple and Pi Gamma Mu National Honorary Society.

WORLEY, ELY ELBERT

Ball Ground. Born 1894 in Fulton Co. Son of Ely Elbert Worley Sr. (b. 1867 near Hickory Flat; Atlanta salesman) and Lena Futrelle Worley (b. 1873 in Cherokee Co.). Grandson of Joel Thomas Worley (Confederate soldier; wounded at the Battle of Kennesaw) and of Abraham Futrelle (b. 1835 in Crawford Co.; served during the Civil War in Phillips' Legion, cavalry; d. 1902). Great-grandson of Wiley Futrelle (b. 1829 in Jasper Co.; d. 1886). Great-great-grandson of Abraham Futrelle (b. 1781 in Halifax Co., N. C.; d. 1843).

Mr. Worley attended the public schools of Fulton Co. Was formerly in business in Atlanta; now connected with Roberts Marble Co. at Ball Ground. World War veteran; member, American Legion. Member, Ball Ground school board. Methodist.

Married, Feb. 18, 1917, in Fulton Co., Mattie Epperson, daughter of Joseph Pharr Epperson, of Cherokee Co., and Elizabeth McElroy Epperson, who came from Gadsden, Ala. The children of Mr. and Mrs. Worley are: Martha, b. Oct. 11, 1918; Ely Elbert III, b. Mar. 8, 1921; Woodrow Wilson, b. Aug. 7, 1924; Joseph Epperson, b. Jan. 26, 1931. The family are all Methodists.

WRIGHT, THOMAS ELLIS

Orange. Born Aug. 13, 1849, at Roswell, Ga. Son of Dotson Bennett Wright (b. Apr. 1, 1824, at Logansville, Gwinnett Co.; Confederate soldier; d. 1865 from wounds received in the war) and Henrietta Sisson (b. Oct. 6, 1827, at Charleston, S. C.). Grandson of Ellis Wright (b. 1799 in Virginia; came to Georgia at the age of 6) and Rhoda Collins Wright (b. Dec. 22, 1792; m. 1818). Great-grandson of James Samuel Wright (b. Feb. 8, 1772) and Rhoda Wright (b. 1772; m. 1792; d. 1835). It is believed that the ancestor of the Wright family came to America with John Wesley and Gen. Oglethorpe to the Georgia colony in 1733.

Thomas Ellis Wright is a highly respected farmer of the Orange community in Cherokee County, to which he came in 1868 from Cobb Co. He has been a deacon in Hopewell Baptist Church for 40 years; is a notary public and justice of the peace.

Married, in 1876, Margaret McClesky, b. 1858 in Cherokee Co., daughter of George McClesky (Confederate major) and Angeline Bell McClesky. Children of Mr. and Mrs. Wright: Mrs. Alma Wright Blackwell; Alvey Dotson Wright; William Tarpley Wright (Canton insurance broker; Mason; Shriner; treasurer of Royal Arcanum for several years; Baptist; secretary and treasurer of Canton Baptist Sunday School for 16 years); Thomas Ellis Wright, Jr.; George McClesky Wright; Henry Fleming Wright.